Fall River Outrage

If I should be m
Rev Mr Avery
know where I a

Naomi Nelson

*my enquire of the
Bristol he will

Dec 20th
S M Cornell*

Fall River Outrage

Life, Murder, and Justice in Early Industrial New England

David Richard Kasserman

upp

University of Pennsylvania Press
Philadelphia   1986

Frontispiece. The note found in Sarah Cornell's bandbox, which aroused suspicions against the Reverend Ephraim Kingsbury Avery. From David Melvill, *A Fac-simile of the Letters Produced at the Trial of the Rev. Ephraim K. Avery* (Boston: Pendleton's Lithography, 1833).

Short passages from the following documents in the collections of the New England Methodist Historical Society, Boston, are reprinted with permission: Asa Kent, 19 July 1836 letter to the Members of the New England Conference; Timothy Merritt, 6 July 1833 letter to Ephraim K. Avery and Charles True.

Short passages from the following documents in the Avery Trial Papers in the Papers of Albert Collins Greene are reprinted with permission of the Rhode Island Historical Society, Manuscript Collections: Grindall Rawson, 19 March 1833 letter to William R. Staples; Dutee J. Pearce, 14 March 1833 letter to Albert C. Greene; Samuel Eddy, trial notes, unsigned and unnumbered booklet, 1833; William Lawless, 27 May 1833 letter to Albert C. Greene; Elihu Greene, 24 June 1833 letter to Mrs. D. Greene (Greene Papers).

Copyright © 1986 by the University of Pennsylvania Press
All rights reserved

Library of Congress Cataloging-in-Publication Data

Kasserman, David Richard.
    Fall River outrage.

    Bibliography: p.
    Includes index.
    1. Avery, Ephraim K., d. 1869—Trials, litigation,
etc.   2. Trials (Murder)—Rhode Island—Newport.
3. Labor and laboring classes—Massachusetts—Fall
River—History.   4. Cornell, Sarah Maria, 1802–1832.
I. Title.
KF223.A94K37   1986   345.73'02523   85-26454
                          347.3052523
ISBN 0-8122-8002-4 (alk. paper)
ISBN 0-8122-1222-3 (pbk. : alk. paper)

Printed in the United States of America

Fourth paperback printing 1993

For Elizabeth J. Kasserman

Contents

List of Illustrations

Acknowledgments

Work on this book was materially assisted by three grants from Glassboro State College and by three grants from the National Endowment for the Humanities, which allowed me to attend NEH summer seminars directed by Solon Kimball (University of Florida, 1976), David Fischer (Brandeis University, 1979), and Ruth Butler (University of Massachusetts, Boston, 1982) where I pursued research related to the case of Ephraim Avery and Sarah Cornell.

I received unfailingly kind and helpful assistance at all the historical societies and libraries in Massachusetts and Rhode Island that I visited while completing this book. Particular thanks are due to the Fall River Historical Society, the New England Methodist Historical Society Library (School of Theology, Boston University), the Library Company of Philadelphia, and the Rhode Island Historical Society for permission to quote manuscripts and reproduce photographs and diagrams in their possession. I also wish to thank Cornell University Press for permission to quote Harold W. Thompson's *A Pioneer Songster*.

Fall River Outrage

Introduction

Sixty years before Lizzie Borden took up her axe, Fall River, Massachusetts, was the scene of another sensational murder. On December 21, 1832, Sarah Cornell, recently employed as a weaver in the Fall River Manufactory, was found hung on the outskirts of town, and Ephraim Kingsbury Avery, the Methodist minister of nearby Bristol, Rhode Island, was implicated in her death. Widespread public indignation was aroused by the crime, and the agitation of Fall River swelled until it engulfed most of the country in varying degrees of intensity for the next year. Local editors enthusiastically printed facts and outrageous improvisations about the murdered woman and the accused preacher, and they had the pleasure of seeing their articles avidly copied in newspapers many states distant. Both the press and the public became aggressively partisan. Riots were threatened, effigies of Avery were hung and burned, and a tireless vigilante organization was created to assist in the minister's prosecution. Songs and plays that condemned Avery became popular, and pamphlets proclaiming either his innocence or guilt flooded the country. His trial, though it took nearly a month and was the longest in American history to that date, was so well attended that even the largest room in Newport's courthouse could not hold the mass of spectators, many of whom spilled onto the street to cluster under open windows.

Public enthusiasm stemmed partly from the case's dramatic particulars; though unmarried, Sarah Cornell was pregnant at the time of her death, and many believed that the minister had seduced her, then killed her to prevent irreparable harm to his reputation. In the hearings and trial that followed Avery's arrest, his lawyers unintentionally played to this interest in a titillating story. They deserve the distinction of, if not discovering, at least bringing a high degree of perfection to the now classic defense strategy that depends on proving that the female victim of a sexually based crime was of such bad character that her assailant could not be culpable. Though their approach was less reprehensible in the intellectual context of the 1830s than it would be today, it was no less entertaining. The court was regaled with an overwhelming volume of unsubstantiated stories depicting the dead woman's dishonesty, promiscuity, deviousness, and incipient insanity. Crowds that attended the trial hoping to witness a memorable show were not disappointed when the defense was allowed to introduce as evidence small-town gossip that was otherwise heard only over backyard fences.

The extent and intensity of general interest, however, had another source in the symbolic and institutional associations of the two people involved. Sarah Cornell was one of the first generation of American women to attain the social and economic independence offered by employment in the cotton mills rising beside New England's streams. The very fact of her death contradicted the assertion of industrial capitalists that the women on whom they depended for labor were as safe in mill towns as they were at home under their parents' care, and the assault on the dead woman's character that figured prominently in Avery's legal defense was an open challenge to the industrialists' claim that factory life did not impede their workers' moral development. The defense of Sarah Cornell, then, easily became a defense of an industrial lifestyle. Although she had lived in Fall River less than three months when she died, that community's capitalists and mill operatives had good reason to adopt her cause as their own and work zealously to avenge her death. In trying to clear her name, they protected their own.

Ephraim Avery, on the other hand, belonged to a church that was in the vanguard of New England's second great awakening. The Methodists preached a novel form of Christianity, based on feeling and free salvation, that had great appeal to the developing working class but posed an ideological threat to the dominant Calvinist Congregational church. The Methodists' emphasis on emotional conversion made their ministry suspect in a society that had always required years of rigorous intellectual training for those who held spiritual authority, while their episcopal government, which centralized power and made them a highly efficient evangelical organization, was at odds with the philosophy of local autonomy that had pervaded New England life for two centuries. Like the Masons, they were castigated as an antidemocratic society, and, worse than the Masons, they were believed to be enthusiasts whose intellects could not always be depended on to control the excesses of their passions. Already viewed with suspicion and engaged in an intense missionary effort, the church could hardly afford the scandal associated with the Reverend Ephraim Avery's possible conviction for murder.

Avery's trial thus became a contest between two emergent institutions, both of which believed that the opportunity for future growth depended on a favorable verdict from the jury. Though lawyers for both sides repeatedly denied any interest in or commitment to the trial's social implications, in their battle the characters and rights of the case's overt principals sometimes became secondary, and one defense lawyer's posttrial comment that he had never really considered the question of the minister's guilt was less cynical than it might otherwise seem. Everyone who followed the progress of Avery's case was aware that the issue had grown beyond a single death. The decision that was reached would not only free or hang an accused man, it would also go far to condemn a way of life.

1. The Outrage

*A*t *nine o'clock* on Friday morning, December 21, 1832, John Durfee took his team from the barn and headed down through the sloping fields of his father's farm toward Mount Hope Bay. The weather of the past few days had been unusually bitter, and the fog—last year's uncut grass—snapped under his boots and his horses' hooves whenever they strayed from the well-worn paths. As Durfee directed his animals across the stack yard where his winter's supply of hay was stored, he noticed an unfamiliar shape huddled against one of the poles supporting the movable roof of the haystack. Suspended from a cord was the cold body of a young woman, her cheek pressed against the rough wood, her toes resting on the ground, and her knees partially bent as though she were frozen in the act of kneeling for prayer.

Momentarily forgetting his team, Durfee ran to the body. The dead woman's hair was wildly disheveled, and the young farmer had to brush it aside to view her face. Relieved to discover she was a stranger, Durfee looked up the hill toward his home for aid. From the stack yard only three vacant windows of the house were visible. Fortunately, Durfee's father, Richard, was standing in the doorway and heard his son's urgent shouts. Hurrying toward the sound, the older man reached the haystack in the company of Benjamin Negus

1. The Durfee farm, near Fall River. In this contemporary rendition of the site of Sarah Cornell's death, artistic license has put leaves on the trees in late December. From Catharine Williams, *Fall River, An Authentic Narrative* (Boston: Lilly, Waite and Co., 1833).

and William Allen, neighbors who happened to be nearby (Marshall and Brown 1833, 12).

The four men who assembled around the body were conscious of the importance of their observations in any coroner's inquest or trial that might ensue. The woman's cloak was almost completely fastened; under its folds, one gloved hand was drawn up to her bosom while the other hung stiffly at her side. Her shoes, one soiled with mud, were neatly set eighteen inches to the right of her stockinged feet. Her handkerchief lay eighteen inches to the left. The ribbons of her calash were caught under the cord that had apparently choked her life away.

When all were satisfied with their initial observations, John Durfee attempted to lower the body to the ground by lifting it so that the cord could be slipped off the top of the pole. His strength and stature were not equal to the task, and his father suggested that the cord be cut. Allen or Negus handed the younger Durfee a knife, the cord was severed about four inches from the body and two inches from the stake, and the four men lowered the corpse to the ground. Frozen in a half-crouching stance, the body defeated all attempt to lay it decorously on its back.

John Durfee was dispatched by the other men to obtain the coroner of Tiverton, the elderly Elihu Hicks. While he was gone others carried the news of the death to Fall River, the nearby manufacturing town where the unfortunate woman had been employed in one of the many cotton factories. Once they learned of the demise of an unidentified working woman, ministers from the local churches rushed to the scene in fear of finding one from their flocks lost. Mill overseers as well—at least those who found a throstle or loom untended in their shops that day—traveled the short distance to Durfee's farm.

Among the first to reach the stack yard from the village was Ira Bidwell, the local Methodist minister who identified the body as that of Sarah Maria Cornell, a "virtuous girl" who belonged to his church (Shove 1833). John Smith, the overseer of a weaving room at the Fall River Manufactory, confirmed the identification, exclaiming that he himself had given her permission to leave the mill early the previous evening and had thus unwittingly sent her to her death. Drawn together by their knowledge of this woman who had neither been in the community long nor had made many acquaintances during her stay, the minister and the mill overseer lingered to discuss the condition of the corpse and the means of her death. Smith first asserted that the cord wrapped around her neck matched that used in his weaving room, then later discovered that he had been mistaken (Hallett 1833b, 3–4).

When news of the woman's identity reached Fall River, her physician, Dr. Thomas Wilbur, was prompted to make the journey to Durfee's farm. Wilbur got to the stack yard a little after ten o'clock that morning (Drury 1833, 7). In the moments before Elihu Hicks brought his coroner's jury of six men to view the corpse, the doctor felt Sarah Cornell's abdomen for signs of pregnancy (Drury 1833, 7). Convinced that she was pregnant, Wilbur recalled his conversations with her as a patient and concluded that she had probably killed herself because of the base treachery of a married Methodist minister, Ephraim Kingsbury Avery, whom she had named as the father of her unborn child. When the coroner had John Durfee remove the body to his house, Wilbur followed. Asked what he knew of the young woman, he recounted her condition and history, not omitting her accusations against Avery.

Coroner Hicks, who had arrived at the scene approximately the same time as Wilbur, had gone first to the Durfee house, where he collected the six men necessary to make up his jury of inquest.

Richard Durfee, owner of the farm, was made foreman over Baulston Brayton, Joseph Cook, Daniel Sherman, Williams Durfee, and Isaac Negus (Hallett 1833a, 191). With the jury selected, Hicks proceeded to the stack yard, where Wilbur had just finished his cursory examination. There he swore in the men he had selected and had them observe the body. It seemed apparent to all that the woman had committed suicide. The contention of self-destruction was supported a short while later when, back in the comfort of the house, the jury heard Wilbur's story of seduction and pregnancy.

After the body had been taken into the house, John Durfee was sent out again, this time to the home of Harriet Hathaway in Fall River where Sarah Cornell had boarded. His mission was to obtain the dead woman's belongings, among which might be found burial clothing. In her locked trunk, the key to which was discovered in Sarah's pocket where Mrs. Hathaway said she habitually carried it, were not only clothes, but also a sealed letter to Ira Bidwell renouncing her membership in the Methodist church and three anonymous letters addressed to Sarah "Connell," which seemed to corroborate Dr. Wilbur's story of seduction.

Convinced that the woman had killed herself, but puzzled and interested by the possibility of foul play, the coroner's jury was released under orders to assemble once again at Durfee's farm at nine o'clock the following morning (Hallett 1833a, 29). In the light of a new day, while arrangements for Sarah's funeral were being made in another room, the reassembled jury came to a verdict of suicide prompted by "the wicked conduct of a married man" (Hallett 1833a, 191). Without further delay, Hicks ordered the body buried.

When John Durfee had learned from Rev. Bidwell of Sarah Cornell's connection with the Methodist church, he had immediately asked the minister if the church would take care of her burial. Bidwell's equivocal reply had been that because she was only a probationary member, he would have to check into church usage in such situations (Marshall and Brown 1833, 167). Either through direct conversation with Dr. Wilbur or through an intermediary, Bidwell soon thereafter learned of the doctor's story of Sarah's seduction by Rev. Avery. Bidwell also may have learned of Sarah's unsent letter renouncing church membership and felt that it released his congregation from further obligation. His original assessment of the dead woman as a virtuous member of his church radically altered, the minister returned to Durfee and coldly informed him that "the deceased was a bad character and the meeting would have nothing to do with burying her" (Williams 1833, 28).

With no relatives in the immediate vicinity and no church to claim her body, Sarah was classified as an indigent, and the community of Tiverton, of which the Durfee farm was part, accepted responsibility for her funeral. John Durfee, both a councilman of Tiverton and one of the overseers of the poor, decided to hold her funeral at his house and inter the body in his family's private burial ground. The Reverend Orin Fowler, recently appointed pastor of the First Congregational Church of Fall River (Fowler 1841, 49), was selected to officiate at the services. Fowler's services were possibly solicited by David Anthony, a prominent Fall River Congregationalist whose corporation owned the mill in which Sarah Cornell had been employed. Thus, while Ira Bidwell traveled across the bay to Bristol to apprise fellow Methodist minister Ephraim Avery of suspicions that had been aroused against him, a Congregationalist pastor—a representative of the sect bitterly criticized by Methodists for taking religion away from the common man—said the final prayers over the dead girl and saw her laid solemnly to rest (Drury 1833, 6).

Sarah Cornell was buried at one o'clock on Saturday afternoon (Marshall and Brown 1833, 13). Almost immediately afterward, information began to accumulate that suggested that the coroner's jury's verdict of suicide was questionable. At the conclusion of the funeral services, Rev. Fowler gave the key to Sarah's trunk to two women and asked that they sift through her belongings to find some indication of living relatives. Susannah Borden and Mrs. Durfee (presumably Richard Durfee's wife) accepted the commission and soon returned with a letter from Sarah's brother that aided in the discovery of her sister and brother-in-law in Connecticut. The two matrons, however, had found something of greater significance in Sarah's bandbox: a scrap of paper on which was penciled, "If I should be missing enquire of the Rev Mr Avery of Bristol he will know where I am Dec 20th S M Cornell."

On Sunday John Durfee took the note to Hicks as new evidence in the woman's death. Combined with the letters found earlier, the note indicated that she had not traveled to the stack yard alone, but had made an appointment to meet Rev. Avery. The suggestion of another party's presence made other anomalous bits of information suddenly meaningful. On Friday Benjamin Manchester found part of what was identified as Sarah's comb lying

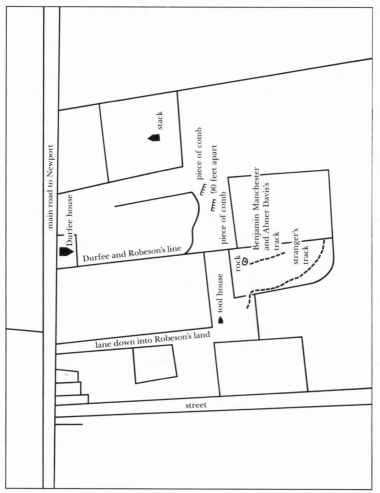

main road to Newport

Durfee house

Durfee and Robeson's line

stack

piece of comb

90 feet apart

piece of comb

Benjamin Manchester and Abner Davis's track

rock

stranger's track

tool house

lane down into Robeson's land

street

2. Site of Sarah Cornell's death, the Durfee and Robeson farms, south of Fall River. After an unsigned sketch in the Avery Trial Papers, in the papers of Albert Collins Greene, Rhode Island Historical Society.

nearly one hundred yards northwest of the stack yard (Hallett 1833a, 45). Two days later, Thomas Hart found the other part of it ninety feet away (Hallett 1833a, 49). When Durfee had discovered her body Sarah's hair had been in such disarray that it obscured her face; however, her bonnet was in place, with the strangling cord encircling its ribbons. Williams Durfee, who had spent his youth as a sailor (Hallett 1833a, 24), noted that the knot that secured the rope around Sarah's neck was a clove hitch, which could not be pulled tight with both ends held together (thus suggesting that the weight of her suspended body could not have tightened the rope around her neck). The matrons who stripped her body in preparation for burial had discovered bruises over the lower extremities, suggesting that Sarah had been "dreadfully abused" immediately prior to her death (Hallett 1833a, 48).

Growing public dissatisfaction with the coroner's jury's verdict, combined with the suggestive web of circumstance woven by these discoveries, pressured Hicks to consider murder more likely than suicide. Could not an unknown assailant have attacked her some distance from the stack yard, near the spot where her broken comb was discovered? Could he not have beaten her to unconsciousness, then strangled her with a cord purloined from the bed of a nearby wagon? Could he not have then carried the dead girl to the stack yard, suspended her from the pole, and left her in the appearance of having taken her own life? Aided by Dr. Wilbur's story of Sarah's accusations against Avery and the tales of the women who had discovered severe bruises on her lower extremities, Hicks imagined an attempt at abortion by the desperate minister, followed by a pain-induced swoon and murder. Certain that the original verdict had been too hasty, Hicks suggested that Durfee visit Dr. Wilbur to get a more detailed statement of his acquaintance with the dead woman (Hallett 1833a, 21) and to request that he perform an autopsy the following morning (Drury 1833, 8).

At nine o'clock Monday morning, Hicks appeared once more at the Durfee farm and asked that Sarah's body be exhumed for the autopsy and observation by a new jury. The old jury and its verdict were dismissed as illegal. Under Rhode Island law, only freeholders—men with landed estates—were enfranchised. Investigation had revealed that two men on the jury, Isaac Negus and Joseph Cook, did not own real estate and thus were ineligible to serve. Their signatures being invalid, Hicks could claim that the original verdict was signed by only four men instead of the required six

(Hallett 1833a, 29). The addition of William Boomer and Isaac Brightman to the jury required that the investigation process be re-instituted. In this way, Hicks's haphazard procedure came to his rescue by providing an easy technique for legally dismissing an unpopular and perhaps ill-advised conclusion.

The new jury watched as physicians Thomas Wilbur and Foster Hooper examined the body in Durfee's barn. Their verdict was never in question. Already convinced that Sarah had been attacked and sexually mauled, some jurors objected when the doctors started to strip the body to determine if she had been raped, or if abortion had been attempted (Hallett 1833a, 31). Their sense of modesty forbade public exposure, even of a corpse, for which they could see no point. Dr. Wilbur's sworn testimony relative to Sarah's explanations of her pregnancy (confirmed that day by dissection) convinced them that Avery had committed murder to cover the effects of seduction.

The jury's conclusion was, in a sense, an anticlimax. On Sunday afternoon, after his conversations with Hicks and Wilbur, John Durfee was certain that the jury scheduled to meet the next morning would return a verdict of murder implicating the Methodist minister at Bristol. With Wilbur's knowledge, and probably at the doctor's suggestion, Durfee set out for Bristol in the company of Fall River's elderly assistant postmaster, Seth Darling. Once at their destination, the two men proceeded to swear out a warrant for Avery's arrest.

The legality of their action was questionable from the start. Only a coroner could make the complaint resulting in a warrant for murder. Without a verdict of murder from a coroner's jury, they were, in fact, accusing a man when no crime had been committed. To further their difficulty, Durfee and Darling first applied to a Mr. Coggeshall of Bristol for their warrant, only to find that he was not a justice of the peace (Marshall and Brown 1833, 60) and that, lacking documentation, neither could remember the Methodist minister's name. Directed to John Howe, who was a justice but, like the Fall River men, did not know the minister by name, they finally swore out a complaint against Daniel Evereth or Everill (Hallett 1833a, 181). It was only after discussion with local people that the last name was corrected to Avery. As the document stood on Sunday afternoon, it implicated a nonexistent man, Daniel Avery, in a nonexistent crime, the murder of a woman who reportedly had committed suicide. Some semblance of legal order was restored only later, when the coroner's jury confirmed the crime on the following day and Avery himself graciously "waived all exceptions to misnomer in the complaint or warrant" (Marshall and Brown 1833, 147).

During the eventful four days between the discovery of the body on Friday morning and the final coroner's jury verdict on Monday afternoon, Durfee and Darling were not alone on the wintry roads connecting Fall River and Bristol. Soon after Sarah Cornell's identification, as the first whispered accusations against Avery were circulating, Fall River's Methodist minister, Ira Bidwell, was hurrying to inform his friend and co-worker of the public hostility and possible legal action that faced him.

Bidwell probably found Avery in the Bristol Methodist Church when he arrived on that Friday afternoon. Drawing the other minister into a side room where a modicum of privacy could be assured, Bidwell informed him that Dr. Wilbur had made statements indicating that Avery had had illicit intercourse with the dead woman. Avery appeared shocked and expressed complete innocence, then requested that Bidwell spend the night at his house, where they could discuss plans to meet possible legal and social repercussions. During the evening Avery convinced Bidwell to accompany him to Lowell, where Avery previously had been stationed and where much of his association with Sarah Cornell had taken place. There, Avery was confident, much evidence could be raised to demonstrate his Christian character—and the whorish disposition of the woman he was thought to have seduced (Avery 1834, 10).

On the following morning Avery wrote to Samuel Drake, the Methodist minister stationed at Portsmouth on the northern tip of Rhode Island, requesting that he come immediately to Bristol. "Your expenses shall be borne," he wrote; "of coming fail not" (Melvill 1833, doc. no. 8). When Drake arrived, Avery explained the situation to him, then admitted that fate had dealt an even crueler blow. Should suspicion of the actual murder eventually be directed against him, it would soon be common knowledge that he had been away from home—and unaccounted for—on the night the dreadful deed had occurred. Avery hoped that Drake would canvass the population of Portsmouth for anyone who had seen him wandering the community's fields and lanes on the previous Thursday. Should such witnesses be found, Avery could substantiate his claim to have been sight-seeing on the island rather than to have been bent on a more sinister mission across the bay. Drake's willingness to help offered momentary relief; while the two ministers were conversing, however, the stage from Fall River arrived, bringing confirmation that Avery was suspected not only of seduction, but also of murder. Although he had recognized the possibility and had begun to prepare for it, Avery was too shaken by the news to preach in the morning and was forced to ask Drake to take his place (Avery 1834, 11).

Avery spent most of Sunday at home, praying and reading the Bible (Avery 1834, 11), but he managed to temper this spiritual fortification with a few worldly preparations. With his appearance in court a virtual certainty, the preacher decided to travel immediately to Lowell to gather testimony. Walking to the stables where the stage teams were kept, he found driver Stephen Bartlett and requested that the young man deliver a message to Ira Bidwell on his next run to Fall River. Bidwell, Avery hoped, would be free to travel to Lowell with him on Monday (Hallett 1833a, 76).

When Bartlett arrived in Fall River on Sunday afternoon, he proved to be a scout as well as a messenger. Seeking Dr. Wilbur, the stage driver attempted to discover the state of agitation and legal activity among the townspeople (Williams 1833, 37). Wilbur, playing his part with skill if not legal authority, had only recently dispatched Durfee and Darling to Bristol to secure Avery's arrest. Aware that the legal cause of Sarah Cornell's death was still suicide, but certain that the autopsy he was to perform in the morning would change that to murder, Wilbur was in no mood to let legal technicalities give a killer the chance to evade justice. Seating the younger man in his parlor, the doctor slowly fed him bits of information, hoping to delay his return until the warrant for Avery's arrest could be drawn up and served.

The conversation between the two men must have been a model of innuendo, careful phrasing, double meanings, and—at least on the doctor's part—significant pauses during which a pocket watch might be repeatedly consulted. Finally, Bartlett informed Wilbur, erroneously, that he had seen Avery at the stable on December 20 (Marshall and Brown 1833, 45), and the doctor reciprocated with news of the warrant (Williams 1833, 38). As the stage driver hurried back to his rig, Wilbur congratulated himself on the clever maneuver by which he had kept Avery unaware of the process against him (of the probability of which the minister had, in fact, learned the day before). By the time Bartlett got back to Bristol, Avery was already in custody.

Arrested as the sun set on Sunday evening (Avery 1834, 11), Avery lost no time calling for a local lawyer, Nathaniel Bullock. After conversing with the justifiably distraught minister, Bullock agreed to take the case, but suggested that his work load would make at least one associate necessary. His choice was Joseph M. Blake, for whom Avery duly sent the following morning. On that same day, Monday, Avery was brought before John Howe and Levi Haile, justices of the peace in Bristol. By the time of his court appearance, the preacher's legal staff included Richard Randolf, apparently recommended by Bullock as another valuable addition. The speed with which events had transpired over the weekend may have been dazzling to Avery, but it was momentarily overwhelming for the prosecution. Dr. Wilbur and his agents, Durfee and Darling, having assumed that no legal action could possibly be taken in Avery's case before the middle of the week, thought there would be plenty of time to get a coroner's jury verdict on which to base the prosecution. Unfortunately, the justices' incredible promptness had placed the hearing before the autopsy and the deliberation of the second coroner's jury. William Staples, who was to be the prosecution attorney, was thus placed in the embarrassing position of prosecuting a man for a crime that legally had not been committed. Faced with public humiliation and undoubtedly cursing overeager civilians, Staples sent a note to the court claiming that the short notice did not allow him to reach Bristol until Tuesday. Much to his relief, the court agreed to postpone the beginning of testimony until the following day (Drury 1833, 3). By that time, the new coroner's verdict of murder was official and the prosecution could begin in earnest.

While Avery's Methodist allies planned his defense and Tiverton's rusty machinery of justice was hastily put into order, the people of Fall River pondered the part they might play in the events transpiring outside their legal jurisdiction. Determined to participate in the punishment of the murderer of one of their numbers, they were checked by the unfortunate circumstances that placed the murder in another municipality and another state. On the Sunday after the body was discovered, few churches in Fall River were well attended; most people who had ventured from home were to be found gathered in little clusters discussing the remarkable events of the last two days (Williams 1833, 36). On the following morning a public meeting was to be held to decide on the community's role in the apprehension and prosecution of the murderer.

Although Fall River had, indirectly, a Puritan pedigree, in

1832 it had only recently become a significant population center. In 1803, when the town of Fall River (what communities outside New England would call a township) was created out of part of the old Freetown, the village itself was comprised of eighteen dwellings housing a hundred people. Ten years later, when the town had changed its name to Troy, the village, continuing as Fall River, had grown to thirty houses and two hundred residents (Fowler 1841, 28). Despite this increase, it lagged behind other growing communities on the shores of Mount Hope Bay (Smith 1944, 8) because it was poorly positioned to compete in the maritime and agricultural economy of the eighteenth and early nineteenth centuries. The village's harbor, at the mouth of the Quequechan River, was shallow and unprotected, making it an inefficient haven for either fishermen or boat builders. The steep slope on which the village lay, which rose over one hundred thirty feet in less than a quarter mile, inhibited inland transportation of goods, a problem that was intensified by the long Watuppa Pond that lay astride the route between Fall River and its eastern neighbor, New Bedford. Badly suited to commerce, the village was equally maladapted to agriculture because of its soil, which was, even by New England standards, thin and rocky (Smith 1944, 17). Its only asset was the granite channel of the swiftly falling Quequechan, a natural mill race on which a series of grist- and sawmills had been built in the eighteenth century.

Fall River's gristmills were sufficiently productive to attract British attention during revolutionary occupation of Newport, but they were a minor industry capable of supporting only a handful of families. It was not until Providence, only twenty miles away, became a center of American cotton-spinning technology, and a generation of young Fall River mechanics had been trained in the Rhode Island mills of men like Samuel Slater, that the natural advantages of Fall River's water power could be fully exploited. In 1813 two cotton-spinning corporations established mills on the Quequechan; nineteen years later, Fall River's population had risen to over four thousand (Secretary of the Treasury 1833, 75), and the economy had diversified to include weaving as well as spinning, woolens as well as cotton, and cloth printing, machinery, and iron manufacture.

Though there had been some wage reductions in earlier years, earnings of Fall River's operatives had risen in 1830 and had surpassed old rates in 1832 (Secretary of the Treasury 1833, 75); this increase, according to one employer, created a community that was "prosperous and happy, possessing the means of a comfortable subsistence" (Secretary of the Treasury 1833, 71). The comfortable subsistence was enjoyed as well by local farmers, who found in the mill community a ready market for their produce, and by capitalists, who, remembering their recent obscurity, could not ignore their dependence on manufacturing. "If manufacturers are under the necessity of abandoning their business," wrote one Fall River industrialist, "they will find no difficulty in employing their capital, for the reason that they will have none to employ" (Secretary of the Treasury 1833, 76). Like the laboring people, the owners would be "destitute of the means of support, . . . brought to wretchedness," and "obliged to live as the first settlers of these shores were, upon fish" (Secretary of the Treasury 1833, 71, 76).

The village that was shocked by Sarah Cornell's death was, then, very much a manufacturing community in which empathy for and identification with a stricken mill girl could be expected to run high. It was also, however, a New England community that was as yet little affected by foreign immigration. The concept of local consensus government was thus strong, both as a model for action and as a justification in the eyes of the larger institutions of the state. Though Fall River's sense of identity might be new, the product of industrial development, the means chosen to express it were as old as New England itself.

It is unclear by whom the Monday morning meeting was called. Its officers—Joseph E. Read as president and George Paine as secretary—were selected at the meeting and played little further role in Fall River's prosecution of Avery. Read was probably brought to the chair because, as a justice of the peace in Fall River (Fowler 1841, 63), he could provide the meeting with a semblance of legal authority. It is suggestive that the meeting was held in the Lyceum, one of the curators of which, Foster Hooper (*Fall River Weekly Recorder*, 18 December 1833), figured prominently in the events that followed. Whoever instigated the meeting, a small boy was sent through the streets of the town, ringing a bell and announcing the assembly (Williams 1833, 36). At this meeting, attended by over two hundred people (Hallett 1833a, 70), two committees were chosen: one with open membership designated a "committee of vigilance," and a five-member "committee of investigation." The committee of investigation, whose members were Nathaniel Briggs Borden, Jesse Eddy, James Ford, Foster Hooper, and Harvey Harnden, was directed to establish contact with the officials of Rhode Island and offer any possible assistance in the investigation of Sarah Cornell's murder (Harnden 1833a, 35). The committee of vigilance—the membership list of which does not survive, but which certainly counted Seth Darling and probably John Durfee among its members—was instructed to act under the guidance of the other committee in collecting information useful in the investigation of the crime and the prosecution of its perpetrator.

The selection of the committee of investigation showed more careful consideration of complementary talents and resources than might be expected from the spontaneous decisions of an unstructured public gathering, and it suggests the direction of a thoughtful, well-informed mind—probably one of the committeemen—behind the public actions. Each of the five men selected occupied a different social and occupational position that made his services particularly useful in the committee's operation.

Nathaniel Briggs Borden, the man who would become the acknowledged leader of the committee of investigation, was born in Fall River's one Revolutionary War shrine: the house of Richard Borden, where a British soldier was mortally wounded in the "Battle of Fall River" (Williams 1833, 12). A member of one of the most socially and financially prominent Fall River families, Borden was both a manufacturer and a politician. After early and unsuccessful attempts at a liberal education (Peck and Earl 1877, 236), in 1821 Borden established himself as the clerk and treasurer of the newly founded Pocasset Company. As the cotton manufacturing establishment's fortunes grew, so did Borden's. By 1832 he still retained his offices in the business and was firmly tied through them to the manufacturers and operatives of Fall River. Using those ties and his social position, in 1832 he was beginning what was to be a long political career that would take him to Boston as a state legislator, to Washington as a congressman, and to the mayor's residence of his own community (Peck and Earl 1877, 236).

Borden served his first term in the state legislature in 1831, and in 1832 and 1833 he campaigned for a second term, which he won in 1834. He was a committed anti-Mason, ideologically opposed to "secret institutions in a free country" (Peck and Earl 1877, 237), which might reinforce aristocratic privilege and immunity from the law. The same impulse that led him to the anti-Masonic party prompted his abolitionism, his lifelong interest in the independent well-being of Fall River's working class, and his attack against Ephraim Avery.

It was not a great step in 1830s New England from opposition to the Masons to opposition to the Methodists. The episcopal government of the church appeared to many to be a corporate body that, like the Masons, could block the operation of public justice. When some ministers in the Methodists' New England Conference openly participated in Masonic rituals, although the Methodist church promptly punished them for it, the damage was done. The identification between the church and the Masons was made. It is hardly surprising, then, that Borden was willing to lend his services in a blow against an organization aligned with his political enemies. The moment Avery's fellow ministers offered their services in his behalf it was inevitable that anti-Masonic politicians would take up the challenge.

Foster Hooper, who may well have been the guiding spirit behind creation of the committee, was an obvious choice for membership because of his medical profession and participation in the examination of Sarah Cornell's corpse. Born in New Hampshire in 1805 (Fall River Historical Society 1927, 64), Hooper settled in Fall River in 1826. Almost immediately he began to take an active interest in public affairs, and was appointed as a member of a committee assigned to locate a poor farm and house of corrections. A large man with a reputation for both personal kindness and great physical endurance, Hooper continued throughout his life to serve the community. As 1832 drew to a close, he had just completed his duties as Fall River's quarantine doctor charged with the important task of keeping cholera, then raging in New York, out of the village. Politically, the doctor, like Borden, was an anti-Mason (Hallett 1833a, 33–34). Where Borden brought to the committee his locally prestigious name and his political skill, Hooper added his expertise as a medical man, first-hand evidence as a participant in the autopsy, and contact with the Rhode Island authorities through Elihu Hicks (who called upon him, along with Thomas Wilbur, to perform the autopsy).

James Ford, eleven years older than Hooper and one of the village's earliest lawyers, was the editor of the *Fall River Monitor* and the committee's choice as communications officer. Born in Milton, Massachusetts, Ford graduated from Brown University in 1814 and settled in Fall River in 1819. During his more than fifty years in the town, he served variously as city alderman, member of the school committee, justice of the peace, postmaster, state legislator, and inspector of the state almshouse (Fall River Historical Society 1927, 10; Fowler 1841, 63). While most of these positions were still ahead

of him in 1832, by that time he had served on the school committee
and had been a central figure in the foundation of the Fall River
Savings Bank (Fall River Savings Bank 1978, 7), for which he had
acted as treasurer in its first two years. Ford contributed much to
the committee of investigation. As a lawyer his skills would be valuable in Avery's prosecution (though he was not officially associated
with the case), and as editor of the *Monitor* he had immediate access
to perhaps the best communication and propaganda tool available
in the village. Further, as a member of the Mount Hope Lodge of
Masons (Fall River Historical Society 1927, 10), he provided a coun-
terbalance to the overtly anti-Masonic Hooper and Borden, and a
defense against the possible charge that Avery's prosecution was an
anti-Masonic witch hunt.

Harvey Harnden, the fourth member of the committee, was in
1832 a deputy sheriff for Bristol County, Massachusetts. An enterprising man nearing forty (Hallett 1833a, 69), apparently always
open to the possibility of financial gain, Harnden provided the
committee with a combination of investigative talents, police authority, and the time necessary for gathering evidence. Outside his
active participation in the Avery case, Harnden remains a shadowy
figure without lasting impact on the Fall River community. Alone
among the committee's members, Harnden did not represent some
important element in the town's social hierarchy. His actions proved
him a dedicated, persevering, enterprising, and sometimes ingenious sleuth; it was this skill that attracted the committee and the
lawyers who employed his services in the prosecution of the Methodist minister.

The final member of the committee was Jesse Eddy. Born in
Northbridge, Massachusetts, in 1801, Eddy got his first experience
in cloth manufacture in Woonsocket, Rhode Island, perhaps in the
mill of Marvel Shove (Bayles 1891, 301). In 1825 he and his brother
John associated themselves with Samuel Shove under the name of
Samuel Shove & Company, and opened a satinet factory in Fall
River (Peck and Earl 1877, 32). It was in this company, from which
the Eddy brothers made sufficient profit to establish their own firm
in 1834, that they were engaged in 1832. John Eddy seems to have
been concerned primarily with the technical aspects of manufacturing, while Jesse demonstrated sound judgment in financial matters and a warm personality that made him an effective company
agent. It is probable that Jesse Eddy's rapport with the workers in
his and other Fall River factories made him the most likely choice as
a representative of the mill operatives on the committee.

Probably having risen from the working class himself, Jesse Eddy seemed to identify with the concerns and orientations of those who labored for him. In lighter moments that concern might express itself by participation in—or at least encouragement for the participants in—the annual snowball battles waged between the "cotton bugs" (boys employed in preparing cotton yarns and who consequently always appeared tufted with bits of the staple) and the "blue niggers" (boys employed in the dye rooms whose faces were stained by dye and oil). In more serious moments, Eddy's concern could be seen in his conversations with employees as they sat around the stove in his factory's finishing room (Peck and Earl 1877, 33). Although there were more successful manufacturers in Fall River, certainly wealthier and more powerful ones, Jesse Eddy was the one man who could represent both the capitalists and the workers and who embodied the ideal of paternal concern for employees that the industrialists sought to portray.

The composition of the committee of investigation showed more than a simple appreciation for the variety of skills that would be needed in its operation; it reflected the political and economic reality of Fall River as well. The industrial development of the town over the preceding twenty years had depended to a large extent on the capital and managerial abilities of two competing groups. One, which was centered in Fall River itself—primarily in the Borden and Durfee families—financed, built, and managed the Fall River Manufactory and the Fall River Iron Works, and controlled the lower portion of the Quequechan River. The other, comprised mostly of Tiverton, Bristol, Warren, Rehoboth, and, later, New Bedford interests, owed its origin to Oliver Chace's fortuitous acquisition of lands on the upper reaches of the Quequechan in 1811 and built the Troy Cotton and Woollen Manufactory (Lamb 1935, V-6). Sharing the power provided by the river's rapid fall, the Iron Works group under the management of Congregationalist David Anthony (married to a Borden) and the Troy group led by Quaker Oliver Chace had contested over the same resources and markets since both organizations began cotton spinning in 1813.

Theirs was not, however, a blind war of personalities; where their interests overlapped, the two groups were capable of cooperation. When the Fall River Bank was chartered in 1824, its corporators were evenly distributed between the two factions, as were those of the Fall River Institution for Savings when it was incorporated four years later (Lamb 1935, VI-18, VI-22). Corporate management of the two banks was likewise divided; David Anthony of

3. David Anthony. Known as Deacon Anthony after he attained that
office in the local Congregational church, Anthony organized the
Fall River Manufactory, where Sarah Cornell worked when she arrived in
Fall River in 1832. Anthony was active in the investigation that
brought Ephraim Avery to trial. From Frederick M. Peck and Henry H.
Earl, *Fall River and Its Industries* (New York: Atlantic Publishing and
Engraving, 1877).

the Iron Works group was president of the Fall River Bank, while Micah H. Ruggles as president and Harvey Chace as secretary, both of the Troy group, dominated the Fall River Institution for Savings. Water, like access to money, was a common problem, and when an engineering project was begun to control the flow of water from Watuppa Pond, which powered all the mills on the Quequechan, it was done under the auspices of the Watuppa Reservoir Company, a corporation formed in 1826 by David Anthony and Bradford Durfee, of the Iron Works, and Nathaniel Borden (allied to his wife's Tiverton/Portsmouth relatives) and Oliver Chace (Lamb 1935, VI-26), both of the Troy Manufactory.

The balance that the two groups tried to preserve in projects important to both was maintained in the committee of investigation. Nathaniel Borden represented the Troy group, while James Ford (married to a Durfee) represented the Iron Works faction. Jesse Eddy appears to have been the balance between them, representing a relatively new force in Fall River—the entrepreneurs who moved in to take advantage of the space and power available in the mill properties of the two original groups. Never firmly allied with either older faction, Eddy's economic career saw him cooperate effectively with both (Lamb 1935, VI-25). Thus the committee was as ecumenical in local politics as it was in national ones, where it balanced Mason with anti-Mason and Jacksonian (N. B. Borden) with Whig (James Ford). Though the contest between Fall River's economic factions would resurface at the close of the committee's work (Lamb 1935, VI-21, VI-22), it must have been clear to the most obtuse resident that for the duration of the investigation no partisan group was going to take over and no local squabble would be allowed to dilute the community's efforts to deal with a common enemy—the murderer of one of their number.

Almost immediately upon their organization, the five members of the investigation committee began to fulfill the duties of their office. Within hours of the meeting on December 24, the committee was informed that Hicks's second jury had returned a verdict of murder. Armed with a warrant for Avery's apprehension, Hicks planned to go to Bristol on the following day to escort the minister back to Tiverton for examination. Unfortunately, Durfee and Darling's precipitous action in swearing out a private complaint against Avery had muddied the legal waters. Hicks knew that Avery was in custody and that he faced a serious problem. Would it be possible, he wondered, to convince the Bristol court of the invalidity of its process while maintaining the legality of his own? The committee of investigation was eager to cooperate with the worried coroner in developing a plan of action that would remove Avery's hearing from a court filled with his friends, acquaintances, and neighbors.

It may have been the importance of the testimony of John Orswell, engineer of the steamboat *King Philip*, that brought Hicks, the Fall River committee of investigation, and, indirectly, prosecutor William Staples together in a grand assault against Bristol on Christmas morning. The month before, Orswell had delivered a letter from Providence to Sarah Cornell in Fall River. Of little importance at the time, the identity of the gentleman who had put the letter into the engineer's hands gained new significance when the paper was found in the dead woman's belongings and its contents appeared to implicate its anonymous author in her pregnancy and death. If Orswell could identify Avery as the letter's bearer, a sturdy link would be added to the prosecution's case.

By chartering the *King Philip* to make a special run to Bristol on Christmas morning, the committee of investigation contrived to bring together all the forces working for the minister's conviction. Hicks was invited to accompany the committee and its boisterous band of supporters; thus the Tiverton official gained the material support of a mob of vocal well-wishers and provided them, in turn, some legal justification for their presence. Orswell, of course, was on the boat, and was persuaded to take advantage of the layover to visit Avery to determine if he was indeed the man who had delivered the letter. Transporting an important government witness gave both Hicks and the committee of investigation an aura of association with the state prosecution that might elevate their legal claims to the minister over those of another municipality—or, at least, so they hoped. An overwhelming show of organization, force, and legal authority might stampede Justices Howe and Haile into a quick capitulation and avoid the interminable legal debate over jurisdiction that might otherwise develop.

When the *King Philip* docked at Bristol on Tuesday morning it carried a heterogeneous crowd of Tiverton and Fall River men bent on a variety of related missions. Like marines establishing a beachhead, they spread through the town. Elihu Hicks, armed with his warrant, went to John Howe and demanded that Avery be released into his custody. The crime, he said, had been committed in Tiverton, not Bristol, and besides, the Bristol warrant was illegally sworn out by private citizens. Howe, having already instituted an investigation into Avery's alleged guilt, was unwilling to give up the case. Later consultation with the minister himself, who was emphatically opposed to being taken to either Fall River or Tiverton, strengthened the justice's resolve to deny Hicks's request. The arguments on which the extradition attempt was made, however, were compelling. Unsure of the proper legal course, Howe promised to make a decision the following day. After Hicks had left, the confused justice wrote a letter to Albert C. Greene, the state attorney general then attending court in Newport, asking for advice in this sticky matter (Howe 1832).

While Hicks debated with Justice Howe, Nathaniel Borden and Harvey Harnden, acting as representatives of the Fall River committee, called upon Avery's lawyer, Nathaniel Bullock. Their request for an interview with the minister was almost a meaningless formality. As they spoke to the lawyer, John Orswell and most of the Fall River delegation went directly to Avery's house and demanded a confrontation with the frightened preacher.

Although Avery had been kept in the custody of the arresting officer on the night of December 23, for the remainder of his examination he was allowed to stay at home (Avery 1834, 18). For this kindness he was appreciative; not only did it save him from the discomforts of Bristol's jail, but also it allowed him free access to his counsel and friends with whom he planned his defense. When the excited mob appeared in the lane before his house, however, he might well have wished for the protection of strong iron bars. If this invasion was generally unopposed, it was not unanticipated. The Reverend John Bristed, Bristol's Episcopal minister, learned of the expedition early that morning and was not tardy in communicating the information to Avery (Hallett 1833a, 62). William Paul, a Bristol County deputy sheriff, was called and stationed himself at the house in the company of some of the local Methodist community's sturdiest men. After having cautioned Avery to retire to the second story of the house, Paul met the crowd on the stairs. It was not he, however, but rather Benjamin Tilley, a local Methodist, who pushed the foremost Fall River man back and declared that they might not take their quarry (Hallett 1833b, 27).

Moving through his supporters, Orswell reached the foot of the stairs and requested that he be given an audience with the minister. The request seemed reasonable, and the threat of physical violence was momentarily checked. With little delay the engineer was ushered upstairs and into Avery's presence; the interview was brief. Upon first viewing the men assembled upstairs, Orswell picked out the minister as the man who had handed him the letter to Sarah Cornell. When Avery tried to shake Orswell's certainty by putting on his spectacles and asking if he still looked like the man, the engineer icily replied, "Sir, your glasses do not alter the features of your face" (Hallett 1833a, 77).

While Orswell spoke with the increasingly alarmed preacher, the crowd, later stigmatized as "wild fellows, mostly Irishmen" (*Fall River Weekly Recorder*, 30 January 1833) by a hostile press, intimidated the rest of the household. Mrs. Avery, terrified by the burly, scowling men who occupied the lane, the yard, and the entrance of her house (Hallett 1833b, 25), fled into a small chamber in the company of Mary Davis, a family friend. Davis, taken up in the excitement of events, probably provided the harried woman little comfort as she recounted overheard threats to take Avery dead or alive and to "shoot him through the window" (Hallett 1833a, 163). More stalwart male hearts were likewise feeling the first tingle of growing fear. Statements that "the Courthouse should not hold him and the town should not hold him" (Hallett 1833b, 25) were inevitably taken by the worried Deputy Paul as threats of vigilante action, and accordingly he sent William Diman, who lived in another section of the house, for aid.

Diman rushed directly to the office of Nathaniel Bullock, where he burst in, drenched in the perspiration of exertion and excitement, shouting that the Fall River people were in town (Hallett 1833a, 161). It was probably in the company of Harvey Harnden, who had not yet left his office, that Bullock made his way back toward Avery's besieged home. Calling to all the men he saw to join him, Bullock hoped to assemble a force large enough to intimidate the mob his imagination and Diman's frenzied report had conjured. Unfortunately, few men were in the street, and even fewer were willing to risk life or limb to defend Bristol's sovereign right to the prisoner (Hallett 1833a, 161). Arriving at the scene without the desired reinforcements, Bullock discovered the degree to which discretion makes up valor, remaining inconspicuously at the edges of the gathering. His surveillance and Deputy Paul's concern were by and large unnecessary. Soon the *King Philip's* hour-and-a-half layover in Bristol was completed (Hallet 1833a, 77), the boarding bell tolled, and the crowd melted away. Much to the townspeople's relief, civil war had not broken out, and damages consisted of frayed nerves rather than broken heads.

The Christmas invasion was generally a failure in that Avery was not taken back to Tiverton for examination and the legal groundwork for such an operation was not established. The optimistic report of the *Fall River Weekly Recorder*, on the following day, that Avery would soon "be brought before the authorities of Tiverton for examination" (*Fall River Weekly Recorder*, 26 December 1832) was premature. When William Staples formally presented the idea of extradition in court on Wednesday, his motion was denied (*Republican Herald*, 29 December 1832). Howe had decided to keep the examination in Bristol. Elihu Hicks later seemed to confirm the right of the Bristol magistrates to consider the case when he handed over his papers to Justice Howe (Hallett 1833a, 29). The original warrant, with all its imperfections, was to be honored. Disappointed and angry, many Fall River men wondered if "the glorious uncertainty of the law" (*Republican Herald*, 5 January 1833) was but another name for total confusion.

However, even if the committee's goals were not reached, at least it had demonstrated its ability to organize a relatively large group and to execute a well-directed campaign. It had also demonstrated its ability to spend money, something that had not been the subject of adequate preparation. On December 31 a second meeting was held, probably in the lyceum, and probably at the instigation of the committee of investigation (Harnden 1833a, 35). Hezekiah Battelle, a Fall River lawyer and justice of the peace (Fowler 1841, 63), was called to the chair. The meeting was essentially about the means to support the prosecution. A subscription was decided upon, and a paper was circulated for the signatures of those who would be willing to bear some part of the cost (Harnden 1833a, 35). This subscription list was still a matter of concern almost two years later. Although most payments had been made by October 1834, the names of delinquent subscribers were kept by the Fall River Bank's cashier, who hoped to have the final payments made as soon as possible (*Fall River Monitor*, 4, 11, 18 October 1834).

By Wednesday, December 26, the confusion surrounding the discovery of the body and the identification of the suspected murderer was resolved. Avery's examination in Bristol, rather than in the openly hostile community of Tiverton, was assured. His fellow Methodist ministers had rallied to his cause and were engaged in a defense effort that would ultimately involve the entire New England Conference of the Methodist Episcopal church. Fall River had responded to the death of one of its heretofore anonymous mill workers by mobilizing its economic resources and its best talent in an effort to gain conviction. Everyone who assembled in Bristol's courthouse to observe the course of Avery's examination was aware that the hearing rapidly became a jousting ground over which the Methodist church contended with the industrial community of Fall River. By what means, they must have wondered, did the Reverend Ephraim Avery become the cornerstone of New England Methodism? By what means did Sarah Cornell, an obscure weaver, become the symbol of the industrial community's rise or fall? The spectators at Bristol, like the thousands who would debate Avery's case in every state of the Union during the next year, wanted to see justice done, to understand why the factions asserting Avery's innocence or guilt aligned themselves as they did, and, perhaps above all, to know through what history this mill girl had come to an early grave and this minister had moved within sight of the hangman's noose.

2. Beginning a Life in the Mills

S*arah Maria Cornell*, whose violent death on a winter-bound hill-side catapulted her into public consciousness, was born on May 3, 1802. Although newspaper reports circulated in 1833 dramatically placed the event at the home of her maternal grandfather in Norwich, Connecticut, where her father had deserted his children and pregnant wife (*New-Hampshire Sentinel*, 20 June 1833), it is more likely that she was born in Rupert, Vermont, where her parents were living out the last days of an unhappy marriage (Williams 1833, 76; Hallett 1833a, 79). In either case, Sarah was the last child of a short-lived union that began in defiance of parental authority and ended in desertion and poverty.

Her mother, Lucretia, was the daughter of Christopher Leffingwell, Connecticut's first paper manufacturer and the affluent descendant of one of the state's premier families. Her future in the genteel society of Connecticut's elite was assured by birth, but she impulsively threw it away when she fell disastrously in love with James Cornell, an adventuresome paper maker in her father's employ. A charming and handsome fortune hunter, Cornell apparently saw his chance not in industry but in matrimony. Against her father's strenuous objections, Lucretia accepted Cornell's attention, and the pair made plans for marriage. Whether the ceremony took place in secret or with her father's reluctant permission, Cornell soon justified his disgusted father-in-law's suspicions by repeatedly prevailing upon his wife to draw large sums from her father's holdings (Williams 1833, 78). Leffingwell tolerated the situation until he decided that Lucretia had used up her rightful share of his fortune, then steadfastly refused to advance another cent. Cornell, who had been living in Vermont (according to some accounts, he had taken his family west), apparently moved to Providence, perhaps to look for work, and finally deserted his wife at her father's doorstep. It was believed that he had fled into the Ohio wilderness, but he was never again heard from.

Lucretia could expect little sympathy or financial consolation from a father whose advice she had ignored. Consequently, the financial disaster precipitated by Cornell's desertion resulted in the dispersal of her three children. Sarah's brother, James, was brought up by relatives; probably apprenticed to a mercantile house, he became a merchant trading in New Orleans. Her sister Lucretia, also taken in by relatives, ultimately married Grindall Rawson, a tailor from Woodstock, Connecticut, who later became a central figure in the religious and educational community of that rural town (Bowen 1926, 277, 395). Sarah, who was an infant at the time her father left, remained with her mother until she was eleven; then she was taken in by her mother's sister Joanna, who had by that time married Charles Lathrop and was living in Norwich.

When Christopher Leffingwell died in 1810, the financial limitations under which Lucretia Cornell labored might have been lifted by the acquisition of her share of his thirty-thousand-dollar estate. In 1809, however, Leffingwell had drawn up a will in which he provided Lucretia with only fifteen hundred dollars—to be held in trust by her brother William (Leffingwell 1811). The interest from this sum, which was ultimately invested in thirteen shares in the Derby Bank, would be sufficient to ward off starvation, but only with industry and frugality. The balance of the estate was divided among Leffingwell's living children—Christopher, William, Elizabeth, Joanna, and Jerusha—and the children of his dead daughter Lydia. The will ensured that while Lucretia would not be destitute, she would remain the poorest of Leffingwell's children, continually dependent on the others for the support denied her by a vagrant husband and a stern father. Thus it was inevitable, and perhaps Leffingwell's plan, that Sarah would not be raised at home.

After four years with Mrs. Lathrop, Sarah was apprenticed to a tailor in Norwich with whom she stayed through the period of her indenture from November 1818 to October 1820 (Williams 1833, 119). During the time in which Sarah was first removed from the control of her maternal relatives, she underwent a religious conversion, joined the church of the Reverend David Austin, a Calvinist Congregationalist (Williams 1833, 79), and remained a member in good standing for two years. One of Sarah's later acquaintances, Lucy Davol, reported that Sarah had admitted having been "bad" since the age of fifteen (Hallett 1833a, 118). If true, and if Sarah's confession referred, as Lucy implied, to her sexual conduct, then Sarah's early removal from the protection of her home and her immediate moral fall were an eloquent warning to New England mothers who thought to send their daughters alone into the commercial world. If Sarah did succumb to the designs of a predatory man, it would help to explain her sudden interest in Rev. Austin's church, where she could both expunge her sin and gain protection from further advances.

In November 1820, with her apprenticeship completed, Sarah moved to Bozrahville, a few miles outside Norwich, where she lived with her mother and worked as a tailor (Williams 1833, 78). She soon moved from her mother's house to that of Deacon Abel, where she boarded throughout the winter, and then to David L. Dodge's, between Bozrahville and Goshen, and within four miles of her mother (Williams 1833, 120). At Dodge's Sarah enjoyed the circumstance of being the only tailor within two miles in any direction. Having succeeded in her trade and having had a steady relationship with the Congregational church, Sarah wrote to her sister, "I desire to be thankful to God for placing me in so pleasant a situation" (Williams 1833, 120).

Barely nineteen years old and yet untroubled, Sarah was impressed by the death of a black servant who resided with Abel's family in Bozrahville. The man, who had worked for Abel twenty years and who "never associated with any but respectable people, as there was but one other negro in the place" (Williams 1833, 120), died after what had seemed an unalarming illness. Reflecting on his sudden death, Sarah wrote: "Sometimes I think *why am I spared* perhaps it is to commit more sin, perhaps for some usefulness. sometimes I think I am no worse than others what have I to fear but God says be ye also ready for ye know not what hour your Lord will come" (Williams 1833, 121).

The events of 1822 and 1823, during which time Sarah earned a reputation as a thief and entered factory work for the first time,

are not completely clear. According to Catharine Williams, a celebrated Rhode Island author who enthusiastically took up Sarah's
cause after her death and interviewed many of her relatives and
acquaintances, the girl's fall began when her mother took her to
Providence to visit her sister, Lucretia, whom she had not seen in
several years. Accustomed to a relatively bucolic existence in Bozrahville and Norwich, Sarah, naturally beautiful and painfully embarrassed by her rustic wardrobe, was unable to cope with the
temptations of urban life; thus she resorted to shoplifting to acquire
the beguiling fashions displayed in store windows. Caught almost
immediately, Sarah returned some goods while her relatives paid
for others (Williams 1833, 130). Charles Hodges, then a clerk in
John R. Carpenter's store, where Sarah stole goods, remembered
that when she was confronted with the deed "she would one moment confess, and be in tears, and the next would laugh" (Hallett
1833a, 131). Although no formal charges had been made, the news
of Sarah's fall from respectability spread rapidly through Providence. Barred from polite society, including that of her relatives,
she was forced to return to Bozrahville, where she hoped to resume
employment as a tailor. Unfortunately, her reputation had preceded
her, and her job was quickly lost. Wandering from place to place,
always viewed with suspicion as a girl who had been "talked about,"
Sarah quit her trade and entered a cotton factory.

In the mill, according to Williams, she found no relief from the
suspicion that surrounded her. Fleeing from the hardened stares
of women in the weaving room, she once again tried her original
profession, but with no more success than before. Finally, hounded
by rumors that attacked her chastity as well as her honesty, she
abandoned the scene of her discomfort and went to Slatersville
where, unknown, she could work in the mills in peace (Williams
1833, 82–84).

While Williams's account explains Sarah's transition to factory
labor, her wandering lifestyle, and her unenviable moral reputation, the story conflicts with Sarah's letters (published in Williams's
book) and testimony given at Avery's trial. In fact, by May 1822, well
before her trip to Providence and her career as a shoplifter, Sarah
had left tailoring in Bozrahville and taken up employment in a
cotton mill in Killingly, Connecticut. The reason for her change
from tailoring to the new occupation of weaver is not recorded.
Williams related a story not directly associated to any specific point
in Sarah's life, but which might provide a clue. Two elderly brothers

who employed Sarah as a tailor were said to have wanted to test her virtue. When both had been firmly rejected, the brothers, fearing what Sarah might reveal to their wives, dismissed her, explaining to their customers that "she was rather too fond of young men" (Williams 1833, 96). Another employee of the two brothers supposedly reported the episode to Williams, adding that "he did not know what proof they had of her being fond of *young men*, except that she did not like *old ones*" (Williams 1833, 96). While probably apocryphal, the story points out a major benefit of factory labor, which took a young single woman out of individual contact with male employers and protected her in the strictly maintained morality of the spinning or weaving room.

Not all Sarah's contemporaries believed that the morals of factory girls were superior to those of their sisters who worked as domestics under the private control of potentially lecherous employers. Her sister Lucretia apparently voiced the most strident opposition to Sarah's new occupation. Responding to what must have been a distressing letter demanding that she leave the factory at once and return to decent society in Norwich, Sarah firmly admonished her haughty sister:

> I received a letter from you soon after I came to this place, in which you murmured at my coming to the factory to work; but I do not consider myself bound to go into all sorts of company because I live near them. I never kept any but good company yet, and if I get into bad it is owing to ignorance.
>
> You wrote me you thought I had better return to Norwich as soon as possible, and that you should not come to Killingly as long as I staid at this factory. You must remember that your pride must have a fall. I am not too proud to get a living in any situation in which it pleases God to place me.
>
> If you do not come to Killingly until I go to Norwich you may not come this year, and I assure you I will never come to Providence first (Williams 1833, 122–23).

Lucretia probably relented, because Sarah was in Providence that winter.

Charles Hodges remembered that his transactions with Sarah were in November 1822, when he trusted her for a silk dress (Hildreth 1833, 71). It was not until January 1823 that the purchase on credit became a theft; in that month Hodges or his employer discovered that Sarah had left town without settling her bill. Traveling to Pawtucket after her, they demanded payment or the return of their unused goods. Samuel Richmond, another Providence merchant, apparently had the same experience when he trusted her for a bonnet and a shawl (Hallett 1833a, 129). Obviously, Sarah felt she needed a complete new outfit that winter, but for what?

The information from Hodges is particularly revealing because it implies that Sarah's departure from Providence was the cause of her reputation as a thief, and not the other way around. Clearly there must have been some other explanation for her sudden exit, but judging from her subsequent behavior it must have been equally unfortunate. After leaving her mother and sister, Sarah traveled the short distance to North Providence where she obtained employment in the factories of Daniel W. Lyman. Taking the assumed name of Maria Snow, she boarded first at the house of Mrs. Hathaway (Hallett 1833a, 140), and then with Mrs. Ide. She reportedly told both families that she had lost her mother and even went as far as to purchase a mourning suit (Drury 1833, 39; Hallett 1833a, 142). Her tenure at Mrs. Ide's house came to an abrupt end when a male visitor from Providence—probably Charles Hodges come to "Pawtucket" to retrieve his goods—exposed her deception (Drury 1833, 39–40). It is easy to understand the girl's confusion and embarrassment, which Hodges later callously attributed to a deranged mentality. Mrs. Ide, however, was not understanding; suspecting the worst of a young woman living under an assumed name, she turned Sarah out of her house. When neighbors refused to take her in, Sarah was forced to leave the community.

The source of Sarah's distressed flight from Providence, in which she changed her name and claimed to have lost her mother, is probably also the source of the awkward lie about the girl's Providence adventure published in Williams's account. In the winter of 1822–23 Sarah was almost certainly competing with her sister for the attention of Grindall Rawson (Marshall and Brown 1833, 96). Stories that Sarah sought the young tailor's interest and resented her sister's ultimate success, which were stoutly denied by the prosecution in Avery's trial, gain considerable support from Sarah's fortuitous residence in Providence at the time of the courtship, her sudden desire for a new and unaffordable outfit, and her apparent banishment from the family for the next two years. In the light of Avery's trial, in which the defense sought to demonstrate that Sarah was a hardened sexual criminal, Catharine Williams's attempt to make much of—and then belittle—an economic crime, which was not really a theft, makes sense. Only in that way could she hope to submerge the more damning social crime that lay beneath it. In the long run, Williams's deception distorted the structure of the girl's life relatively little. By January 1823, her "theft" had caught up with her, forced her out of North Providence, and lowered her into a twilight world of social suspicion from which she could never quite emerge.

From North Providence, Sarah moved to Jewett City, Connecticut, just a few miles north of her home in Norwich. There she was employed in a weaving room overseen by Thaddeus Bruce (Marshall and Brown 1833, 91). Bruce, to whom Sarah asserted that she was still a member of the Congregational Church in "Bosworth," was concerned about her character after he saw her leave a building late in the evening accompanied by a young man. While Sarah never admitted any wrongdoing, neither did she take steps to correct the appearance of it. As a result, she was dismissed from the factory after a tenure of about three months.

It was probably in the spring of 1823 that Sarah moved to Slatersville, Rhode Island, where she found employment in the factory of Almy, Brown, and Slater, a secure home, and an apparent end to her troubles. After almost two years of steady employment that produced "a comfortable living, with economy and prudence" (Williams 1833, 124), early in 1825 Sarah felt that she had overcome her earlier difficulties and that her family might finally be willing to forgive her transgressions. The birth of Lucretia's first son, Edward, could be expected both to cement the Rawsons' marriage and to make the new mother receptive to the overtures of her repentent competitor. Offering cautious congratulations to her sister for her marital success, Sarah sought the chance to reenter the security of the family circle. In a letter to her mother and sister, she wrote:

> *While I am writing perhaps you have long since forgotten you have a daughter Maria—but stop dear mother, I am still your daughter and Lucretia's only sister. God in his mercy has shown me the depravity of my own wicked heart—and has I humbly trust, called me back from whence I had wandered.*
>
> *I want to see Mother and if any of you desire to see me—write and let me know and I will try to come and spend a few days with you before long—but whether I ever see you again or not, I want you should*

forgive me and bury what is past in oblivion and I hope my future good conduct may reward you (Williams 1833, 124–26).

The attempt to bring about a reconciliation was a success, and Sarah enjoyed a pleasant visit at her sister's home in the summer of 1825.

Sarah's social regeneration at Slatersville was not the simple product of steady employment. While Sarah hoped for ultimate readmission to her family, she was working toward a more important absolution. Though she was painfully aware that her earlier sins had "caused Jesus to open his wounds afresh" (Williams 1833, 124), she wrote serenely to her sister: "I feel that I have an evidence within my own soul that God has forgiven me, and I have an unshaken trust in God that I would not part with for ten thousand worlds. . . . I have enjoyed some precious seasons in this place" (Williams 1833, 125). Such spiritual assurance in a socially convicted sinner would have been impossible under the dour Calvinism of Sarah's original Congregationalist faith, but was easily attainable among the Methodists she met in Slatersville. Like many of her contemporaries, Sarah was moved and heartened by the message of a series of dynamic Methodist missionaries that preached in her neighborhood. "Elder Tailor preaches here half the time," she wrote to her sister in 1825; "he is a powerful preacher, reformation follows him, wherever he goes he draws about as many hearers as ever John N. Maffitt did" (Williams 1833, 127).

The two preachers she mentioned, whose efforts figured prominently in her conversion to Methodism, were dramatic characters who personally typified the message of evangelical Methodism in New England. "Elder Tailor" was the Reverend Edward T. Taylor who later gained national fame as the sailor preacher of Boston. A born orator, Taylor as a child reportedly impressed his elders in Richmond, Virginia, by the power and eloquence of the eulogies he preached to neighborhood slave children on the deaths of their kittens and chickens (Daniels 1887, 563). After a career as a sailor, during which—Methodist and nautical folklore combine to assert—he learned to outshout a hurricane, Taylor took up residence in Saugus, Massachusetts, where a wealthy Methodist recognized his innate oratorical abilities and provided both the encouragement and the financial backing necessary to train him for the pulpit. Taylor was admitted to the New England Conference of the Methodist Episcopal church in 1819 and remained a circuit preacher until he was appointed chaplain to the seamen, under the auspices of the Boston Port Society, in 1829 (Daniels 1887, 565). His disdain for the rules of grammar, his extemporaneous style, and his sailor's vocabulary made him an instant success among working-class people, who found in him a man after their own hearts.

Taylor's appeal to Sarah Cornell almost certainly transcended his earthy diction and boisterous style. A crusader for spiritual democracy, Taylor was a loudly self-proclaimed soldier in the attack on the doctrine of salvation of the elect, which was basic to Sarah's own Calvinist church. For Sarah, there could be little spiritual comfort in a society of saints from which she, by her transgressions, was barred. In Taylor's sermons—in the doctrine of Methodism—she found the basis for reestablishing her feelings of self-worth. The Methodists, who were enthusiasts demanding an emotional conversion experience, believed in the Arminian concept of the salvation of all souls through faith in Jesus Christ (Scudder 1870, 531). Among them, the fallen sinner could rise again. Although this doctrine brought criticism down on them as a sect that actually encouraged backsliding, it is easy to see its appeal to an unfortunate woman who had recently been turned out of genteel Calvinist society for a relatively minor infraction. Combined with an energetic and noisy social style—one that suited Sarah's ardent disposition—the doctrine of universal salvation through faith must have played an important part in her decision in 1825 to renounce her Congregationalist associations and join the Methodist meeting at Slatersville.

John N. Maffitt, whom Sarah had heard preach prior to Taylor, and whom she would make special trips to Boston to hear in 1827, was another of the New England Conference's unlikely, flamboyant preachers. Born in Dublin and educated as a tailor (an obvious attraction to Sarah), Maffitt immigrated to the United States where he professed religion and attached himself to the Methodist church. Accepted on trial by the New England Conference in 1822 (the same year as Ephraim Avery), Maffitt was almost immediately in trouble because of his flippant style and excessive gallantry to the ladies (True and Green 1823). Never accused of originality or philosophical depth, Maffitt owed his success in New England— and later in the nation's capital—to his physical charm, his oratory style, and his uncanny ability to make the hearts of otherwise stable women beat a little faster.

The foppish Maffitt and the earthy Taylor might be worlds

apart in personality, but they presented Sarah with a consistent and enticing picture. Methodist meetings obviously provided an entertaining spectacle not to be found in more staid congregations. Whether in the form of the hulking Taylor or the dandy Maffitt, the preacher, elevated only slightly above the common stock from which both he and his flock came, was tangibly human and made church attendance physically as well as spiritually gratifying. Further, both men were generally uneducated. The religion they professed and preached was one of faith and feeling, something that their uneducated followers could understand and experience. While the Methodist church organized itself on an episcopal model, its practices—particularly the camp meetings that would become a major part of Sarah's life—recognized intimate contact between divinity and the individual through faith, not education or social position.

The relatively high status of women among the Methodists must also have contributed to Sarah's determination to convert. John Wesley himself had led the way toward the practices of the Apostolic church by allowing women to become religious teachers and "even to speak in an assembly of men" (Scudder 1870, 490). He further scandalized some of his contemporaries by creating exclusively female classes with female class leaders and supervisors; although none of the classes to which Sarah belonged ever fell into this category, the example of others and the possibility of female elevation to positions of authority must have appealed to her. As the church developed in Europe and America, women were encouraged to speak in class meetings as preparation for more demanding oratory in love feasts and social prayer meetings, where female exhortation became common (Scudder 1870, 491). Although still subordinate to an exclusively male ministry, Methodist women were not faced with the dull prospect of an unrelentingly passive role in organized religion. In her association with the church, Sarah apparently took advantage of opportunities for public discourse. It was later reported that Sarah boasted that she "could pray and exhort, as well as any of them" (Hallett 1833a, 110) and eventually became a leading member of the classes at Lowell because of her demonstrated talent (Hallett 1833a, 135–36).

Sarah's trip to visit her sister in the summer of 1825 was combined with her first experience at a Methodist camp meeting, this one held at Woodstock, Connecticut. Her brother-in-law, Grindall Rawson, generally found the meetings foolish, and although he

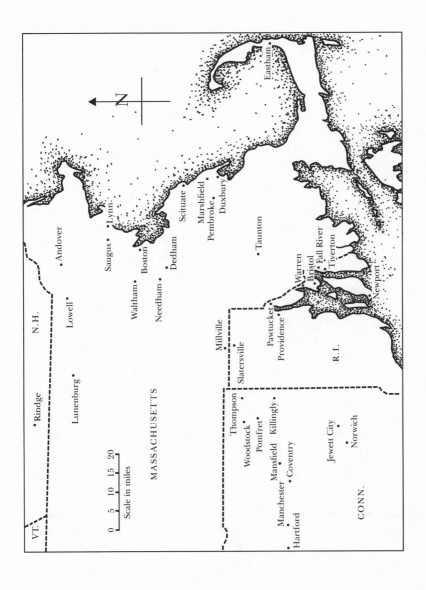

4. Map showing primary locations in the lives of Sarah Cornell and Ephraim Avery.

aided Sarah in attending them, he did not hesitate to voice his opinion (Williams 1833, 141). Sarah, however, was not to be dissuaded, and her experience at Woodstock was followed by attendance at camp meetings throughout New England every year—with one probable exception—for the rest of her life.

Although they are often considered primarily a frontier phenomenon, camp meetings had become by 1825 a central feature in the yearly cycle of New England Methodism. By June of each year, the *Zion's Herald*, a Boston newspaper published under the auspices of the New England Conference, would begin to announce camp meetings to be held that summer. While most meetings seemed to be held in July and August, the season extended from June through September. By July the *Herald* would fill its columns with reports of the successful camp meetings thus far completed. These testimonials, eagerly awaited by those who had taken part in the camp experience, were published well into the winter months and filled with news of powerful preaching and saved souls:

> The meeting was attended by five travelling and seven local preachers, who delivered their discourses in the power and demonstration of the spirit; and Jehovah, who is everlasting strength, manifested his power in the conviction and conversion of souls, in arousing the slumbering sinner to a sense of his guilt and danger, and in encouraging the believer to "press towards the mark of the prize of his high calling" (*Zion's Herald*, 26 October 1825).

Meetings usually lasted four days, with days added at the beginning and end for arrival and departure. Their sylvan setting and circles of tent dwellings had multiple meanings to their members. Reminiscent of the camps of Israel wandering through the wilderness, Methodist camp meetings were a conscious attempt to recapture the pristine spiritual intensity of the roots of Christianity. The division of the congregation into residential tents by geographic origin paralleled the tribal organization of the migrating Israelites. The very impermanence of the physical community (although the same camp sites were used for years) was a constant reminder of man's temporary residence on earth. Sarah explained this Methodist concept of worldly impermanence to her sister when she wrote, "I am with them in sentiment believing with the Apostle that we should be as strangers and pilgrims having no continuing city or abiding place, but seek one to come" (Williams 1833, 138). The Methodist belief that promoted participation in camp meetings

was equally useful in justifying the migratory lifestyle of mill operatives, for whom market fluctuations, low water, fires, and labor disputes made long-term residence in any one location unlikely.

The symbolic significance of a camp in the wilderness was combined with a sort of boot-camp psychology that asserted, with
reason, that spiritual conversion was more easily attained in an environment in which individuals were removed from all contact with
their usual lives. Even detractors, who found the camp meetings
more ridiculous than sublime, were impressed by the psychological
impact of the settings selected by the Methodists. "I can aver,"
wrote one critic, "that I have never seen a Methodist encampment
but in a situation well adapted to inspire feelings of awe and melancholy" (*New England Galaxy*, 29 August 1823). The Methodists
themselves, ignoring charges that conversions accomplished in ar-
tificial isolation could not withstand a return to daily life, appealed
to the Bible for justification:

> Having left their worldly concerns behind them for a season, and
> having retired into the shades of wilderness—they have a better
> opportunity to call to remembrance their sins and transgres-
> sions—to meditate upon the merciful forbearance and loving
> kindness of Jehovah—and to "dedicate their souls and bodies
> anew to Him and his service, in a holy, righteous and godly life."
> In the stillness of the forest and in the retirement of nature, it is
> well known, from experience, that religious discourses often
> make the most lasting impression upon the human heart. And
> indeed, our blessed Savior, availing himself of this circumstance,
> "*went up into a mountain*," where he preached that celebrated ser-
> mon recorded by St. Matthew (*Zion's Herald*, 25 August 1824).

Sarah's discovery of Methodism, with its offer of salvation for
the fallen and its community that would accept a repentent sinner,
made her experience in Slatersville initially positive. With work
steady and social connections more secure than she had known recently among her own kinsmen, Sarah hoped to spend her life employed at Slater's mill (Williams 1833, 138).

In December 1825, after having been out of the mill a week
due to illness and one Saturday to attend a Methodist quarterly
meeting, Sarah wrote to her mother that she could not visit home
because her overseer did not want her to take additional time away
from the factory. Her concern for her job, while commendable, was
soon made meaningless. On the afternoon of February 1, 1826, the
heating ducts of Slater's mill overheated and set the building on

fire. The factory, on which there was no insurance, was completely destroyed (*Independent Chronicle*, 4 February 1826), and Sarah was left without employment for the period in which the mill would be rebuilt.

Unwilling to leave Slatersville, where she had established social ties, Sarah moved to the nearby Branch Factory. With the distance to Slatersville negligible, she maintained her membership in the Slatersville meeting. Her employment at Branch Factory continued until mid-July, when low water and the scarcity of materials made weaving impossible (Williams 1833, 129). Still looking forward to an ultimate return to Slatersville, Sarah was forced to move farther away, this time to Millville (also called Mendon Mills), just across the Massachusetts border, where she was employed weaving blue satinet. Although working with wool did not appeal to most cotton weavers, Sarah took the job happily, knowing it would be temporary—until Slater's mill was completed—and would keep her within walking distance of the Slatersville Methodist meeting, upon which she depended for social interaction.

By the summer of 1826 her relationship with the Methodists was deteriorating. Sarah apparently had been admonished by William Holmes, her class leader in the church, for lewd behavior after reports were circulated that she called for lodgings at a local tavern in the company of a young man (Hallett 1833a, 127). Holmes, whose position required him to be well informed about her moral condition and "to advise, reprove, comfort, or exhort, as occasion may require" (Winebrenner 1849, 359), apparently let the matter drop at that point, hoping for the best.

Unfortunately, the best did not occur. At the end of August, Sarah joined a group of Methodist friends from Mendon Mills (Williams 1833, 129) and attended her second camp meeting, once again at Woodstock, where she was seen leaving the grounds with a young man (Hallett 1833a, 128). When she returned to the Slatersville Methodist meeting she was faced with both the old charge of lewdness and a new one of walking out with a nonprofessor.

Her position was made even more precarious by the arrival of the Bruces from Jewett City, where Sarah had used the name of Maria Cornell; at Slatersville and Mendon Mills she was known as Maria Snow. With the arrival of Thaddeus and Zilpah Bruce, Sarah employed the confusing tactic of using both names to avoid charges of using a pseudonym to escape her reputation (Marshall and Brown 1833, 93). Her ploy solved nothing; suspicious of a girl with multiple names, the Methodists brought her to church trial. The charges against her were not recorded in church records (Hallett 1833a, 128), and thus their exact nature remains uncertain. Zilpah Bruce, whose language was colorful, reported that Sarah told her of two "acquisitions brought agin her" (Hallett 1833a, 127): lewdness and walking out at a camp meeting. Holmes later remembered that she had been tried and expelled from the church for fornication and lying (Marshall and Brown 1833, 93).

The truth or falsity of the charges brought against Sarah is impossible to determine. Elizabeth Shumway, who boarded in the same house with Sarah at Slatersville, remembered that she had been despondent over her sister Lucretia's marriage to Grindall Rawson (Hallett 1833a, 122). Perhaps Sarah did, then, allow her next suitor excessive liberties in the hope that he would not be taken from her "by art and strategem" (Hallett 1833a, 122). The charge that she walked out of the Woodstock camp meeting with a nonprofessor must be seen in light of the fact that the meeting was near the homes of her mother, sister, and brother-in-law. That Sarah found an acquaintance in a community she had visited before is not surprising. The charge of lying, if it resulted from her use of the name Snow, would be true but hardly damning of the character of a young woman trying to make a new life after losing family affection and peer acceptance.

After her expulsion from the meeting, Sarah left Slatersville temporarily; she probably spent the month following her church trial at the home of Joanna Lathrop, the aunt who had raised her in Norwich (Hallett 1833a, 127). Encountering a cold reception from her former Methodist friends upon her return, she remained in the area only a short time. In the winter of 1826–27, she left Mendon Mills for Providence, where she met her mother (Williams 1833, 130). Attempts to settle in the area were foiled by Thaddeus Bruce, who was instrumental in the Pawtucket Methodist meeting's rejection of Sarah's application for membership (Hallett 1833a, 127). Even without Bruce's intervenion, the Methodists of Pawtucket and other Providence suburbs were probably already aware of Sarah's bad reputation stemming from the shoplifting charges several years before.

Fortunately, Sarah had retained the friendship of Lydia Knight, a young woman who had worked with her in the mill at Slatersville, and probably also at Branch Factory and Mendon Mills. Lydia apparently wrote to her suggesting that they go together to seek employment at Lowell (Williams 1833, 86). Arrangements were made to meet in Dedham, Massachusetts. In the spring of 1827 their planned meeting took place, but instead of traveling to Lowell, they took employment in the Dedham Mills. The situation turned out to be less than satisfactory. There was no Methodist meeting in Dedham, and Sarah was forced to board in a house with sixty other women (Williams 1833, 131). Neither situation was to her liking. After four weeks in Dedham Sarah moved on to Dorchester, Massachusetts.

In Dorchester, Sarah fared much better. She was readmitted to the Methodist church, and being only four or five miles outside Boston, was again able to hear the sermons of John N. Maffitt, who was preaching at the Bromfield Lane Chapel (Williams 1833, 131). Perhaps because she had seen no one she knew other than Maffitt, Bartholomew "Oathman" (Otheman, another Methodist preacher), and Lydia Knight since she had left Pawtucket, Sarah could report to her mother that "the good people of Dorchester have treated me with the greatest respect" (Williams 1833, 132).

Although Sarah planned to go to the Ashford camp meeting in September 1827, and to visit her mother and sister on the trip (Williams 1833, 131), the expenses of the long journey proved too formidible, and she went instead to the closer Lunenburg, Massachusetts, meeting. A contingent of forty Boston Methodists, with Sarah among them, rented six private carriages for the trip (Williams 1833, 132). The camp opened on Tuesday, August 28, and services "from the stand" began the next day. Ultimately, over twenty ministers and as many as five thousand persons attended. Sarah ambitiously placed the number of converts at forty, but the minister who recounted the camp experience for the *Zion's Herald* (26 September 1827) more cautiously claimed twenty or thirty.

By anyone's reckoning, Lunenburg was a success. There observers were confronted with the sobering spectacle of "the brothers and sisters struggling as if in the pangs of death to be delivered from inbred corruption and saved from all sin. Oh, what lingering groans and heartrending agonies were extorted from the bosom!" (*Zion's Herald*, 26 September 1827). On Friday, the last day of the meeting, a mass celebration of communion with Christ was held. "A circle was formed in front of the tents, all around the ground, two, and in some places, three deep, all kneeling to receive from the hands of Zion's watchmen the sacred symbols, while the congregation were generally within" (*Zion's Herald*, 26 September

1827). Sarah found it an impressive scene and predicted that "it will no doubt be remembered by hundreds through time and eternity" (Williams 1833, 132).

In September Sarah toyed with the idea of leaving Dorchester and moving to Boston where she could find employment once again as a tailor (Williams 1833, 132). The planned move would have brought her into closer contact with the Boston Methodists with whom she had spent many pleasant hours. It never materialized, however, and Sarah spent the winter of 1827–28 working in the mill at Dorchester. The money was good, but the work was exhausting: Sarah ran four looms, weaving a total of 120 to 130 yards of cloth a day. At the rate of a half cent per yard, a good week could mean an income of about three and a half dollars. Unfortunately, Sarah did not have many good weeks. Her health was poor through the winter and she rarely worked a month without losing time to sickness (Williams 1833, 133).

With room and board relatively expensive in Dorchester and her income sporadic because of her poor health, Sarah must have had moments when her ability to support herself seemed doubtful. Her association with the Methodists was jeopardized when she was accused of resorting to theft as the easiest way out of her financial difficulties. The charges, while finally dropped due to lack of evidence (Hallett 1833a, 118), could have had no other effect than to reduce her security in the church at Dorchester. During this time she wrote to the Reverend David Austin, whose Congregational church she had abandoned several years before, but received no answer (Williams 1833, 135). It is possible that, fearing a second expulsion from the Methodists, she hoped to effect a reconciliation with her former pastor.

The combination of an exhausting work load and a tenuous position within the church eventually became too much for her to bear. Abandoning her problems in Dorchester, on May 17, 1828, she arrived at Lowell—her original destination—hopeful of finding employment and a home. In the fall of 1827 Lowell had boasted six cotton mills with 25,000 spindles and 150 looms. These establishments, employing twelve hundred people, each year turned over a million pounds of raw cotton into over five million yards of finished cloth. With three new mills under construction and the hope of adding two more each year through an indefinite future, the prospects of Lowell were bright (*New-Hampshire Sentinel*, 30 November 1827).

By modern standards the hours at Lowell were long. While at least one factory called its operatives to labor as early as three o'clock in the morning (*National Intelligencer*, 19 June 1833), the workday for most extended from five in the morning to after six in the evening, excluding a half hour for breakfast at seven and an hour for lunch at half past twelve. Viewed from a distance, the operatives seemed as regulated as the machines at which they labored. When the five o'clock bell rang in the morning, "The girls swarmed out from all the streets and avenues which led from their boarding houses, and directed their steps toward a single point, where they became concentrated in a dense mass, at the bridge leading to the entrance of a range of factories" (*National Intelligencer*, 19 June 1833). The scene was repeated with clockwork precision at seven o'clock and half past twelve, when the operatives went to and from their boarding houses for meals. Life for these workers, however, was not as grim as it might have been. Prior to management changes in the early 1840s, which made Lowell more profitable to its owners but less an experiment in democratic manufacturing, the operatives were paid by the piece rather than by time. As a result, the speed of their labor was, within limits, a matter of personal choice, and many could indulge in moments of leisure:

> We noticed groups of these factory girls, as they were in attendance upon the looms and spinning frames. They were in the freshness and bloom of life, generally about twenty years of age. Sometimes, when half a dozen in a neighborhood had put their looms in order, they would leave them to their own exact and rapid motions, and assemble in little squads at some favorite place of resort, where there was a looking glass, at which they arranged their curls or adjusted their combs, tattled all the gossip, and found out who was who and what was what (*National Intelligencer*, 19 June 1833).

If the image of Lowell in its first ten years as a utopian establishment is visionary, so too is the image of Lowell as the den of wage slavery. The city to which Sarah went in 1828 was an ambitious, hopeful community in which the process of molding industrial production to the needs and prejudices of Yankee America was well started.

Sarah used her certificate of membership in the Dorchester Methodist meeting to gain admittance to the Lowell church (Drury

5. Lowell, Massachusetts, the premier manufacturing village of New England, where Sarah Cornell first met Ephraim Avery. From John Warren Barber, *Historical Collections* . . . (Worchester: Warren Lazell, 1839).

1833, 45), then under the ministry of Abraham D. Merrill, at whose house she apparently found lodging (Hildreth 1833, 67). Her first employment, probably with the Merrimack Company, was uninterrupted until the following January. On the fifth of that month (the third, according to Sarah) Merrimack Number Two caught fire and burned to the ground, taking with it all its machinery and representing an uninsured loss of approximately one hundred thousand dollars (*New-Hampshire Sentinel*, 9 January 1829). Like the Slatersville mill that Sarah had watched burn in 1826, the Merrimack mill was the victim of its heating system (Williams 1833, 136). Fortunately, at a major manufacturing center like Lowell, where several corporations owned multiple mills, loss of a single factory did not mean loss of employment. After the fire Sarah moved to "the other side of the river, about half a mile distant" (Williams 1833, 136), and continued as a weaver until May.

In May 1829, shortly after writing to her sister that her reputation as a "moving planet" was largely undeserved, Sarah left Lowell and went to Boston, where she found employment as a tailor. Her explanation to her mother that the move was "on account of my health" (Williams 1833, 140) can probably be taken at face value since there is no evidence of discord in either her occupation or her relationship with the Methodists. In August she attended her first seaborne camp meeting, sailing with a group of Boston Methodists to Eastham on Cape Cod. Sarah described the expedition, which took eleven days, to her mother: "Had about twelve sermons preached on board, and one on the shore—dug clams—had plenty of good codfish, crackers and coffee—and on the eleventh day reached Boston wharf in better health and better spirits than when I left—having had but about six good hours sleep in ten nights" (Williams 1833, 140). Although she had been seasick on the voyage, Sarah was convinced that the salt air had done much to improve her general health (Williams 1833, 142).

In October, without explanation—which may have been unnecessary if she indeed had left Lowell only to escape the factories during the sweltering summer months—Sarah returned to Lowell and found a position in an Appleton Corporation mill. Her employment was short-lived; barely two months after she got the job, she negligently damaged her loom and was dismissed by overseer Brooks Shattuck (Hildreth 1833, 62).

If her career as a weaver was entering rocky times, her social life showed promise. The often-repeated claim that responsible

young businessmen sought wives among the mill girls of Lowell
seemed a reality. Sarah met a young man, a counting-house clerk
(Hallett 1833a, 110) with ambitions to rise in the mercantile world,
on the stagecoach from Boston to Lowell (Hallett 1833a, 117).
Sarah firmly believed that the courtship would end in marriage
(Hallett 1833a, 124), but others were not so certain; by June, stories
that could damage her reputation were beginning to circulate in
Lowell. Some said that on the Sunday after their chance meeting,
Sarah and her admirer rode to a tavern in Andover where he plied
her with alcohol (Marshall and Brown 1833, 80). Others claimed
that they made regular trips to a tavern in Belvidere (Hallett 1833a,
117) or held their assignations in his counting room after hours
(Marshall and Brown 1833, 87). Whatever the truth in these stories,
by June Sarah had broken up with the young man and all hope
of marriage had ended. The separation was not amiable because
Sarah claimed that the rumors about her chastity were nothing
more than spiteful reports raised by a disappointed and vengeful
suitor (Hallett 1833a, 129).

In fact, the truth of the accusations was immaterial; their very
existence made her position in Lowell precarious. It is probable
that her employment in the mills was terminated, or at least seriously threatened, because of them. Needing employment as well as
security from slanderous gossip, in July Sarah sought to solve both
problems by applying for a position as a domestic in the household
of Lowell's newly arrived Methodist minister, Ephraim Kingsbury
Avery.

3. Ending a Life in the Mills

Under the circumstances, it made sense for Sarah Cornell to seek entry into Ephraim Avery's domestic circle; employment by the minister would be both a testimonial to her innocence and a pledge of her continued good behavior. However sensible her reasoning, she encountered difficulty almost immediately. Avery later asserted that because his wife did not like her looks she was never hired (Avery 1834, 11). He was contradicted by Catharine Williams, who claimed that she was employed for about a week, until Avery's excessive attention to his attractive servant goaded his normally docile wife into demanding Sarah's departure (Williams 1833, 90). The Reverend Samuel Drake, one of Avery's associates, confirmed the basic fact of Williams's version under oath when he testified that Avery had informed him that Sarah had lived in his household at Lowell for a short period (Staples 1833, 16).

Whether she was initially denied employment by Avery or spent a week in his house before his wife (perhaps hearing rumors) demanded her removal, Sarah's plan failed. Undaunted, she approached another minister. Remembering the kindness of the Reverend Abraham D. Merrill, who had admitted her to his church and his home when she arrived in Lowell, Sarah followed the minister to his new assignment in Lynn, where she asked for a position in his household. Unfortunately, even her flattering explanation that she had come to Lynn for the "religious privilege" (Hildreth 1833, 74) of being in his flock was ineffective; Merrill had already employed a satisfactory girl (Hallett 1833a, 134). Merrill, however, unaware of Sarah's problems in Lowell, aided her in getting a position in a neighbor's house. Three weeks later her employer suspected her of theft and went to Merrill with the charge (Drury 1833, 45). Formal proceedings against her were forestalled only when the minister was informed that she had quietly left town.

Sarah's hope of entering the Lynn community before word of her character could come from Lowell had been dashed; ironically, she was faced with the problem of how best to salvage something from Lowell before word got back from Lynn. Her solution was to return to Lowell and request that Rev. Avery give her a certificate of good standing that would allow her to enter a church in another community. She attributed her haste in requesting the document to her intention to go to camp meeting—once more in Eastham on Cape Cod—and from there travel to Killingly, Connecticut, where she had begun her career as a mill girl. Her decision to attend the Eastham camp meeting was probably influenced by her learning from Lydia Pervere that Avery would be at a Weston camp meeting and thus be unable to monitor her movements (Hallett 1833a, 118). With no job waiting in Killingly, and only a poor prospect of getting one in a community from which she had fled in disgrace seven years before, Sarah probably had no intention of going to Connecticut. With the provisional certificate that Avery gave her as security, after the meeting at Eastham she quietly returned to Lowell.

It was clear that she could not go back to the employment she had enjoyed during her unfortunate romance, so she applied to Brooks Shattuck for a second chance in the Appleton weaving room (Hildreth 1833, 62). Shattuck agreed to take her back on the condition that she be more attentive to her work (Marshall and Brown 1833, 76); however, stories about her loose behavior soon came to Shattuck's attention, probably from the clerk of the Appleton Corporation (Drury 1833, 4). In the confrontation that followed, Sarah apparently admitted her relationship with her past suitor and declared a desire to reform, keep her job, and stay in Lowell. Shattuck, himself a Congregationalist, agreed to keep her on for a few days if she would use the time to see her minister, Ephraim Avery, and work out the problem with him (Hallett 1833a, 115). Sarah's position was thus once again made delicate; she could not seek an audience with Avery without demonstrating to him that she had not gone to Killingly as intended, yet she had to consult with him to keep her job. After several days in which she did nothing, Shattuck took it upon himself to visit Avery and inform him of the rumors and Sarah's confession. Probably told of this interview by Shattuck or a Methodist acquaintance, Sarah went to see Avery a few days later.

At first confessing only to improper behavior with a single suitor, under Avery's insistence that she had slept with two or more men she finally admitted to numerous affairs (Drury 1833, 4). These confessions, like the ones she wrote to Avery over the next year, were probably exaggerations designed to convince him of her total repentance and thus pave the way for her readmission to the Lowell meeting. Unfortunately, Avery did not respond to her confession with great sympathy. Instead, he advised her that a church trial would have to be held—one in which the outcome was made inevitable by her admission of guilt—and that, because of the delicate nature of her offense, it would be better if she left Lowell during the proceedings (Drury 1833, 4). He asked her for the certificate he had given for her proposed trip to Killingly, but, unwilling to surrender her passport into Methodist society elsewhere, Sarah told him it had been lost at Eastham (Drury 1833, 4).

Sarah's confession only guaranteed her a swift, efficient execution. She was dismissed from the Appleton mill as a woman of low character. Without any hope of being rehired in Lowell, she left the city on September 21, 1830, and traveled to Dover, New Hampshire. Two weeks later, Nathan Howard, Sarah's class leader at the Lowell meeting, took charges prepared by Avery and formally preferred them before the congregation (Hallett 1833a, 116). Although he mistakenly believed Sarah to be attending a camp meeting on Cape Cod at the time of the trial, he knew and approved of the minister's advice that she be absent during the embarrassing procedure of expulsion (Hallett 1833a, 116). By this time Avery had learned that Sarah still had his certificate in her possession; thus the charges included lying as well as fornication. The charge of theft that prompted Sarah to leave Dorchester—and the similar charge in Lynn—could have been added, but Nathan Howard judiciously decided that the question of theft was not germane (Marshall and Brown 1833, 75). Witnesses against her were Brooks Shattuck, who could relate the rumors he had heard and

Sarah's confession, and Ephraim Avery, whose testimony included Sarah's confessions to him and the reports of Doctor William Graves.

Graves, one of several physicians working in Lowell, had come to Avery ostensibly to discover Sarah's whereabouts to collect an unpaid bill. The story he told the minister, however, was more useful to Avery than any information the preacher could return. According to the doctor, Sarah had visited his office seven times between August 30 and September 20 (her last day in Lowell). Her disorder was diagnosed as a venereal disease (Hallett 1833a, 110), and when Graves refused to believe that a Christian woman could be so afflicted, she had shown him her certificate of good standing in the Methodist church, signed by Avery. The doctor and his patient debated over more than relative morality; when asked for payment Sarah was supposed to have named a young man, a clerk or messenger in a Lowell counting room, who was the author of her disorder and to whom the doctor should go for his fee. When Sarah left town the money was still uncollected, and Graves was prompted to visit not the clerk but the minister whose name he remembered from the certificate.

Sarah Cornell told a different version of the story, saying that at the Cape Cod camp meeting she had caught a cold that developed into "humours" demanding treatment (Hallett 1833a, 129). With her daytime hours filled, she was forced to go to the doctor's office late in the evening, alone, after attending class meeting. The doctor, reportedly delighted by this nocturnal visit from an attractive girl whose reputation for chastity was not good, "put his arm around her neck, and kissed her, and said that she was a pretty girl" (Hallett 1833a, 129). Sarah then admonished him, presenting her church certificate as proof that she was a Christian woman who could not be so abused. Convinced that she had cooled his ardor, Sarah made a subsequent visit to his office, at which time Graves was supposed to have locked the door, made further advances, and offered free medical treatment for physical favors (Hallett 1833a, 129). Furthermore, he threatened to report her as a victim of the "particular complaint" if she did not comply (Hallett 1833a, 126). Sarah escaped, steadfastly refused to pay the bill of this medical lecher, and left Lowell.

Without additional testimony from other sources, it is impossible to determine which version—if either—is true. Both would legitimately explain the future behavior of Sarah and the doctor. Sarah's refusal to pay Graves's bill might have stemmed either from the belief that her ungallant and unhealthy suitor was responsible for it or from unwillingness to pay for being treated indecently. Whichever account was closer to the truth, Graves's version was the one heard by Avery and, through Avery, by the Methodists; thus the minister's testimony of Sarah's confessions, and Shattuck's report of the rumors in the mill, seemed substantiated, and Sarah was formally expelled from the church.

Although Avery had advised her to visit her friends during the church proceedings against her, Sarah had chosen instead to move to the unfamiliar community of Dover, a major manufacturing center where jobs were plentiful and Sarah would be unknown. As a stranger bearing a certificate of good standing in the church, Sarah hoped to enter Methodist society, thus ignoring her expulsion from the meeting at Lowell.

Arriving at Dover in the last days of September 1830, Sarah took a position weaving in one of the factories that were reportedly so impressive as to be almost sufficient to convert South Carolinians, widely known for their hot-headed opposition to the protective tariff, into advocates of the "American System" (*New-Hampshire Sentinel*, 1 February 1828). Her admission into the local Methodist church did not go smoothly. The minister, John G. Dow, noticed the August date on her certificate of good standing and, thinking the time between issue and use excessively long, granted her only a trial membership (Hallett 1833a, 126). Shortly thereafter, Dow received a letter from Avery—who had heard of Sarah's use of the certificate—in which her expulsion from Lowell was reported and the history of the certificate explained. Avery noted that she was guilty of fornication, lying, and theft (the charge that Nathan Howard had considered unproven and irrelevant to the Lowell proceedings). Adding Dr. Graves's information that Sarah had the "foul disease," Avery ended his letter by saying, "Now if you want her in your church, you may have her" (Hallett 1833a, 126).

Dow, of course, was appalled by this information. When he next saw Sarah, she informed him of a letter she had received from Avery, demanding the return of the certificate and notifying her of her expulsion. Sarah's version of the story was not convincing to the justifiably suspicious minister, and Dow told her she could not expect to gain admittance to his church (Hallett 1833a, 126). Without

Methodist affiliation Sarah was uneasy in Dover, and her stay was correspondingly short. After only two months she moved again, this time to Somersworth, Great Falls, New Hampshire.

Only five miles from Dover, Somersworth, like Lowell, had been a wilderness in 1820. Its first mill was built in 1822, followed by another in 1824 and another in 1827. The industrial center that developed was, like Lowell, a social as well as an economic experiment.

> [A visitor in 1827 had] inquired particularly as to the morals of the hands, and was assured they were better than those of the same class, employed in agriculture and other pursuits. For their physical appearance I can speak for myself, for I saw nothing but rosy contentment and comfort; and I hesitate not to say, there are no farmer's daughters, in any country, who live better in every sense of the word. To such an extent do they carry this, that good dry paths are kept, in winter, from the boarding-houses to the mills; and, in very stormy weather, they are taken to and fro in carriages and sleighs. The curfew bell (as they call it) gives, at ten o'clock, the summons to retire for the night, and is strickly [*sic*] observed (*New-Hampshire Sentinel*, 7 December 1827).

Somersworth offered major employment possibilities, but, for Sarah, was haunted by the events of Lowell.

Sarah first boarded at the house of Timothy Paul, but left after confessing to him the story of her removal from Lowell (Hallett 1833a, 126). The circumstances of this confession are unclear, but it may have been related either to her continuing medical treatment or her attempts to join the local Methodist meeting (which inevitably brought her past history to local knowledge). When Sarah left Paul's house, she boarded with a Mr. Hovey or Honey, with whom she stayed for the remainder of her residence in Somersworth, from March 1 to August 7, 1831.

Noah Martin, a physician practicing in Somersworth, treated Sarah during the first two months of 1831, according to his later testimony at Avery's trial, for gonorrhea (Hallett 1833a, 112). Sarah visited his office six or seven times before treatment of the disease was successful. During this time, he said, she became increasingly loquacious and confided to him that her disorder had been the fault of her Lowell suitor. She blamed her inability to gain admittance to the Dover church and her difficulty with that in Somersworth on Ephraim Avery, whose knowledge of her disease had led him to advise both congregations to reject her (Hallett 1833a, 112).

The accuracy of Dr. Martin's account is questionable. What is certain, however, about Sarah's stay in Somersworth is that her religious situation seemed to be improving. Her relationship with Rev. Dow's church in Dover might have been irredeemable, but she found her prospects brightening in Somersworth. The Reverend George Storrs raised her hopes by telling her she could work her way back into Methodist fellowship. Church policy stipulated that while members expelled for an aggravated offense would not be re-admitted, those expelled on lesser charges could work their way back into the church by confessing their crimes and undergoing six months' probation (Drury 1833, 38).

Sarah was informed that by gaining certification of the Lowell congregation's forgiveness she could free herself of past sins that would otherwise keep her from beginning a new life in the church. Recognizing that the defiant or unrepentant could not be forgiven, Sarah confessed all charges in two letters to Avery (Drury 1833, 5), both of which were unanswered. Losing hope that Avery would send the needed certificate, she decided to return to Lowell in the first week of June 1831 to gain the forgiveness—and signatures—of her former Methodist brothers and sisters (Hallett 1833a, 124).

Armed with a prepared certificate stating that those who signed would have no objection to Sarah's admission to the church in Somersworth, Sarah made the rounds of Lowell, confronting embarrassed Methodists with her emotional confessions and her pleas that they sign her document. Nathan Howard met her at the meeting house; to his recollection her document stated that her acceptance would be contingent on future good behavior (Hallett 1833a, 116). Brooks Shattuck saw her at the same place, while Lucy Davol, Ellen Griggs, Lucy B. Howe, and Sarah Worthing met her at various other locations (Hallett 1833a, 116–18, 121). A few signed her certificate, but others did not. Sarah's confession to Sarah Worthing was typical; confessing to the charges brought against her at Lowell, Sarah went on to admit an unholy attachment to her brother-in-law, stealing, drunkenness, and—to emphasize her need for the signatures on the certificate—self-destructive impulses (Hallett 1833a, 120). Sarah Worthing's reaction was not what Sarah had anticipated; instead of sympathy, it expressed revulsion: "I considered her a very vile girl, and refused to sign her certificate. She called me a hard hearted girl, and wept bitterly" (Hallett 1833a, 121).

Sarah's luck with Avery was somewhat better. Although by ignoring her letters of confession he seemed unwilling to forgive her, when she accosted him in person he signed her certificate. His reason for signing was that George Storrs already knew of her behavior at Lowell and, since she had been under his ministry for several months, might have reason to believe her to be reclaimed (Avery 1834, 13). Adding the pious note that his forgiveness was nothing if not compounded by the forgiveness of the Lord, Avery sent her on her way.

If Sarah was elated by her apparent victory over her hard-hearted classmates in the church at Lowell, the feeling was not long-lived. The day after Avery gave his signature, he wrote to Rev. Storrs revoking it and asserting that "we should all of us here be opposed to her joining anywhere" (Melvill 1833, doc. no. 2). The basis for his opposition was that "alas! alas!! alas!!! this morning direct information was brought us that she had told a *known willful* falsehood—her standing being as it is I have not taken any pains to enquire into the cause" (Melvill 1833, doc. no. 2). Considering the impulses that led Sarah to Lowell, it is not surprising that some exaggeration, misinformation, or contradiction could be found in her statements. If nothing else, her cat-and-mouse game with the irate Dr. Graves during her short stay in Lowell must have given the Methodists new cause to wonder about her character. By unfortunate circumstance, Graves met Sarah at Mr. Howe's boardinghouse, where she was visiting Mary Anne Barnes; when Sarah refused to pay anything on her account, the doctor went to get the sheriff. By the time he returned, Sarah had vanished, wearing a borrowed calash and a plain dress she had been carrying with her (Hallett 1833a, 117). Her disguise was so successful that several times during the day she passed the doctor without being recognized (Hallett 1833a, 121).

Whatever the details of the accusations that Sarah had told a falsehood, the mere rumor was too much for her already blighted character. Upon receipt of Avery's letter, Rev. Storrs refused to admit Sarah to his church (Storrs 1833). He further barred her from semipublic church celebrations, such as the love feast (Drury 1833, 63), a communion with bread and water in which members and selected nonmembers celebrated Christian brotherhood and recounted the edifying stories of their conversions (Robbins 1824,

6. Ephraim Avery's letter to George Storrs revoking his signature on Sarah Cornell's certificate of forgiveness. Avery's "alas! alas!! alas!!!" was widely parodied by his critics. From David Melvill, *A Fac-simile of the Letters Produced at the Trial of the Rev. Ephraim K. Avery* (Boston: Pendleton's Lithography, 1833).

168). The product of Sarah's attempt to rejoin the church was ultimately only her public admission of a series of crimes that she had
denied before and would deny again. Caught in a vise between the
Methodist requirement that she confess her crimes to gain forgiveness and the general abhorrence with which her confessions were
greeted, Sarah found church membership in Somersworth just as
impossible as it had been in Dover. Sometime during summer of
1831, probably shortly after her trip to Lowell, Sarah left Somersworth and moved to Waltham, Massachusetts, where she boarded
in three houses in as many weeks; unable to find comfortable lodging, she left (Hallett 1833a, 113).

The year had hardly been a success for Sarah. Beginning with
her expulsion from the church in Lowell, she had been forced to
move to three other villages, and had taken the time she would
otherwise have used to attend camp meeting in a fruitless journey
to seek forgiveness from Avery's flock. She must have been pleas-
antly surprised, then, when her fortune seemed to reverse itself in
Taunton, Massachusetts. Now thirty years old and an experienced
weaver, Sarah obtained a position "hooking up, and folding cloth
and keeping the weaving room books" (Williams 1833, 142–43).
The job involved considerable responsibility, and while it gave her
two or three hours of leisure daily, it kept her closely tied to the
mill. In March 1832 Sarah wrote to her mother that visiting would
be difficult because her employer was unwilling to excuse her from
the mill for even a single day (Williams 1833, 143).

Late in May, Sarah did manage to escape the mill for a few days
and visit her family in Providence (Williams 1833, 143). The trip
proved to be more than recreational; meetings with her sister and
brother-in-law led to a job offer as a tailor in Grindall Rawson's
Woodstock shop. Sarah's previous objection to living in Woodstock—there was no regular Methodist meeting there—had been
removed by the construction of a meeting house in West Woodstock
after an 1829 revival led by Methodist ministers John Lovejoy, Ira
M. Bidwell, and Onesiphorus Robbins (Bowen 1926, 314). The
possibility of access to this new Methodist congregation forming
under the direction of Reverend Charles Vergin, combined with
the pleasant opportunity to live with her family and ply her original
trade, made her brother-in-law's offer impossible to refuse.

On her return trip to Taunton to collect her belongings and
settle her accounts, Sarah took the steamboat from Providence
to Fall River, intending to transfer to the Boston stagecoach that

would carry her the rest of the way. Her long experience with un-certain employment prompted her to look over the thriving indus-trial village as a possible future home. Instead of lodging at the local tavern, Sarah called on the Methodist minister, Ira M. Bidwell (who had aided in establishing the Methodist presence in West Woodstock three years before), for aid in securing a respectable place to stay for a few days. Presenting her class certificate from the Taunton church as identification, Sarah was not disappointed by the minister's efforts. Although he was unable to offer lodgings him-self, he procured a place for her in the home of Edward Mason, a member of his congregation. The following Sunday he noticed her in the meeting house as he preached (Staples 1833a, 12).

By the second week of June Sarah was settled in the Rawsons' home in Woodstock where, after three weeks' vacation, her employ-ment began (Hallett 1833a, 85). Grindall Rawson, who was teach-ing her the "rules of cutting" (Hallett 1833a, 89), found her an expert seamstress and a competent businesswoman. When he trav-eled that summer he left her in charge of the business with full power to settle accounts and receive money (Drury 1833, 27). Her integration into the Methodist community was going just as smoothly. Reverend Vergin accepted her certificate—signed by her class leader, not the minister, at Taunton—without question.

She had found, apparently, a solution to her problems with the church. By gaining admission to a class meeting at Taunton without asking for full church membership, Sarah reestablished Methodist connections without the review of her past that attempted transfer of membership had always provoked. Her certificate, obtained when she traveled to Providence, identified her only as a person seeking salvation, not one who had found it. With that certificate, which could be obtained on the grounds of her recent behavior alone, she could travel freely in Methodist circles, as demonstrated by her interview with Rev. Bidwell in Fall River. Perhaps Sarah left Taunton precisely because her certificate could open doors to full membership elsewhere. When her brother-in-law's offer materi-alized, the benefits of her position at Taunton were outweighed by the social and religious potential of a move to Woodstock.

Woodstock provided Sarah with many opportunities for social interaction. Living at her sister's home, she was able to use her fam-ily connections to gain entrance into many households in the com-munity (Drury 1833, 26). John J. Paine remembered that during her residence in Woodstock he saw her only at parties at the Rawsons' house (Drury 1833, 26); he implied that she was socially acceptable but appropriately modest and retiring.

As August approached, Sarah began to make arrangements to participate in the Thompson camp meeting, which was conveniently located only five miles from the Rawson house. Several times she had one of her brother-in-law's apprentices, Benjamin Saunders, post letters for her to Bristol, Rhode Island (Hallett 1833a, 87). Although Saunders could not recall to whom the letters were addressed, she might have been arranging a meeting with Avery (by then stationed in Bristol) to retrieve her self-incriminating letters, whose publication in Methodist circles would seriously damage her newly won position in Rev. Vergin's congregation. The facts that she apparently knew no one else in Bristol (Hallett 1833a, 86) and that she was remarkably impatient to get to the camp meeting on time support this supposition.

With the meeting approaching, Sarah asked her brother-in-law to obtain transportation for her to the camp grounds, a task that was more difficult than Rawson expected. His first choice, the Presbyterian minister William Mason Cornell, was delayed by a protracted meeting at Ashford (Staples 1833a, 15). Rawson then considered asking another neighbor, Colonel Bowen, to take the family on Wednesday, but Sarah was adamant that she reach the camp grounds as soon as possible.

Rawson finally obtained a ride for her with John J. Paine on Tuesday, August 28. Giving Sarah money for her night's lodging and advising her to take care of her health, he sent her off with Paine at one o'clock in the afternoon (Drury 1833, 27). Once at the campground, Paine cared for his horse and wagon in the parking zone about a quarter of a mile away from the grounds while Sarah proceeded on foot. She had previously asked Rev. Vergin if she might find accommodations in the Thompson tent (residential tents at the camps were organized by geography and controlled by tent masters who determined the composition of their population). Once on the grounds, however, she found that no space had been saved for her. Polly Horton, an elderly woman, was helping Sarah search for a tent in which to stay when Paine caught up with them (Hallett 1833a, 140). Uncertain of her chances for success, Sarah had Paine leave her trunk at Mr. Elliot's nearby tavern where she feared she might be forced to lodge (Drury 1833, 26). Fortunately, she found a place in the Muddy Brook tent, located in the outer range of two concentric circles of tents surrounding the meeting

grounds (Staples 1833a, 15), and it was there that the Rawsons
found her when they came for a few hours' visit the next day.

One of the first ministers Sarah met on the camp grounds was
Ira M. Bidwell, from Fall River, who expressed surprise that she
should come from Woodstock rather than Taunton (Drury 1833,
21). After explaining to Bidwell her move to her "mother's" residence in Woodstock, she seems to have attracted little attention.
Inviting the Rawsons to dine at Muddy Brook tent with her, she
offered her bed to her sister as a welcome retreat from the afternoon heat and later introduced them to several Methodist friends
(Drury 1833, 27–28).

On Thursday her confrontations were more dramatic. Finding
Rev. Merrill, from whom she had fled at Lynn, Sarah accosted him
in his tent with an impassioned "Brother Merrill, will you forgive
me?" (Drury 1833, 45). When the embarrassed preacher managed
to move her away from the people in the tent, Sarah emotionally
confessed her previous "wicked" behavior. Merrill's response was to
admonish her that confession was meaningless without a "continued course of well doing" (Drury 1833, 45).

Later that day Ephraim Avery saw her in the crowd as he stood
on the preachers' stand; he reported to other ministers that when
she saw he had recognized her, she "dropped as though she had
been shot" (Hallett 1833a, 136). Avery's feeble attempts to get her
banned from the grounds were unsuccessful; although numerous
undesirable persons were escorted off the grounds, Sarah was not
among them (Hallett 1833a, 136). His attempts, however, may have
contributed to the slanderous remarks directed at her. When Henry
Mayo saw Sarah walking with two other women he amused himself
and his companions with the observation that "she ought to be married to save her credit" (Hallett 1833a, 137). Mayo's wife, Betsy, who
had known Sarah in Lowell before she was married, rebuked him
for the comments and asserted that there was nothing in Sarah's
physical appearance or her actions to indicate that her credit needed
salvation (Hallett 1833a, 138). But something must have prompted
the jovial Rev. Mayo's remark.

Betsy Mayo's friendly disposition toward Sarah resulted in an
embarrassing rebuke by another minister, less jovial than her husband, before the day was over. Later in the afternoon she met
Sarah and had a brief conversation with her about their time in
Lowell. Returning to her tent, she pointed Sarah out to several
others as the "Miss Cornell with whom Mr. Avery had trouble in

Lowell" (Hallett 1833a, 138). When Avery heard of her comments, he reproved Mrs. Mayo for conversing with Sarah and for mentioning her in connection with him (Hallett 1833a, 138).

The events of Thursday evening, August 30, because they had a major bearing on Avery's motive for murder, were hotly debated at his trial. According to the minister, his only contact with Sarah was visual, on Thursday morning when he saw her in the congregation. According to Sarah, as she related events to her family, there was much more to tell. During the day, Avery supposedly arranged to meet her at Elliot's tavern when the evening horn blew. The purpose of the interview was to determine how she might retrieve her letters of confession and insure her continued good reputation with her new congregation. When the tavern proved too crowded for an intimate conversation, Avery sent her out alone and, after discreetly following a few moments later, walked with her arm in arm into the forest surrounding the camp-meeting site. Grindall Rawson later recounted Sarah's description of what followed:

> They sat down; some conversation followed about Avery having burned the letters. He said he had not, but would on one condition, and settle the difficulty. At that time he took hold of her hands, and put one into her bosom, or something like it. She said she tried to get away from him, but could not. She said he then had intercourse with her, and they returned to the camp. He promised to destroy the letters, on his return to Bristol (Hallett 1833a, 86).

The following day both Sarah and Avery left the camp. Sarah returned to the Rawsons' house in the company of Benjamin Saunders, whom Rawson had sent to pick her up. Arriving home at dusk, Sarah resumed her position as seamstress and office manager for her brother-in-law. Whether or not Avery had extorted sexual favors from her at the meeting, her peace was soon disrupted.

As September drew to an end, Sarah became suspicious and increasingly apprehensive that she was pregnant. Working up enough courage to confide in her sister on the evening of September 21, Sarah related the story of her seduction at the camp meeting and its probable consequences (Williams 1833, 99). Any doubts Lucretia might have had about the time when Sarah's child was conceived (and thus about the father's identity) were swept away by her certain knowledge that Sarah had been "unwell as females are" eight days before the camp meeting (Hallett 1833a, 79). This information came to her because she did the household laundry and was later confirmed by Ruth Lawton, another of Rawson's seamstresses, who slept in the same bed with Sarah (Hallett 1833a, 79). Thus reasonably certain that the story was true, Lucretia immediately consulted her husband, who was initially uncertain about the proper course to follow. Rawson in turn went to his minister, Rev. Cornell, for advice. Cornell was as unsure of proper action as Rawson, so the case was put to a local lawyer, Mr. Lellan (Marshall and Brown 1833, 52). The opinion of these three men was that it would be best for Sarah to move to the state where Avery resided and there press for support, ultimately, if necessary, at law. The solution was a relief to Rawson because he was concerned about Sarah's influence on the young people in his shop when it became apparent that she was pregnant (Williams 1833, 99).

Sarah agreed with their advice and proposed to move to Fall River, which then straddled the Massachusetts–Rhode Island border. There she would be able to support herself in the factories while negotiating with Avery. If Fall River's position on the border seemed to make it a questionable location for a woman seeking Rhode Island residence, it also had advantages. Fall River was the most convenient manufacturing center near Bristol, and Sarah had established contacts there in May. Her only other possible choice was Providence, where employment and acceptance were unlikely because of her unfortunate history in that city. Consequently, on October 1 (or 2, according to Lucretia Rawson) Grindall Rawson transported his sister-in-law as far as Providence (Hallett 1833a, 85), where she obtained passage to Fall River.

In Fall River Sarah found lodging in the home of Elija Cole (Drury 1833, 16). Her tenure at Cole's house lasted eight weeks and four days—from October 1 to December 1. On Friday, October 5, Sarah presented herself at Ira Bidwell's church and applied for admission. Still using her certificate from Taunton, Sarah was given probationary membership (Drury 1833, 22). Where she first found employment is uncertain, but by November 1 she was employed weaving sheetings in the Fall River Manufactory managed by David Anthony (Fall River Manufactory 1832). Hours were long in Fall River, as they had been in the factories of Lowell, Taunton, and Slatersville. The workday began at five o'clock and lasted until half past seven in the evening with a half hour at eight for breakfast and forty-five minutes at noon for lunch. The men in some of the mills were fortified by a serving of New England rum at eleven o'clock each day, but the female operatives could expect no such benefit (Borden 1899, 482).

Boarding at Mr. Cole's was increasingly uncomfortable for Sarah. Contending with what must have been nausea related to the first months of pregnancy, Sarah was sick eleven working days in October and barely made enough to pay her expenses (Hallett 1833a, 190). Elija Cole remembered later that sometimes she had been melancholy and absentminded, but seemed determined to show a greater cheerfulness than she actually felt (Drury 1833, 16).

Throughout her career Sarah had always preferred quieter, smaller boardinghouses; at Fall River that preference took on increasing importance. On November 30 Sarah approached Lucy Hathaway, a girl she had met the week before in Anthony's mill, and asked about the possibility of lodging in her mother's house. Lucy replied that she would ask her mother at noon, but Sarah, unwilling to wait even that long, went directly to Mrs. Hathaway. Harriet Hathaway deferred to her daughter's judgment, and Sarah reported to Lucy that her room was assured if Lucy did not object (Drury 1833, 14). Lucy was not intimate with Sarah—they worked in the same room but in different aisles—but she knew of no reason to reject her; thus Sarah moved to the Hathaways' residence on Spring Street the following Saturday, December 1. While in their house, Sarah provided an air of mystery with questions about female responsibility in cases of seduction, tantalizingly strange letters, and dark hints about improper behavior among the religious at camp meetings (Drury 1833, 15). If Sarah's conversation made her a source of household gossip, her behavior was unexceptional. She led a quiet life, never going out in the evenings except Tuesdays and Sundays to attend Methodist observances (Drury 1833, 15).

On October 19 Ephraim Avery came to Fall River in an exchange of ministerial services with Ira Bidwell, who left for Bristol the next day and stayed until Monday, October 22, the duration of Avery's visit (Hallett 1833b, 19). For Sarah, who had not yet communicated with Avery about her condition, the minister's sudden appearance was a mixed blessing. She needed a chance to confront him, which his arrival provided, but she ran the risk of disturbing the delicate balance of her association with the Fall River Methodists. Waiting until the evening meeting ended, Sarah followed Avery and Bidwell to the doorway of Edward Mason's house, where Avery was to spend the night (Drury 1833, 5). Bidwell had already discussed Sarah with the visiting minister, asking if she were the girl that he had expelled at Lowell. Because she had used her middle name, Maria, at Lowell and was using Sarah in Fall River, there was some question. When Bidwell recognized her outside Mason's door, he discreetly withdrew in order for Avery to converse with her and determine if she were the same person (Hallett 1833b, 16). As a result, their short interview was overheard by no one. Avery's rendition indicated that Sarah feared he would expose her character in this community as he had done elsewhere:

> She said I have come to live in Fall River where I am not known, and dont want you to expose me. I told her I had no disposition to injure her, and it would depend upon her behavior whether I exposed her or not. Dont, says she, ruin me here, you have ruined me in Lowell and Dover, but dont here. I told her I had not ruined her she had ruined herself. She said she had joined a class on trial, and if I did not tell Brother Bidwell about her conduct, it would not be known. She urged me not to expose her. I replied as before and left her. This conversation could not have lasted more than five or ten minutes. The Sabbath following I preached in Fall River and noticed her in the congregation. I have never seen her since (Drury 1833, 3–4).

Sarah's version of the same event is predictably different. Drawing him aside at Mason's doorstep, she demanded an interview and threatened to go to Bristol if it were not granted. The short conversation that ensued was devoted to arranging a meeting the following evening (Hallett 1833a, 190).

When night fell on Saturday, October 20, it was so dark and stormy that those stepping out even a short distance were obliged to carry lanterns. The Methodist meeting for that evening, which Avery was to conduct, was held at the home of George Davol (Hallett 1833a, 89), and began, as was accepted practice, at half past seven. When Avery concluded shortly before nine o'clock, at least one of the congregation thought it a hurried affair (Hallett 1833a, 85). Lucy Spink was further surprised to see the minister leave the hall immediately at the end of services instead of following the more usual course of staying to converse with members (Hallett 1833a, 85). Her curiosity aroused, she looked after the departing minister and saw him meet a short woman whose "figure made a singular appearance" (Hallett 1833a, 85). Avery and his mysterious companion disappeared into the darkness.

The minister worried more than one of the Fall River Methodists. By twenty minutes after nine, Nancy Bidwell, Ira's wife at whose house Avery was expected to spend the night, was concerned enough to call on John E. Green to discover if he knew the where-abouts of her missing guest. Green, thinking Avery had had suffi-cient time to reach the Bidwells' house, told the upset woman that Avery must have gone somewhere else for lodging (Hallett 1833a, 179). Such was not the case, however; shortly after Mrs. Bidwell re-turned to her home Avery appeared at the door explaining that he had been to Warren's stables to observe the horses (Hallett 1833a, 87). Mrs. Bidwell had no watch, but was informed by Avery that the hour was about half past nine.

Sarah's account of Avery's activities that night placed him with her rather than with the horses at Warren's:

> He came and I spent an hour with him. He said as I told he would, that if that was my case it was not his, and said I must go to a doctor immediately; said he had burned my letters—if he had known what would have happened he would have kept them—said I must never swear it, for if that was my case he would take care of me—spoke very feelingly of his wife and chil-dren—said I must say it belonged to a man that was dead, for, said he, I am dead to you—that is I cannot marry you. He owned and denied it two or three times. He left me by saying that I might wait a few weeks, and then I might write him (Melvill 1833, doc. no. 4).

The implication of the interview, as Sarah described it, was that they should wait for the passage of time to confirm that the basis for her present distress was not some physical irregularity other than pregnancy.

As October drew to a close, Sarah decided to get confirmation of her pregnancy from a physician. She chose Thomas Wilbur, who kept an office at the corner of South Main and Borden Street. Wilbur was tall and slender, thirty-seven years old, a native of Rhode Island, and a graduate of Yale Medical School. His career, prior to setting up practice in Fall River in 1828, had included medical study in Philadelphia, a position as principal of a Friends school in Providence, and a short-lived practice in Swansea, Rhode Island (Peckham 1927, 65–66). If his chronic stomach trouble ever af-fected his disposition, it was not apparent to Sarah, to whom he was unfailingly courteous and sympathetic. How much of that sympa-thy stemmed from kindly feelings for the girl, and how much from his dawning awareness that her story damned the Methodist minis-try whose episcopal government his own Quaker affiliations preju-diced him against, is impossible to say.

The exact time of Sarah's first visit to Wilbur is debatable. Wilbur himself placed it "some seven or eight weeks, before her death" (Hallett 1833a, 35). Catharine Williams, more precise, wrote that it occurred on the evening of October 8 (Williams 1833, 19). Either date is possible. The eighth was one week after Sarah arrived in town and may have been her first opportunity to seek medical advice. On the other hand, Wilbur's calculation, which would place the event roughly between October 22 and 31, suits Avery's alleged suggestion on the twentieth that Sarah confirm the pregnancy before further negotiations, and with the end of the second month of Sarah's interrupted menstrual cycle.

Wilbur's conversations with his patient about the source of her pregnancy were later barred from Avery's trial as hearsay evidence. Outside the courtroom, however, the doctor made no secret of what had transpired. Essentially, Wilbur said, Sarah came to see him five times (Hallett 1833a, 14). Under his relentless but kind cross examination, though she was unswervingly committed to the preservation of Avery's reputation and the elevation of the Methodist people (*Painesville Telegraph*, 12 April 1833), she finally divulged the source of her misfortune. The "artless, candid & unassuming" girl told Wilbur that Avery had seduced her partly by force and partly in exchange for the destruction of her confession letters. Her inhibitions broken down, she also confided in the doctor that Avery had prescribed oil of tansy as an effective agent to induce abortion (Hallett 1833b, 14). Wilbur was horrified to discover that the minister had, according to Sarah, told her to take thirty drops, a dosage that would almost prove fatal to her as well as to the fetus (Williams 1833, 24).

These stories, although they could not be entered into the minister's trial because Sarah was neither under oath nor in her dying moments when she made the assertions, did much to convince the general public that Avery was both the father of her unborn child and a willful murderer who acted in desperation when his plot to have Sarah kill herself was foiled. While Wilbur's Quaker affiliations made him hostile to the established clergy of which Avery was a part, it would be presumptuous to assert without further proof that the doctor had lied. Avery's defense attempted to reduce the damaging effects of Wilbur's story by asserting that Sarah had been involved in an elaborate plot to discredit Avery, and thus lied to the doctor to further her devious aims. While the plot theory remained unproven and became increasingly fantastic as the web of interaction between Avery and Sarah was more clearly drawn, it was not disproven. As in many of the last events of Sarah's life, the truth is elusive.

What is incontrovertible is that Sarah did consult Wilbur five times during October and November about her pregnancy, and that she inquired about the use of oil of tansy to induce abortion. If the story of her interview with Avery on the cloudy night of October 20 is true, then Sarah's reported anxiety that Avery not be exposed gains credibility (because he had promised to support her through her pregnancy and birth if he were not exposed). More certain of her pregnancy after medical consultation, Sarah wrote to Avery in the beginning of November informing him of her assurance (Hallett 1833a, 190). A hasty reply dated November 13 was soon in her hands enjoining her to keep quiet and "write me as soon as you get this nameing some time and place where I shall see you and then look for answer before I come and will say whether convenient or not and will say the time" (Hallett 1833a, 189).

Sarah, encouraged by his reply, wrote to her sister and brother-in-law that all was progressing well. Knowing that her settlement depended on the preservation of Avery's good name, Sarah instructed her family not to mention Avery's part in her condition to anyone; the most they could say was that "it belonged to a Methodist minister, but that we settled it, and that I do not choose to tell whose it is" (Hallett 1833a, 190). With the problems of economic survival through her confinement all but solved by the minister's eagerness to comply, Sarah began to plan her future. Thinking that she could save six dollars a month through the winter if the low water of November improved in later months, Sarah planned to work until March 1 before retiring to await the baby's arrival. Having learned that there was a girl employed in the mills who boarded her illegitimate child for fifty cents a week, Sarah hoped to be able to do the same. "It will not," she wrote, "make half the noise here that it would in the country" (Hallett 1833a, 190).

Determined to keep her child, Sarah must have recognized that childbirth out of wedlock could only result in reexpulsion from the Methodist church. In order to forestall the investigations that expulsion proceedings would entail, she wrote an undated letter to Ira Bidwell in which she renounced her church affiliation:

> I take this opportunity to inform you that for reasons known to God and my soul I wish no longer to be connected with the

Methodist Society When I came to this place I thought I should enjoy myself among them but as I do not enjoy any Religion atall I have not seen a well nor a happy day since I left Thompson Campground You will therefore please to drop my name from Mr. Greens class and I will try to gain all the instruction I can from your public labours I hope I shall feel different some time or other The Methodists are my people when I enjoy any Religion To them I was indebted under God for my spiritual birth I once knew what it was to love God with all my heart once felt that God was my Father Jesus my friend and heaven my Home but have awfully departed and sometimes fear I shall lose my soul forever I desire your prayers that God would keep me from this (Melvill 1833, doc. no. 2).

The letter was never sent, but was discovered, sealed, among Sarah's possessions after her death.

Upon receiving the letter of November 13, Sarah wrote again, offering times for potential meetings (Hallett 1833a, 190). Still plagued with hopes and fears, she waited for a reply that would confirm the appointment. It came on November 27 in the form of a pink letter delivered by John Orswell, engineer on the steamship *King Philip*, who claimed to have taken it from Avery on the docks of Providence that very morning. Signed "B. H." for Betsey Hills, Sophia Avery's invalid niece, the letter requested that Sarah come to Bristol December 18 or 20 (Hallett 1833a, 189). If it were impossible for her to get to Bristol on either of those evenings, "B. H." indicated a willingness to come to Fall River. The decision on what course to follow in what was certain to be a delicate negotiation probably troubled Sarah; Elija Cole's daughter, Betsey, saw Sarah presumably lost in thought with the pink letter and two others in her hands on Thanksgiving (Hallett 1833a, 78). Her mind finally made up, possibly with the aid of Dr. Wilbur, who suggested that she not travel to see a man who had once threatened her life (Williams 1833, 24), Sarah replied to "B. H." that he would have to come to Fall River. Her move from Elija Cole's house to the "more retired" house of the Hathaways, which occurred at this time, may have been related to the desire to set up a safe, secluded meeting point.

The final meeting was confirmed in a terse note, posted in Fall River on December 8, which said simply, "I will be here on the 20 if pleasant at the place named at 6 oclk if not pleasant the next Monday *eve* Say nothing &c" (Melvill 1833, doc. no. 7). When Sarah— whose habit of frequently inquiring for letters had been noticed by the postal clerk (Hallett 1833a, 91)—picked it up that same day, the stage was set for the confrontation that ended in her death.

The letters that Sarah claimed to have written in this correspondence were never found, presumably because their recipient destroyed them. The letters of November 13 and December 8 and the one received November 27, which were found in Sarah's possessions, were unsigned or signed "B. H." Though attributed to Avery by Sarah (and later by the prosecution in his trial), they were never proven to have originated at the minister's hand. The prosecution did demonstrate that Avery was in Providence when Orswell allegedly received the pink letter from him, and in Fall River on December 8 when the final note was sent. Thus, while authorship was not positively established, the web of circumstances that linked him with the fatal correspondence was strong.

A week before December 20, Sarah told her friend Lucy Hathaway of her plans to leave the mill early that day. She hoped, she said, that the weather would be fair and that her overseer, John N. Smith, would be reasonable (Hallett 1833a, 66). Whether or not he was reasonable, she was determined to go, even at the cost of jeopardizing her position (Hallett 1833a, 66). When the appointed day arrived, Sarah asked Mrs. Hathaway at noon if she might have her dinner early, before dark. Back in the mill for the afternoon, Sarah finally approached her overseer and, in the diffident manner that she always employed when asking a favor, requested an early release (Marshall and Brown 1833, 157). Smith's answer must have been so full of qualifications and discourses on the impropriety of leaving the mill before half past seven that even he was uncertain if she understood that permission was given. At a quarter to five Smith went to Sarah at her loom and asked if she understood that she could leave. She said she did, and soon she departed (Hallett 1833b, 3).

When Lucy Hathaway had borrowed some money from Sarah earlier in the day to purchase an apron for another girl, Sarah had requested that she buy one for each of them as well so they could wear matching outfits the following week. Five minutes before she left the mill, Sarah walked over to Lucy's window and, while combing her hair, gave her further last-minute instructions (Hallett 1833a, 67). She wanted her loom, which was out of order, to be stripped of its web so that it would be ready for new operations by Monday. She also asked that Lucy wind some waste yarn for her—a benefit provided free by the mill—for knitting. With the last of her preparations for a happier future completed, she left her friend.

Sarah ate supper alone at Mrs. Hathaway's house. Her mood was reportedly better than usual as she ostensibly made preparations to go to class meeting at Job Durfee's (Hallett 1833a, 66). After her meal she went upstairs, where she probably penciled the note found in her bandbox: "If I should be missing enquire of the Rev Mr Avery of Bristol he will know where I am Dec 20th S M Cornell" (Melvill 1833, doc. no. 5). Putting on a better cloak than she usually wore to the mill, Sarah informed Mrs. Hathaway that she would be back soon—in no case later than nine o'clock. She did not, however, keep her word. The older woman waited for her until ten o'clock and then, leaving the door unlocked, went to bed. The following morning her body was found suspended from a stake in John Durfee's stack yard on the south side of town.

4. The Minister

When *Ephraim Kingsbury Avery* stood before Justices Howe and Haile at Bristol, he was thirty-six years old, an ordained minister of the Methodist Episcopal church, and a man whose checkered history had neither expelled him from polite society nor allowed him to rise to the levels of honor and respect that, above all, he wished to attain. Arrayed in the somber dress of his profession—most noticeably defined by the severe cut of his dark, single-breasted coat and the wide brim of the hat he had worn on the short walk to the courthouse—the minister appeared self-possessed, almost aloof. His eyes, which might have betrayed the workings of his mind at the outset of his ordeal, were partially obscured by a pair of colored spectacles. Well built, with a full head of dark hair, a broad forehead, and features thought handsome by many (if marred by a trace of corpulence and what some called a "sensuous" mouth), Avery attracted the attention of all and the sympathy of many. When he described to the court the incidents during his acquaintance with Sarah Cornell, he opened a public interest in and scrutiny of his life that in the following months traced him back through an active career to his very origins.

Avery was born in Coventry, Connecticut (Rawson 1833), a small town about twenty miles east of Hartford. His father, Amos, was a farmer, and young Ephraim, soon initiated into the drudgery of agricultural life, developed a not uncommon distaste for tilling the soil. Hoping to better his position in the world—almost desperately eager to escape the back-breaking labor of rural life—Avery spent the years of his young adulthood experimenting with a variety of other professions. Neither storekeeping (Hallett 1833a, 178) nor schoolteaching in East Hartford (Hallett 1833a, 169) proved consistent with his aptitude and inclination. For a young man seeking to rise to a public station above manual labor without family connections, wealth, or extensive education there were few other options. Avery finally chose medicine (Hallett 1833a, 169, 178). His education in the art of healing began, probably through apprenticeship to a local physician, but was never completed. Sometime during his initiation into the mysteries of "physic," his ambitions once more shifted their course; responding to an inner call, Avery abandoned his medical studies in favor of becoming a Christian minister.

By the time Avery decided to enter the clerical world, he was married and in his midtwenties. Combined with his minimal formal education, these factors arose as a major obstacle to the launching of his ministerial career. Gaining a pulpit in a Congregationalist church, then still the overwhelmingly dominant denomination in Connecticut, required a lengthy formal education for which he had neither the background nor the time and money. Fortunately, the first decades of the nineteenth century had seen the rise of a new and energetic church in New England that did not place such formidable barriers between the uneducated and the pulpit. It was to this church that the young man turned.

The Methodist Episcopal church offered young men (and, although in a subordinate status, young women) a religious forum without the pains of a long and perhaps emotionally irrelevant apprenticeship. Basing their ministry on the desire and ability to preach combined with an acceptance of the church's dogma—particularly the concept of free salvation through faith—the Methodists relied on their highly centralized organization to ensure the theological conformity that Congregationalists might hope to enforce only by long periods of indoctrination (or by tendencies toward presbyterianism, which had been fought in New England since the seventeenth century). Secure in the expectation that they could control the potential for deviation that lack of religious instruction innocently produced, the Methodists could encourage emotional commitment rather than intellectual education and readily reward innate speaking ability with a pulpit.

To Avery—as to many young men who felt the need to express their religious experiences—the value placed on his zeal and the opportunities for an immediate ministry that he found among the Methodists must have had great appeal. In fact, a comparison of a physician's career, purchased at the price of long apprenticeship and marred by the objectionable aspects of treating bodies that made doctors socially suspect, with the career of a Methodist minister, who might rise to unsullied social prominence in the course of two or three painless years, may have prompted Avery's decision to abandon care of the flesh for that of the soul.

7. Ephraim Kingsbury Avery. The artist called his portrait a "good Likeness," but Avery's friends labeled it a cruel caricature done to impress upon the public that he was a "savage and libidinous monster." From Marshall and Brown, *The Correct, Full and Impartial Report . . .* (Providence: Marshall and Brown, 1833).

The ministry to which Avery aspired could never make him as wealthy as the medical practice he did not pursue. A Methodist minister's yearly salary was one hundred dollars for himself, one hundred dollars for his wife, sixteen dollars for each child under seven, and twenty-four dollars for each child between seven and fourteen (Robbins 1824, 168). As little as this might be, it was not even guaranteed by the church. Each minister's pay was made up by the collections on his circuit; those whose congregations did not adequately supply them had no claim on the Methodist organization to make up the deficit in their pay. Only in special cases the quarterly meeting might levy a bonus for preachers working in depressed areas that could not support them (Winebrenner 1849, 374). Undeterred by these monetary limitations, in 1822 Avery took his wife, Sophia Hills, to Mansfield, Connecticut, where he had obtained a probationary assignment under V. R. Osborn, the local Methodist preacher.

As an assistant to the preacher on a Connecticut circuit, Avery found himself to be something of a second lieutenant in the Methodists' spiritual war of conquest. In the 1820s, Methodism was scarcely thirty years old in New England. Long a bastion of the doctrine of predestination, an intellectually elevated clergy, and the "curse of State-churchism" (Daniels 1887, 539), the New England states presented an irresistible challenge to men like Francis Asbury and Jesse Lee, who brought Methodist ideology and organization into the area in the last years of the eighteenth century. Their evangelical zeal was rewarded with success not only because of the appeal of the concept of free salvation, but also because of the closely knit structure of the Methodist organization. Every community in which Methodists lived constituted a society, which was broken down into classes of approximately twelve to twenty people. Each class was supervised by a class leader, a layman whose obligation was to monitor the Christian progress of his charges and report on them to the minister in charge of the society. Classes were further subdivided into bands containing three or four persons of the same sex and nearly the same social condition. Bands, like classes, met once a week to discuss religious topics, pray, and exhort one another to greater religious perfection (Robbins 1824, 167).

A number of societies spaced conveniently close to one another formed a circuit, to which two or three preachers were appointed, one the superintendent and the others his staff. A presiding elder had charge of a district composed of several contiguous circuits. A bishop had administrative control over a series of districts that comprised his conference. Special extraclerical posts were established to administer the wealth of the church (stewards and trustees) and to officiate at meetings when clergymen were not available (exhorters).

Coordination in the administrative hierarchy of the church was ensured by a series of regular meetings. Societies met at least once a week, and often more frequently. All the class leaders of a single district met regularly to report progress, turn over collections to stewards, act upon probationary members, and discuss administrative problems. Quarterly meetings of all the officials of a single district allowed the presiding elder frequent contact with his widely dispersed staff. An annual assembly was held for each conference of the church, in which aspiring ministers' qualifications were examined and disputes were settled. At the general conference, held every four years, representatives of all the conferences gathered to legislate temporal and spiritual matters (Winebrenner 1849, 372).

Coordination and communication were the keystones of the Methodist church. No Methodist community, no matter how small, was isolated. Besides the formal meetings system, the Methodists employed frequent four days meetings, in which local ministers came together in a single community to reestablish bonds among themselves and to present a united front to the local populace. Exchange of preaching services was also employed to keep neighboring circuits in touch. As the nineteenth century progressed, camp meetings became another popular mechanism by which Methodists enhanced communication among their many scattered societies. The itinerancy of the Methodist clergy also figured in maintaining the channels of communication on which the church's cohesion depended. Stationed on one circuit for no more than a year or two, no minister could become exclusively attached to one church, knowledgeable of only one congregation, and independent of all others. The church, rather than the congregation, controlled his life. While this might have led to a certain disdain for local custom and opinion, it had the powerful effect of promoting the conformity to dogma and the loyalty to chain of command that made the Methodists an effective evangelical force.

Avery's introduction into the highly organized and tightly coordinated world of the Methodist clergy was apparently satisfactory. With his first probationary year at Mansfield safely and unevent-

fully behind him, in June 1823 the aspiring young minister was assigned under Elias Marble to Pomfret, Connecticut (Whittaker
1912, 21). Pomfret was then a manufacturing village, completely
owned by the Pomfret Manufactory (Stanley 1833). The local
Methodists, with neither a meeting house nor the funds necessary
to construct one, were allowed by the company to hold their meetings in the community's schoolhouse. It was under that simple roof
that Avery preached his first sermon to his new congregation.
While the text of his presentation does not survive—most Methodist sermons were extemporaneous—Avery seems to have chosen
some controversial topic on which his views did not conform to
those of many of the flock. Conspicuous among his critics were
Sylvester Stanley, his wife Nancy, and their daughter. It was this
family that became the center of the first controversy of the new
preacher's career.

On the basis of Avery's schoolhouse sermon, Stanley decided
not to attend his further discourses. The state of hostility that was
generated between the Stanleys and the minister lasted from July,
when Avery arrived in the village, until September, when a sudden
and serious illness drove Sylvester from the fields of contention.
As the stricken man declined, he must have had bitter regrets concerning his harsh treatment of the young Methodist minister who
laid aside personal hostilities in favor of Christian compassion.
Throughout Stanley's last days, Avery comforted him as best he
could and managed the well-being of his family.

At Sylvester's death in the first week of October, his widow and
orphans gratefully accepted Avery's offer of further assistance.
Sophia Avery and Betsey Hills, Mrs. Avery's chronically ill niece who
periodically resided in the preacher's house, aided in funeral preparations. Avery preached the mortuary sermon at the "grove" and,
after tea at Mrs. Stanley's, took the widow to probate court and
helped her settle her husband's estate.

The amiable relations that had been established between the
bereaved Stanleys and the Averys was short-lived. On October 20
Mrs. Stanley was shocked by the news that Avery had been discussing charges against her oldest daughter with Elias Marble. Shortly
thereafter, the young woman was turned out of the church as a
person of low character (Stanley 1833). Unwilling to accept such a
humiliating verdict from the church, Mrs. Stanley immediately began a campaign to clear her daughter's name. Charges against character, however, were more difficult to refute than charges against

behavior. By April of the following year, Mrs. Stanley had had no success. In fact, her position had deteriorated under the impact of charges of lying, which threatened her expulsion from the church. Enraged and frustrated in her attempts to see justice done, the desperate woman confronted Avery in person, demanding a full church trial for her daughter and herself. Avery replied that he thought such an action unwise. In his opinion, the trial would only publicly prove the disreputable morals of mother and daughter and ensure that they might never re-enter the church.

Disgraced and humiliated, Mrs. Stanley considered bringing a civil suit against Avery for slander, but never followed through. The church, which might have punished or expelled the probationary preacher on the mere appearance of wrongdoing, took a lenient view of Avery's actions and upheld him against his enemies. Rather than ejecting him as contentious and vain (an opinion of his character held by Mrs. Stanley for years afterward), the New England Conference quietly reassigned him in June 1824 for a final year of probationary service with Elisha Frink at Warwick (Whittaker 1912, 35). His service there was unexceptional, and the following year he was duly admitted in full connection with the church.

As a preacher Avery was licensed to expound on the meaning of the Bible and the doctrines of the church, but not to baptize or to administer the Lord's supper (Winebrenner 1849, 372). His first assignment in his elevated capacity, to Eastham, Cape Cod (Whittaker 1912, 47), passed uneventfully. In June 1826 his service was rewarded with promotion to the position of deacon. Now holding a parchment from a bishop of the church that entitled him to perform marriages, baptisms, and burials and to assist an elder in administering the Lord's supper (Winebrenner 1849, 372), he was reassigned to the Marshfield and Pembroke, Massachusetts, circuit. A minor scandal was whispered in that year that Avery had made indecent overtures to a young woman in Duxbury (Borden 1833), but nothing was proven that could injure his reputation. It was not unusual, after all, for young women in enthusiastic religions to develop crushes on handsome ministers and to hide their embarrassment at rejection with tales of imaginary advances.

Avery was ordained an elder of the church at the 1827 annual conference and reassigned to Marshfield (Whittaker 1912, 70). His new status gave him the right to administer the Lord's supper (Winebrenner 1849, 372); thus he was empowered to carry out all church ordinances and had reached the first rung of the administrative ladder of its organization. Further elevations would result in greater temporal power in church administration but no further religious abilities.

The Marshfield circuit included Scituate, where Avery preached often; there he met Miss Fanny Winsor, who stirred up the second minor controversy of his short career. In 1827 Miss Winsor was a spinster of forty-five who had gained a position of considerable influence and respect in the local Methodist community (Williams 1833, 102). Whether or not, as Catharine Williams claimed, Avery was immediately threatened by her local esteem, the relationship between the two was never a happy one. What was already a tense situation reached crisis when Miss Winsor thoughtlessly repeated Avery's ill-considered comment that a local man who had recently lost his wife would soon drown his sorrow in liquor (Williams 1833, 103). Avery, naturally upset that such a slip was made public, retaliated by attempting to get the woman expelled from the church for "lying and unchristian conduct, and exercising ungodly and unholy tempers" (Williams 1833, 104). The case was hotly debated. Long accustomed to taking care of herself, Miss Winsor was able to rebut the charges made against her. Admitting to her mistake in repeating Avery's words (Williams 1833, 105), she steadfastly refused to accept a single thoughtless error as grounds for dismissal from the church. The matter was finally referred to Scituate's parent church at Duxbury. The Reverend Enoch Mudge, then stationed at Duxbury, looked into the matter and awarded Fanny Winsor complete exoneration in the form of a certificate of good standing in the church (Williams 1833, 104). Although Avery's attempts to remove Miss Winsor from the church were unsuccessful, his superiors viewed his actions as reasonable and asserted that his character remained unblemished (Hallett 1833a, 169).

In July 1828 Avery was assigned to the Needham circuit (Whittaker 1912, 79). During this sojourn he made his home at Marlborough, Massachusetts (Hallett 1833a, 133). Perhaps because the controversy with Fanny Winsor was still going on, the minister carefully avoided further complications at his new post. He was not so lucky in his next assignment, at Saugus, Massachusetts (Whittaker 1912, 98).

On the coast to the north of Boston, Saugus seemed an ideal location. Avery filled his spare time wandering along the scenic beach at Nahant, "a place of great resort" (Hallett 1833a, 135). The religious environment seemed as plentiful as the physical one; the congregational society at Saugus, bereft of a permanent minister, invited Avery to address its meeting (Williams 1833, 108). The opportunity for proselytizing was not lost on the determined preacher, and he eagerly accepted. However, another Methodist preacher, Thomas F. Norris, soon accepted a similar invitation and also began to offer services. Norris was a minister of the Reformed Methodist church, a splinter group that owed its existence to the secession of fourteen persons from the Methodist congregation of Whitingham and Readsborough, Vermont, in 1813 (Winebrenner 1849, 383). Very similar to the Methodist Episcopal church in doctrine, Reformed Methodists distinguished themselves by operating under a congregational organization that eliminated original Methodist hierarchy.

Probably fearful that Norris would steal the congregational flock from him because of his church's political structure, Avery struck at his opponent through the avenue most immediately open to him. Taking for his text a passage in Job 32 : 10—"I also will declare mine opinion"—Avery attacked Norris from the pulpit, accusing him of being a man of low character and a thief (Williams 1833, 109). Norris predictably asked for a retraction and an apology; when they were not forthcoming he filed a slander suit (Norris 1833). Held in East Cambridge, Massachusetts, in 1830, the civil action against Avery resulted in a verdict of guilty (Williams 1833, 109). Judgment was arrested by a legal maneuver, and Avery settled with Norris out of court for one hundred and ninety dollars (Norris 1833).

The Norris affair, like Avery's exchange with Fanny Winsor, although the court's verdict exonerated Avery's opponent, did not result in censure of his character or ministerial behavior by Methodist leadership. While the justification for their refusal to sanction the preacher for his attacks on apparently inoffensive victims was not stated, it seems most likely that both events were considered by Avery's superiors to be the actions of a man dedicated to the advancement of his denomination. It was, after all, the minister's obligation to preserve the integrity of his flock; if that required him to press charges against those who might later be cleared—as in the case of Fanny Winsor—his zeal in the prosecution of his duties could hardly be counted against him. In the case of Rev. Norris, Avery's opponent represented a doctrinal and structural threat to the Methodist Episcopal church. While some might construe Avery's attack on Norris as a personal matter, the Methodist administration might easily view it as simply a skirmish in a legitimate war against schism.

In 1830 Avery was assigned to the manufacturing village of Lowell, Massachusetts. If removal to the interior came as a relief to the minister, whose assignments at Marshfield and Saugus had resulted in discord, his feelings were premature. From Scituate, Fanny Winsor still pursued him for what she considered slander on her good name (Williams 1833, 105–6). Her muttering about possible legal action probably did not stop until the following year when her certificate of good standing from Rev. Mudge cleared her. Thomas Norris likewise followed Avery to his new post, and in a more dramatic manner. When the slander suit was filed in East Cambridge, Norris had the sheriff of Lowell apprehend Avery to answer the charges. The minister was visibly shaken when Mr. Kimball, the local law officer, interrupted a prayer meeting to serve him with a summons (Williams 1833, 144). Although some suggested that Avery's reaction at being taken into custody was disproportionate to the seriousness of the charge (Williams 1833, 144), his dismay could be explained by the humiliation suffered by a man intensely concerned with his social status. That Avery was such a man is a reasonable assumption in view of his record of attacks on those who threatened his elevated position as a minister of the gospel.

On June 1, 1830 (Avery 1834, 11), Avery arrived at his new post in Lowell, haunted by persistent specters of past controversies but determined to make a new start in a new community. He originally took lodging in a house owned by a Mr. Lamb, but, probably by the end of the month when he expected a visit from Betsey Hills, moved to the larger quarters in the upper story of a house owned by a Mr. Abbott (Marshall and Brown 1833, 143; Hallet 1833, 178). Besides its greater size, the Abbott property offered a more convenient floor plan; Avery had a study—or ministerial office—with an outside door. Widely publicized by Avery's critics at his trial as an obvious den of seduction, the office provided a legitimate service to church members who might desire a private consultation, and to his family, who would be spared the disruption of strangers passing through kitchen and parlor.

When Sarah Cornell knocked on Avery's door in July 1830, neither she nor he marked the significance of her act. During the initial phase of their relationship—from July through September 1830—it was probably viewed by Avery, his flock, and his clerical peers as nothing more than the usual process of separating the wheat from the tare. By the next summer, after extensive if one-sided correspondence and Sarah's remarkable return to Lowell seeking forgiveness, Avery himself admitted that the situation was exotic. Attending a camp meeting at Ashford, Connecticut, Avery remarked to Elias C. Scott, a fellow minister, that the stories Scott told of wicked females could not hold a straw to the history of Sarah Cornell (Hallett 1833a, 133).

Avery ended his two-year assignment to Lowell—the longest allowable to a traveling preacher—in June 1832 (Whittaker 1912, 133). He arrived at his next station in Bristol, Rhode Island, with his reputation intact (Upham 1891, 67), but with his ankle broken or dislocated by a fall suffered only a week before (Hallett 1833a, 178). Undaunted by his minor physical handicap, Avery managed to win the approbation and affection of his new congregation (Upham 1891, 67). "The prospect in the things of religion," he wrote in the first week of August, "are brightening with us, and we are looking for better times. To God shall be the praise" (*New England Christian Herald*, 15 August 1832, 182).

Scarcely two months after his arrival in Bristol, Avery left to attend the camp meeting at Thompson, Connecticut. His critics later suggested that his decision to go to that meeting was prompted by communication with Sarah Cornell, who had written to him asking that her letters of confession be returned (Hallett 1833a, 87). However, even though the minister was not scheduled to take part in the proceedings at Thompson, it was not unreasonable for him to attend. Like the annual conference, camp meetings offered Methodist ministers an opportunity to reestablish contacts and bonds of friendship with other clergymen and members of their earlier congregations.

Though the camp meeting began on Monday afternoon with a sermon by I. Jennison from John 4:14—"But whosoever drinketh the water that I shall give him, shall never thirst" (*New England Christian Herald*, 12 September 1832, 198)—Avery did not start for Thompson until the morning of the next day, August 28. His late start for the camp grounds may have resulted from a sudden impulse to attend, prompted, perhaps, by Sarah Cornell's letters; however, if he had arranged to meet young Rev. Horton at Cady's tavern twenty miles past Providence to give him a ride on the last leg of the journey (Marshall and Brown 1833, 97), it is more likely that pressing business at home had forced him to schedule a late departure. In any case, Avery, who had left Bristol for the forty-mile trip alone, arrived in Thompson in the company of Rev. Horton and Jonathan Cady, whom he had fortuitously met at Cady's tavern as well.

It was near sundown when Avery reached Thompson, and it seemed to the weary preacher that lodgings should be his primary concern. The immediate vicinity offered two houses where rooms might be had: "old Mr. Elliot's," owned by David Elliot, and "young Mr. Elliot's," a mile distant and owned by David's son John. Leaving Cady at the elder Elliot's door, Avery drove his carriage to the barn to see if shelter was available for his horse. Unfortunately, the stalls were already filled with the tired animals of other travelers, and the minister was forced to make the journey to the younger Elliot's (Marshall and Brown 1833, 98). Sophia Elliot, John's wife, later remembered that Avery arrived at her house at "early candlelighting" (Hallett 1833a, 131), found room for his animal and himself, and remained all night.

On Wednesday morning Avery arose early, breakfasted, and at about sunrise was met at the house by Jonathan Cady (Hallett 1833a, 131), who had presumably lodged at the elder Elliot's. The two ministers proceeded to the camp grounds, about three quarters of a mile distant, together. Once there, Avery sought out Elias C. Scott, who, at Avery's request, found the newly arrived preacher a tent to which he could go for "refreshment" (Hildreth 1833, 72). Avery was among a number of ministers who sought only board for the day on the grounds, having taken rooms at local taverns. Although Scott procured him a place in the Plainfield tent, Avery happily accepted when Milton Daggett, master of the Weston tent, offered him board (Marshall and Brown 1833, 109). He later took some meals with the Plainfield contingent, but spent most of his time with the people of Weston, whom he had come to know when he preached in their community five years before.

While making his arrangements for the day, Avery fell into conversation with Peter Sabins, another minister who preferred a bed and roof to a cot and canvas. A few minutes after nine, the two preachers walked back to the younger Elliot's to engage a bed for the following night (Hallett 1833a, 131). With both room and board thus secured, Avery returned to the camp grounds for religious services.

Although he was not to take part in the public services of the meeting, as a preacher Avery had access to the special accommodations of the ministry. Thus, instead of standing anonymously in the crowd, he spent the morning at the preachers' stand in the company of an agreeable fellow minister, Henry Mayo (Hallett 1833a, 137). After having dined at the Plainfield tent, Avery returned to the preachers' stand for the afternoon sermons. At about two o'clock Jonathan Cady met him there (Hallett 1833a, 131), and the two discussed the sermon being delivered by Rev. Griffin (Marshall and Brown 1833, 97). Avery was back at the Weston tent by four that afternoon (Hallett 1833a, 141). During the half hour he spent there, or immediately afterward, he met the Reverend Abraham D. Merrill, who alerted him that Sarah Cornell was on the camp grounds. The two decided that they should warn the community that she—and other women of bad repute—were attempting to mix with the decent people (Hallett 1833a, 134). Although Avery and Merrill took tea with Milton Daggett immediately after their conversation (Hallett 1833a, 141), Daggett was not informed of Sarah's unacceptability.

Henry Mayo and his wife Betsy were also in the small party that took tea in the Weston tent that afternoon (Hallett 1833a, 137–38). After tea, Henry walked to young Mr. Elliot's, returned to the tent, and sat conversing with Avery until the horn blew, at seven twenty-five, to announce evening services (Hallett 1833a, 137). At Avery's urging, Mayo accompanied him to the preachers' stand at the beginning of services, then into the preachers' tent as the sermons began. Mayo stayed with Avery until about fifteen minutes before the preaching ended at half past eight (Hallett 1833a, 137). After the close of services, Avery returned to the Plainfield tent, where he conversed with Elias Scott for a few minutes (Hallett 1833a, 132). Near nine o'clock he was seen leaving the grounds (Hallett 1833a, 139), and he was soon back at Elliot's for the night (Hallett 1833a, 132).

Thursday morning found him back on the grounds, at the preachers' stand from eight until ten (Hallett 1833a, 133). While at the stand he was met by Elias Scott, who, like Merrill the day before, informed him of the presence of bad women on the grounds (Hallett 1833a, 133). Avery agreed that there were indeed some questionable females attending, noting that he had earlier seen Sarah Cornell in the congregation. From half past ten until noon Avery was in the ministers' tent (Hallett 1833a, 137). He left for dinner, intending to eat at the Weston tent in the company of Rev. Merrill and Milton Daggett (Hallett 1833a, 141). On his way to his meal, he met Phineas Crandall, with whom he spoke about the possibility of his taking Peter Sabins's place at Elliot's (Hallett 1833a, 133).

In the early afternoon Avery conversed with the Reverend Samuel Palmer in the Grafton tent (Hallett 1833a, 139), then attended the afternoon services beginning at two o'clock and ending at half past three (Hallett 1833a, 133). By five o'clock he was back at the Weston tent, where, hearing his name mentioned in connection with Sarah Cornell, he reproved Betsy Mayo for her loose tongue (Hallett 1833a, 138). A few minutes before tea, Avery left Weston and went to the Plainfield tent (Hallett 1833a, 133), perhaps to avoid the questions that Mrs. Mayo's conversation might prompt. By six he had returned to officiate at the opening of a prayer meeting. Avery called the meeting to order, prayed once or twice, then turned the activities over to Milton Daggett and other exhorters (Hallett 1833a, 142). He stayed at the service until the candles were lit (Hallett 1833a, 138), and when the horn blew for the public evening meeting was helping Daggett repair the tent (Hallett 1833a, 141). Excusing himself, he left his friends and moved off toward the preachers' stand.

Sarah Cornell claimed that Avery went directly to the inn, where he had agreed to meet her, then to the forest where the seduction took place. Avery's ministerial friends told a significantly different story. Phineas Crandall remembered meeting Avery as he left the Weston tent and making arrangements to join him after services for the walk back to Elliot's (Hallett 1833a, 134). Henry Mayo recalled that he stayed in the preachers' tent with Avery throughout the evening until Crandall was finished preaching at about half past eight (Hallett 1833a, 137). At nine o'clock Crandall found Avery waiting for him at the appointed spot. The two ministers went back to the preachers' tent to pick up Crandall's possessions, walked to Elliot's, conversed for about an hour, then went to sleep (Hallett 1833a, 134).

The last sermon of the meeting was to be preached on Friday afternoon by Abraham D. Merrill (*New England Christian Herald*, 12 September 1832, 198) from 1 Timothy 4:8. The power of Merrill's discourse, however, which netted twelve converts, was missed by Avery, who had left the grounds several hours before. Early that morning the preacher, anxious to get home, retrieved his horse and chaise from the barn, where they had stood unused throughout the meeting (Hallett 1833a, 131), and prepared to return to

Bristol. By seven o'clock he was ready to go, impatiently waiting for Phineas Crandall to return from the grounds with a forgotten cloak. When Crandall was still nowhere in sight after Avery had exchanged a few words with Elias Scott (Hallett 1833a, 133–34), the minister took advantage of the delay to seek out Milton Daggett at the Weston tent and bid him farewell. By then his passenger was ready to go, and Avery could set out for home.

That evening saw Crandall deposited in Providence and Avery safely returned to his family in Bristol. If his wife or his congregation asked, he could report the meeting an unqualified success. Under fair skies, thirty-six tents—three devoted to blacks and Indians—had held the core of a crowd that swelled to five thousand on Wednesday, and which, ministered to by twenty-three traveling and six local preachers, produced seventy converts to Christ. The only complaint aired about the orderly crowd was amusing: The Reverend S. W. Coggeshall, stifling a yawn, commented that loud prayer meetings lasting late into the night had disturbed the sleep of others and demonstrated "religion without mercy" (*Christian Herald*, 12 September 1832, 198).

Once home from the camp meeting, whether or not with a clear conscience, the minister returned to his daily rounds. In September he hosted a four days meeting in Bristol to which he invited Ira Bidwell, then stationed at Fall River (Hallett 1833b, 15). It was probably during this visit that the two men decided to exchange ministerial services in the coming month. The exchange would be useful to both: Bidwell, who had previously been stationed at Bristol, would have the opportunity to renew old ties, and Avery would be introduced to a new community where he might someday be expected to take over clerical duties. It would also serve to strengthen the bond between the two preachers—a bond that Bidwell apparently valued. A native of Connecticut like Avery, Bidwell was seven years his junior but roughly his equal in the church (Allen 1880). Although he had been an elder of the church since 1828, the younger minister seemed occasionally unsure of his duties and looked to Avery for advice.

Avery arrived in Fall River on Friday, October 19, ready to take over the congregation for the next three days. Bidwell was there to greet him, introduce him to the flock at services that evening, and guide him to his lodgings at Edward Mason's house, where Sarah Cornell had stayed during her visit the previous spring. The following morning, after spending a restless night (Lawless 1833;

Aristides 1833, 79), Avery saw Bidwell off to Bristol where, of course, no introductions were needed. That evening he officiated at a prayer meeting at George Davol's home (Hallett 1833a, 89), expounding on a chapter from Matthew before others rose to pray and exhort (Avery 1834, 15). When the meeting concluded before nine o'clock, Avery left the congregation to its own devices and disappeared from sight until his delayed appearance at the door of the worried Mrs. Bidwell. On Sunday he preached to the assembled congregation, and on the following Monday he returned to Bristol.

Avery's rendition of his Fall River trip indicates that he had one interview with Sarah Cornell—on the night of the nineteenth on the steps of Mason's house—in which she begged him not to expose her character in Fall River as he had in Lowell and by letter in Dover (Drury 1833, 3–4). The minister's critics latter suggested that the short interview of the nineteenth precipitated both Avery's sleeplessness that night and a longer conversation with Sarah following the next evening's prayer meeting (Hallett 1833a, 190). Avery, of course, stoutly denied it.

In the weeks that followed, Avery spent several days away from his church in Bristol. At the end of the first week of November he attended a four days meeting in Portsmouth (Staples 1833a, 16). Earlier in that week he had been seen by the Reverend Abraham Holway in the streets of Warren, the town immediately north of Bristol. By the middle of the month he was in Warren again, describing this second venture to Holway as a shopping trip for a new stove (Hallett 1833a, 152).

Avery's final expedition of November took him to Providence for a four-day meeting. His stay in Providence became, during his trial, a matter of great interest to both his critics and his friends. His movements were of particular concern because on the morning of November 27, the second day of the meeting, the engineer of the steam packet *King Philip*, then at berth on South Water Street in Providence, received a letter addressed to Sarah "Connell" at Mrs. Cole's house in Fall River. That anonymous letter, which was later found in Sarah's possessions, began the negotiations that led to her death on December 20. It was of particular importance, then, to determine if Avery might have been—as engineer Orswell claimed—the man who sent the letter.

On Monday, November 26, Avery took the mail stage from Bristol to Providence. Arriving between four and five o'clock in the afternoon, just as night began to fall, Avery left the stage at the

doorstep of a Methodist baker, Pardon Jillson, who had offered
him a room (Hallett 1833a, 143). Jillson served his guest tea, then
accompanied him to a prayer meeting, presumably at half past
seven. The two men returned to the baker's house together. At
about half past nine Avery took a candle and went upstairs to bed
(Hallett 1833a, 143). The next morning, the minister appeared
shortly after daylight. After sitting with Jillson for a few minutes,
he observed that dawn was approaching and left to attend a sunrise
prayer service (Hallett 1833a, 143).

At the prayer service Avery met the Reverend Jotham Horton,
who requested that he take charge of the nine o'clock prayer meeting to follow. Horton had expected to preside over it, but was called
away on an errand that would occupy him past the opening hour
(Hallett 1833a, 146). Avery agreed to perform the opening cere-
monies. Shortly after eight o'clock the sunrise service broke up, allowing the faithful time to get breakfast before the nine o'clock
meeting began. Five minutes later Avery was back at Pardon Jillson's
house where the baker, returning from his morning rounds, found
him awaiting a meal (Hallett 1833a, 143). By half past eight Avery
had eaten breakfast and excused himself to visit Rev. Holway, the
minister from Warren lodged nearby at Mr. Fuller's (Hallett 1833a,
143). The Reverend Joseph Ireson, who had accompanied Avery
home from the sunrise service, was delegated the responsibility for
morning prayers at Jillson's house.

At Fuller's, Holway was just finishing preparations for the day.
While he shaved, he and Avery occupied themselves with a banter-
ing disagreement over the meaning of the report brought by spies
from Canaan (Hallett 1833a, 149). Avery's purpose in visiting, however, was more mundane than theological dispute; he hoped to get
a ride home—or at least to Warren—with Rev. Holway (Hallett
1833a, 149). Apparently they could not coordinate their schedules
because when Avery left the following day he took the stage back to
Bristol.

After talking with Holway, Avery walked back alone to the
meeting house for the prayer meeting. (It was during these unobserved moments that Avery was supposed to have hurried down
to the *King Philip* and handed his letter to the engineer.) He was
late; Horton, who had asked him to open the meeting to avoid delay, had arrived before him. Irritated to find the meeting not yet
underway at five past nine, Horton took over (Hallett 1833a, 146).
Avery appeared at the end of the opening hymns and immediately

offered a prayer—but no explanation (Hallett 1833a, 153). After its faltering first moments, the meeting was orderly and uneventful.

At the conclusion of the prayers, near half past ten, Avery stepped outside momentarily with Samuel Palmer. After a short intermission, the two preachers returned for morning services, preached by Joseph Ireson (Hallett 1833a, 153). Collecting another minister, Joseph A. Merrill, Avery and Palmer took their lunch at the house of Hezekiah Anthony. Avery and Palmer then attended the afternoon service, which ended with a prayer by Palmer at about four o'clock. In all, Avery and Palmer had been together in a continuous series of prayer meetings and services for seven hours.

Where Avery took his supper that evening is not recorded. He did not eat at Jillson's. Probably the ministers at any four days meeting tried to distribute their meals among the congregation to avoid placing an undue burden on the few in whose houses they stayed. After evening meeting Avery returned to Jillson's house for the night (Hallett 1833a, 143). On the following morning Avery went to the new market to a barber, returned to Jillson's, and waited for the afternoon stage to take him back to Bristol (Hallett 1833a, 143). On the next day he celebrated Thanksgiving with his own congregation (Avery 1834, 16).

If Avery were indeed not the man who sent the letter to Sarah Cornell by the *King Philip* on the morning of November 27, he was certainly among the most unfortunate of individuals to have been so conveniently in Providence at that time. Whoever the letter writer was, the days that followed must have been filled with tension while Sarah digested its contents and composed a reply. That she chose, of the meetings offered, Fall River at six o'clock on the evening of December 20 (early enough to avoid the throngs of operatives who would still be in the mills and late enough for darkness to provide some protection from discovery) was apparent from the confirming note she received on December 8. Mailed in Fall River, the note of the eighth added to the impression of Avery's involvement because, as in Providence, he was on the scene when this final letter was dropped into the manufacturing village's mailbox.

On the morning of December 7, between eight and nine o'clock, Avery arrived in Fall River by stage. His destination was not Fall River, he told Ira Bidwell whom he happened to meet while waiting for the stage journey to continue, but New Bedford, where he hoped to find a foundry that could supply some brasswork for his church. Bidwell changed the traveler's plans by suggesting that

8. North Main Street, Fall River. Sarah Cornell moved to this manufacturing village, then lying on the Massachusetts–Rhode Island border, in October 1832 to be near Ephraim Avery, who was stationed in Bristol, Rhode Island. From John Warren Barber, *Historical Collections . . .* (Worchester: Warren Lazell, 1839).

there were local brassworkers who could fill his order. Besides, Bidwell added, the Fall River congregation would welcome Avery at their services. The invitation was accepted, and the two men sought out the local brassworks. Unfortunately, by the time Avery discovered his needs could not be met in Fall River, the stage for New Bedford had already departed. Disappointed, he accompanied Bidwell to his home, where they shared lunch. During the early afternoon, Avery apparently loitered about the house while Bidwell visited the sick. Upon Bidwell's return, the two went to the house of Edward Mason, who had invited them to tea. That evening, commencing at eight o'clock, Avery held services at the newly enlarged Methodist meeting house on Central Street. Invited to spend the evening with one of the congregation, Avery chose to remain at the Bidwells' for the night (Drury 1833, 20; Staples 1833a, 10).

Bidwell's pleas for a longer visit were unsuccessful, and the rainy morning of the eighth found both men in Iram Smith's variety store on Pleasant Street, waiting for the New Bedford stage that would carry Avery back to Bristol. The two ministers arrived at the store shortly after ten o'clock and, aware that the stage was not due at nearby Lawton's Hotel for half an hour, apparently amused themselves by perusing a copy of the November 28 *Fall River Weekly Recorder*. A discussion of the paper's contents ensued, and Avery decided to write a letter to the editor in protest (Hallett 1833b, 19). Exactly what the preacher was protesting is uncertain; Avery later described it vaguely as some "exceptional matter" in the paper's editorial columns (Melvill 1834, doc. no. 6).

Nothing in the paper's contents was precisely incendiary, but, whatever article was the focus of the minister's attention, he was too agitated—or too bored by his wait for the stage—to delay composing the letter until he reached home. Avery called on the shopkeeper for paper and a sealing wafer (Hallett 1833a, 73). Unclear in his mind about the request for paper, Iram Smith was later certain about the wafer; he remembered that his stock had been depleted and that it was necessary for him to go next door to the shop of Content Parry to get one. Although Smith thought it was a common red wafer that he handed to the preacher, Mrs. Parry was sure that she had provided an unusual purple one (and identified it on the letter of the eighth that was discovered in Sarah Cornell's possessions) (Hallett 1833b, 2).

On that same morning, Mrs. Parry was awaiting her husband's return from an errand; thus she found herself staring expectantly out the window from time to time. Her husband did not come immediately into view, but she observed Rev. Bidwell leave Smith's store for a few moments—moments in which Smith was also away. Avery was thus left in the store unattended and could have taken a half sheet of paper, written a quick note, and closed it before either Bidwell or Smith returned. The storekeeper could not be sure, but he believed that he might have seen Avery at his desk when he returned to his shop (Hallett 1833a, 73). Jeremiah Howland, who went into the store that morning, had no doubt that he saw Avery with a piece of white writing paper in his hand (Hallett 1833a, 75).

If Avery had composed a letter in the shop, no one actually saw it. The minister accepted the wafer he had called for, and the subject was dropped. As the hour for departure of the stage approached, Avery and Bidwell left the store, Bidwell to return to his home and Avery to go to the boarding station at Lawton's tavern. The short walk from Smith's to Lawton's did not take the minister past the post office. However, he continued up the street, past Lawton's, to the stables where the young stage driver, Stephen Bartlett, was hitching the team (Hallett 1833a, 76). Informing Bartlett that he would be taking the stage back to Bristol, Avery returned to Lawton's door to await the fully prepared vehicle. The post office stood on his route back to the tavern. Joseph Lesure, a postal clerk, thought he recognized Avery as he passed, heard a letter fall into the mailbox, and, upon retrieving it, found it to be addressed to Sarah M. Cornell (spelled "Connell") (Hallett 1833a, 91). Avery boarded the stage at Lawton's door and was home in time for dinner, his brasswork unobtained and apparently forgotten. Two Sundays later he preached a sermon attacking the Reformed Methodists who had separated from the Methodist Episcopal church, taking his text from II Kings 45 : 16: "Fear not, for they that be with us are more than they that be with them" (*Providence Journal*, 1 January 1883). Fighting other battles, if he felt any nervous anticipation about the following Thursday—December 20—he gave no sign.

The events of Avery's life that linked him to Sarah Cornell were hotly debated at his trial, in the public press, and in the streets of most towns on the eastern seaboard. Even with the remarkable assemblage of witnesses brought by his defense to testify to minute details in the sequence and timing of behavior that was unexceptional at the moment of occurrence, Avery was unable to demonstrate conclusively that his version of the events of 1832 was accurate. He was at the Thompson camp meeting and could have met and seduced Sarah. He was in Fall River on October 19 and 20 and could have had two interviews with her. He went to Warren in the middle of November and could have mailed the letter Sarah received postmarked from that town. He was in Providence on the morning of November 27, was suspiciously late for prayer meeting, and could have delivered the letter into Orswell's hand. He was in Fall River on December 8 and did pass the post office where Sarah's final letter was deposited. It is small wonder that his harried defense proposed a conspiracy theory that assumed a conscious plan to make him look guilty.

The events of the day of Sarah's demise, predictably, share in the uncertainty of the months that preceded them. Avery stoutly asserted that his absence from home during the hours in question was the product of a spur-of-the-moment excursion combining the business of procuring winter fuel with the pleasure of sight-seeing. The people of Fall River attributed his journey to another motive. According to the minister, the subject of Rhode Island coal had come up in casual conversation at the four days meeting that had been held on the northern tip of the island—at Portsmouth— in the second week of November. Samuel Drake's passing comments about the benefits of the local product caught the ear of more than one thrifty preacher. Because the coal was cheap and could be mixed with better-burning, more costly coal to produce a good, inexpensive fuel, Avery was determined to inquire further about its purchase. Abraham Holway, stationed at Warren, agreed to accompany him on some future expedition to the island to secure a supply, but as the weeks rolled by he continued to put off the trip (Avery 1834, 16). Fearing that cold weather would catch him unprepared, Avery decided to take the first pleasant day he could spare for an excursion to the island. His interest in the trip was increased by letters from his father that described the older man's service on Rhode Island during the Revolutionary War. On Thursday, December 20, Avery found himself unemployed for the afternoon and the weather "remarkably pleasant" (Avery 1834, 16). At about two o'clock he set out on foot for the ferry two miles from his house that would take him to the island.

William Pearce, the ferryman on the Bristol side, took Avery across the bay and directed him toward the mines. For a moment the minister considered calling on an acquaintance on the island for company, but reflecting that the errand would take him out of his way and use up much of the remaining daylight, he decided to make his ramble a solitary one. Following the road south for a short distance, he left the right of way beside a windmill and started off to the southwest. Near the mines he encountered a man carrying a gun whom he asked if coal were being produced; the man's negative reply ended his pleasant daydreams of an economical winter. His trip now reduced to a simple sight-seeing excursion, Avery considered renewing some of the acquaintances he had struck up at the Portsmouth meeting. His intention to visit the Freeborns, who lived nearby, was soon canceled by a short conversation with a small boy who left his sheep and cattle long enough to inform Avery that the family was not at home (Avery 1834, 17).

Widow Wilcox, who lived only a short distance farther south on the island, had asked Avery to call on her when they met early in November (Staples 1833a, 16); hoping that he could remember the complicated directions to her house, the minister made one more attempt to visit an island friend. His progress, however, was slowed by the uneven ground, approaching darkness, and his tender an-

kle, which had not completely mended from the injury suffered in
Lowell. By the time he had come out of the pastures to the road,
nightfall had made discovery of the Wilcox house unlikely. Giving
up on this last social impulse of the day, Avery turned back toward the ferry. Following the roads made his return journey easier.
Shortly after nine o'clock he made his way into the sinkroom of the
ferryman, Jeremiah Gifford, and requested the passage that would
take him to the warmth of his own fire. Gifford would not comply
because of the lateness of the hour, and the minister was forced to
spend the night as the ferryman's guest.

Next morning, Gifford's daughter, Jane, remarked to the
preacher that she had not heard that he was to preach on the island
the previous night. Avery replied that he had been there on private
business and should have stopped at brother Cook's had he known
the hour when he sought passage over the bay. Shortly afterward,
Jane's brother rowed the eager minister across to Bristol's shore
(Avery 1834, 18). Avery was safely home with his family in time for
morning prayers (Hallett 1833a, 72).

In the months that followed, a massive search directed by the
minister's legal counsel and the Methodist organization itself failed
to locate either the man with a gun or the boy herding his animals—the only persons who could substantiate Avery's story. Faced
with little more than the preacher's word for his whereabouts on
the twentieth, many came to believe that he had lied and had in fact
followed a quite different course.

On December 18, the Tuesday prior to Avery's journey, Nancy
Gladding, a Bristol Methodist, invited the minister and his family
to her house on the twentieth. Avery declined the invitation, claiming that Thursday would not be as convenient for him as Friday
(Hallett 1833a, 72). Although one of Avery's four children was ill
during that week, and the minister might legitimately have been
putting off the visit until the child recovered, some skeptics looked
at his determination to move the visit from Thursday to Friday as
an overt attempt to keep the twentieth open for his excursion. Remembering the letter posted in Fall River on the eighth, which set
the meeting between Sarah and her correspondent at six on the
afternoon of the twentieth, the minister's opponents found his
freedom from obligations in Bristol on that afternoon less than
accidental.

Jane Gifford threw another shadow on Avery's story by her account of his conversation with her on the morning of the twenty-

first. According to the ferryman's daughter, Avery had informed her that he had been on the island "on business at brother Cook's" (Hallett 1833a, 65) and would have stayed there all night had he known it was so late. Since neither Cook who lived in the area— William or John Earl—had seen Avery that night, if Miss Gifford's testimony was correct, the minister had lied about his whereabouts on the island.

Avery's prosecution hoped to prove that the minister had not stayed on the island at all, but had crossed Howland's stone bridge to the mainland and traveled to Fall River in the late afternoon, remaining on the outskirts of town until darkness had sufficiently advanced to make his discovery by acquaintances unlikely. While sitting on a stone wall on Andrew Robeson's property, Avery had noticed a cart used by Abner Davis and Benjamin Manchester to hold their equipment as they blasted rocks. In the cart were several coarse bags, laced together with the cord that would supply him with his murder weapon. Shortly after six, the minister supposedly entered town, took a hurried meal at Lawton's, then met Sarah at the appointed location. Directing her to the south, where he had seen Durfee's farm yard with its sheltering haystack, Avery tried to convince the worried young woman that an abortion would be in the best of interests of everyone. When his crude and cruel attempts at manually stimulating a miscarriage failed, he took the opportunity offered by Sarah's debilitated condition to run to the cart, withdraw a cord, return, wrap it twice around her neck, secure it with a clove hitch, and strangle her. Tying the corpse to a pole in the haystack, he hoped to simulate suicide. Once the illusion was established, with fear of discovery and death spurring him on, he hastened from the scene and made his way to Gifford's ferry, the last obstacle between him and the security of home.

Whether the minister had been on the most innocent of errands or the most murderous, sunrise of December 21 found him trudging up from the ferry toward his home and family. Probably met by a worried and questioning wife—who nonetheless had good news about their child's health—Avery was home in time to officiate at morning prayers. After an unexceptional day performing mundane tasks, that afternoon he took his family, including his convalescent son, to their appointed tea at Nancy Gladding's. Perfectly at ease, the preacher engaged in polite conversation, offered a prayer, then took his leave by six o'clock (Hallett 1833a, 72). It was the last untroubled social call of his ministerial career.

5. Preliminary Engagements

For a man of Ephraim Avery's temperament, the night of December 23, 1832, must have been an ordeal. In the custody of the arresting officer, whose vigilance was a tacit assertion that the minister was expected to flee from justice, and charged with a crime "to name which would chill one's blood," (Avery 1834, 11), Avery was unsure of the degree of sympathy he would face when the examination began in the morning. Had they been forthcoming—and they seem not to have been—no assurances of legal security from his lawyer could have completely allayed his fears, which focused on public censure and loss of ministerial status as well as on criminal conviction and punishment.

The opening of the hearing before Justices John Howe and Levi Haile the following morning proved something of an anticlimax. In their remarkable zeal to bring the truth to light, Howe and Haile had far outstripped both the prosecution and the defense. Nathaniel Bullock had been involved in the case for less than twenty-four hours when the hearing convened, and was still trying to assemble a legal team (to include Joseph M. Blake and Richard Randolf). William Staples, assigned as prosecutor in the absence of State Attorney General Albert C. Greene, had not yet arrived in town. Faced with an unprepared defense and a nonexistent prosecution, the justices could do little but defer the case until the next day.

9. Bristol County Courthouse, Bristol, Massachusetts. Here, on Christmas day 1832, Ephraim Avery declared himself innocent of Sarah Cornell's murder. The examination that followed resulted in his discharge by the court and intense agitation in Fall River.

Before they adjourned, however, they offered the grateful minister a small portion of his lost freedom. Convinced that Avery would not attempt to escape, Howe and Haile freed him from close arrest and confined him to his house for the remainder of the hearing. Momentarily saved from the humiliation and restraint of prison, Avery returned home, where he and Bullock met with Joseph Blake to plan their strategy. Blake listened to Avery's explanation of his condition, then advised him that he might make such a declaration at the opening of the proceedings in court. It is probable that the lawyers spent much of the day refining the text of the preacher's voluntary statement.

The twenty-fifth, not then a legal holiday in Rhode Island, saw both the dramatic arrival of William Staples, accompanied on the *King Philip* by the Fall River Committee and its supporters, and the opening of the hearing's actual testimony. Advised by the court that he was not required to make a statement and that his statement, if proven false, could be used against him, Avery chose to occupy the first day with his carefully prepared text. The minister's lawyers had concluded that they would be hard-pressed to prove Avery's whereabouts on the twentieth. Unless Rev. Drake could come up with an accidental witness to Avery's island excursion, the best they could hope for would be to cast doubt on the inevitable prosecution assertion that he had traveled to Fall River. Their most profitable course, then, was to ignore the details of the day of the murder and focus on preconditioning events. Were Avery shown to be a man of unblemished moral character, and Sarah Cornell a deranged whore—and were the minister cleared of any suspicion of authorship of the letters that had sent the young woman to her death—then the prosecution's circumstantial evidence would lose its force and the charges would have to be dropped.

It was hardly surprising that when Avery stood before the justices—surrounded by a throng of curious people from Bristol, Tiverton, and Fall River—he failed to mention the critical December 20 and instead detailed three years' acquaintance with the unfortunate failings of the deceased woman. Implicitly a denial of "improper connexion" and murder, Avery's statement was much more directly an assertion of relative moral worth (Drury 1833, 3–6). Sarah Cornell was presented—unhappily by a minister who had failed to save her—as profane, unchaste, untruthful, devious, dishonest, and afflicted by a "foul disease," a woman outside the bounds of normal social intercourse who sought by trickery and de-

ceit to insinuate herself, for un-Christian purpose, in Christian society. On the other hand, Avery painted himself as a modest and
humble propagator of the faith whose good opinion of his fellow
man sometimes led him too far in offering the penitent sinner an
opportunity to reform. His relationship to Sarah—in which he provided her a certificate of good standing in the church even though
he was aware of rumors detrimental to her character, forgave her
sins against him and the church, and agreed to let her prove her
reformed character when he found her living in Fall River—pointed
consistently to his Christian willingness to aid in the salvation of a
wayward soul.

Interestingly—and here the influence of Avery's lawyers is apparent in the direction and emphasis of his statements—the only
two times in which Avery admitted reversing his charitable position
toward Sarah were those around which major points of his defense
would revolve. He was first adamant that she must be tried for
adultery when rumors began to circulate in Lowell in 1830. His
participation in the case both led him to the startling discovery that
she was suffering from venereal disease (which, of course, would
preclude any thought of exploiting her sexually) and established
the motive for her dramatic quest for revenge against him. He rejected her a second time at the Thompson camp meeting, where he
warned others that Sarah was unfit for Christian company, and
where, significantly, their physical encounter was alleged to have
taken place. While inconsistent with his later decision to let Sarah
reside in the Methodist community at Fall River undetected, both
actions were defended as the legitimate activities of a minister seeking to maintain his flock's security. Thus Avery portrayed himself as
a minister who sought the sinner's ultimate salvation while attempting to protect the congregation's purity. His statements challenged
Justices Haile and Howe to consider not only if a minister might be
tempted to seduction—and through its unfortunate consequences,
murder—but also if a man aware of a woman's disease would still
seek her favors and if a plotting adulterer would bring the object of
his ambitions to the attention of his closest clerical associates.

The prosecution's case was opened the next morning. William
Staples, aided by a number of Fall River and Tiverton people bent
on gathering evidence (*Fall River Weekly Recorder*, 26 December
1832), hoped to forestall a long proceeding of doubtful outcome by
transferring the hearing to Tiverton. The first suggestion that this
be done had been presented to Justice Howe on the twenty-fifth by

Elihu Hicks and Harvey Harnden. Staples was aware that Howe had appeared indecisive and had agreed to make a determination on the matter later. Seeking to achieve by force of argument what had not been accomplished by a show of force on Christmas, Staples opened his case by calling John Durfee, who had discovered the body, Dr. Thomas Wilbur, who had first examined it, and Elihu Hicks, who had selected the two coroner's juries. Hicks explained the circumstances of his investigation, then presented the court with the letters that had been discovered in Sarah Cornell's trunk and had implicated Avery in her condition (Drury 1833, 3). Staples's last witness for the day was John Orswell, who identified one of the letters and pointed out Avery as the man who had given it to him for delivery.

Staples was confident that he had demonstrated that a crime had been committed, in Tiverton, and that there was reasonable suspicion that Avery was its perpetrator. It could only be a matter of form for him to request that the hearing be moved to the jurisdiction in which the crime had been committed. The *Fall River Weekly Recorder* felt the same confidence and reported that the trial was soon to be brought to Tiverton (*Fall River Weekly Recorder*, 26 December 1832). When the court convened at half past nine on the morning of the twenty-seventh, John Durfee was recalled to clarify a point of his testimony, then Staples moved that the court decline jurisdiction in the case. Rather than a quick agreement, the prosecutor found himself faced with an argument of several hours' duration, at the end of which Howe and Haile determined to hear the case. It was a serious defeat; through its decision, the court had voiced skepticism about both the existence of a crime and Avery's participation in it.

That afternoon, Staples called Benjamin Manchester and Thomas Hart to testify to the discovery of the broken fragments of Sarah's comb scattered over the hillside (Drury 1833, 10). Seth Darling followed, asserting that the knot at Sarah's throat was a clove hitch, which cannot be tightened with the ends of the rope parallel—as they must have been if she hanged herself. Darling further noted that the corpse's hair had been wildly disheveled, indicating a violent attack before her calash was put back on her head and its ribbon caught under the cord that choked her life away (Staples 1833a, 5).

All of Staples's ground was not so easily won. Having gained at least a reasonable suspicion that Sarah's death had not been self-inflicted, he asked the court's permission to present witnesses who could establish that Avery had indeed been in Fall River on the afternoon of the murder. It would have been better for him if he had not been granted his request: Leonard Rice, who had seen a stranger in town on the twentieth, could not identify Avery and instead picked out Rev. Horton, a man shorter and heavier than Avery, on the basis of his "built" (Drury 1833, 11). Margaret Hambly was no better, and her fumbling attempts to pick out Avery brought howls of derisive laughter from the crowd.

Staples followed these unfortunate witnesses with Foster Hooper, whose medical testimony about the condition of the corpse and the "half grown" fetus he had discovered in Sarah's uterus could be certain to still the boisterous spectators. The day ended with testimony from Peleg Cranston, keeper of Howland's bridge, that a tall stranger had crossed to the mainland on the afternoon of the twentieth and that footprints in the sand indicated that a man had returned to the island sometime that night, and with Jeremiah Gifford's statement that Avery had arrived at his house between half past nine and a quarter to ten (Drury 1833, 12–13).

On Friday morning Bullock opened with a request that Hooper be called again to describe the cord that had been found around Sarah's neck. The physician obligingly identified the rope as marline, but was unable to say if it could have come from the cotton factory in which Sarah had been employed (Drury 1833, 13). The prosecution resumed, after this inconclusive attempt to link the girl to the murder weapon, by calling Harriet Hathaway, who could describe the last day Sarah had boarded in her house, and then by bringing Lucy, Harriet's daughter, to the stand. Lucy's testimony ended with an emotional bombshell:

> A week or a fortnight from the Sabbath before her death, in the morning [Sarah] asked me this question: "Lucy, don't you think it is possible for an innocent girl to be led away, by a man that she has confidence in, and rather looks up to?" I hesitated and said—"I don't know." She then said—"But what can an innocent girl do, in the hands of a strong man, and he using all kinds of argument." I never suspected she was in a delicate situation then, or at any other time; she had made similar suggestions as those before to me; she was not visited by any young man during her living at our house, and never went out evenings, but Tuesday to go to class-meetings, and Sabbath evenings. Said she had been to many camp-meetings; said she would never go to any more. I

says—"Why, Sarah?" "Why," says she, "because I have seen things transacted there that would condemn them to my mind." I then asked her what it was? she said it was between a church member and a minister, and a married man, too (Drury 1833, 15–16).

Staples followed the Hathaways with Elijah Cole, who, from his experience with Sarah when she boarded at his house, could substantiate what the two women had said. Sarah, he reported, "had a melancholy appearance on her countenance, and appeared to feign cheerfulness, as though something troubled her" (Drury 1833, 16). The morning ended with testimony from Abner Davis, John Durfee, and Benjamin Manchester that they had all seen a stranger, one who well might have been the Methodist minister—although they were not sure—loitering near the Durfees' stack yard on the afternoon of the twentieth. Through Staples's careful juxtaposition of witnesses, the prosecution's case took on an aura of strength.

The afternoon session was begun by calling Elihu Hicks to the stand to testify to the five letters that had been found in Sarah's trunk after her death. A succession of witnesses followed—including Seth Darling, Fall River's assistant postmaster who was forced under cross examination to admit that he was a member of the town's committee of vigilance—that tried, inconclusively, to link Avery to the correspondence (Drury 1833, 18–19). Stymied by honest witnesses whose "impression of mind" was not strong enough to send a man to the gallows, Staples read the pink letter Sarah had received from Providence by the hand of John Orswell into evidence (Drury 1833, 19). Needing some way to bring Avery and the other letters together, the lawyer was forced to call his first obviously unfriendly witness, Avery's friend Ira M. Bidwell, who began a five-hour ordeal on the witness stand, describing his knowledge of Avery's movements and relationship to the dead woman. At adjournment his testimony was still not complete.

On Saturday morning, instead of simply calling Bidwell back to the stand, Staples chose first to question Williams Durfee about the rope used in the murder. If Durfee's evidence was redundant, it still served a purpose; after hours of discourse by one of Avery's friends, Staples wanted to bring the justices' attention back to the horror of the crime. No one in the courtroom could fail to be struck with sickened fascination by Durfee's account of how the cord was so deeply embedded in the victim's neck that it could not be cut out without also slicing her flesh (Drury 1833, 23). With the ghastly

No 5

10. Incorrectly dated 1831 instead of 1832, this letter, written on pink paper, was delivered to Sarah Cornell by John Orswell, engineer of the steamboat *King Philip*, who later swore that Ephraim Avery had handed it to him in Providence. From David Melvill, *A Fac-simile of the Letters Produced at the Trial of the Rev. Ephraim Avery* (Boston: Pendleton's Lithography, 1833).

crime reaffirmed, the prosecution serenely called Bidwell to finish his testimony. The day was ended, after Bidwell was finally released, with an attempt, through the testimony of Jeremiah Howland and store-owner Iram Smith, to demonstrate that Avery, on the morning of December 8, had had the opportunity at Smith's store to compose the letter that led Sarah to her death on the twentieth (Drury 1833, 24–25).

The court did not meet again until the afternoon of Tuesday, January 1, when John J. Paine, then of Providence but previously Grindall Rawson's apprentice in Woodstock, was called to vouch for Sarah's good character while she was employed by her brother-in-law (Drury 1833, 25–26). After Paine's testimony, Staples had to plead for an adjournment until Rawson and his wife could arrive from Woodstock. The justices agreed, and the proceedings were put off until nine o'clock the next morning.

When Grindall Rawson took the stand on Wednesday morning, his testimony went smoothly as he detailed Sarah's movements in the months she had lived with him and his wife. As he neared the end of his tale, Staples casually asked him: "Did you hear Maria, before she left your house for the last time in October last, say what her situation was?" (Drury 1833, 27). Before he could reply, describing Sarah's confession and accusation of Avery, the defense objected. No declaration of the deceased, Bullock asserted, ought to be heard by the court because it was neither spoken under oath nor a dying statement. The court agreed, and the testimony of both Rawson and his wife was neatly eviscerated. Not allowed to recount what her sister had told her, Lucretia Rawson was only on the stand for a few moments.

Staples had a last chance. Sarah had named Avery as the father of her child to one other person, Dr. Wilbur, to whom she had gone for medical advice in Fall River. Calling Wilbur back to the stand, the lawyer cautiously asked the court if it would be proper to have the witness describe Sarah's statements about her symptoms (Drury 1833, 28). Not so easily circumvented, the justices replied that he might describe her symptoms but not her declarations. Under that injunction, like the Rawsons before him, the physician had little to say.

Undismayed by the setback, which any lawyer would have expected, Staples patiently set out on another course. Establishing by the testimony of William Pearce and William Gifford that Avery had gone to Rhode Island on the twentieth and returned to Bristol on the twenty-first, the prosecutor called the Reverend Samuel Drake to the stand to describe Avery's trip. The court apparently saw no inconsistency in allowing Drake to testify to Avery's description of his journey on the island immediately after refusing to allow three witnesses to testify to Sarah's explanation of her condition. Staples let the minister assert that Avery had not left the island that day, then called George Lawton to swear that he had seen "a tall man" cross Howland's bridge to the mainland (Drury 1833, 31). It was a weak gesture, but the best that Staples could muster.

The diligence of Harvey Harnden gave the prosecution one more trump to play. On Saturday no one had denied in court that Avery was in Iram Smith's store on December 8, but there was no real evidence that he had written a letter there. That afternoon, Harnden went to Smith's store and carefully sifted through the supply of writing paper. His search was rewarded by the discovery of a half sheet of paper that, when microscopically examined, matched perfectly—fiber, watermark, and tearline—the paper of the letter received by Sarah. With this evidence, Staples hoped the court would accept the letter as proof that Avery was involved with the dead woman. Bullock, however, took the new evidence in stride. Even if the paper matched, he told the court, it did not identify the writer. The letter was still unsigned, and the defense still contended that it was not in Avery's handwriting. The court agreed, the letter was not admitted as evidence, and Harnden's detective work went unappreciated (Drury 1833, 31–33).

The prosecution's case was completed by the testimony of the matrons who had prepared Sarah's body for the grave. All the women agreed that bruises on the corpse's abdomen showed that Sarah had been "very much abused" immediately before death (Drury 1833, 34). Almost as an afterthought, Staples called Annis Norton to testify that she had seen a man heading from Howland's bridge toward Fall River on the twentieth, and, when court reconvened on Thursday afternoon, four other witnesses to corroborate points of detail in previous testimony. The prosecution rested its case.

Nothing in what the prosecution had managed to present forced the defense to make a major change in its strategy. Orswell's stubborn insistence that Avery was the man who had given him the pink letter in Providence would require answering, but the force of Bullock and his staff's argument would still center around casting doubt on the circumstantial evidence on which Staples relied, factually where possible and otherwise through a comparison of the characters of the minister and the mill girl he was supposed to have seduced and murdered.

The Reverend Joseph A. Merrill opened the defense by testifying that Avery's character, for the ten years he had known him, was unblemished, while Sarah had been read out of the church in 1830 for "lying and fornication" (Drury 1833, 36). When cross examined, Merrill admitted knowledge of Thomas Norris's successful slander suit against Avery, but maintained that Avery had been given a clean bill after a subsequent ecclesiastical trial and thus kept his reputation untarnished.

Bullock quickly followed with a string of witnesses whose combined testimony was designed to discredit Orswell's statements by proving that Avery could not have been at the *King Philip*'s berth on the morning of November 27. Jotham Horton reported seeing Avery at sunrise meeting on that day until ten or fifteen minutes after eight. When Pardon Jillson came home for breakfast, near quarter after eight, he found Avery at his house awaiting a meal. Jillson stated that Avery left his house at about quarter to nine, bound for Joseph Fuller's. At Fuller's Avery was picked up by the Reverend Abraham Holway, who reported his arrival at between half past eight and nine and remembered the term of his stay at between twenty and thirty minutes. Joseph Fuller confirmed Holway's story, adding that Avery could remain almost until the opening of the nine o'clock prayer meeting because his house was only two hundred feet from the meeting house. Just to be on the safe side, Bullock finally called Samuel Boyd, who had seen Avery at the prayer meeting from nine o'clock until twenty minutes before eleven (Drury 1833, 37–38). By that time, the *King Philip* had departed on its run south.

When Joseph Merrill was recalled to the stand to reaffirm Sarah's bad character by recounting the contents of her letters of confession to Avery, Staples objected. The contents of her letters, he said, could not be proved without showing the letters themselves. Merrill's account was only acceptable if the letters were first demonstrated to have been destroyed (Drury 1833, 39). The defense countered with a series of reverend witnesses who testified that they usually destroyed unimportant letters when they left a station. The only Methodist preacher to disagree was the uneasy Rev. Holway, who admitted that he kept his letters, then tried to reclaim his rash statement by adding that he did not know if he would have preserved *those* letters (Drury 1833, 39). His qualification was too late; the court was forced to conclude that the letters might not have been destroyed, and Merrill was not allowed to recount their contents.

The defense, however, was more than adequately prepared for the court's refusal to let Sarah's missing letters condemn their author. Bullock had collected four female witnesses who had personal knowledge of Sarah's depravity. Upon discovering what was to be the nature of their testimony, Justices Howe and Haile considerately withdrew from the crowded courtroom to take the women's statements in private (Drury 1833, 39). Mary Ide recounted to the attentive justices how Sarah had boarded at her mother's house in North Providence under an assumed name, had admitted she was unchaste, and had behaved badly before male visitors. Catharine Blake, who knew Sarah at Lowell, agreed that she was indeed an unsavory character and added her opinion that the girl was insane (Drury 1833, 40). Mary Ann Barnes amplified the appearance of Sarah's sexual laxity with stories of drunken orgies at taverns outside Lowell, and Lydia Pervere reinforced the notion of Sarah's insanity by reporting that she had once appeared for work at the mill dressed entirely in white (Drury 1833, 40–41).

After this flood of damning gossip, Staples managed to bring forth a witness, Jane Gifford, who could testify that Avery had lied about the purpose of his trip to Rhode Island on December 20. Here, too, the defense was prepared and replied with a barrage of witnesses testifying to Jane Gifford's bad character and dishonesty (Drury 1833, 41).

The last defense witness called on Friday afternoon was David Davol, a Portsmouth blacksmith who claimed to have made the footprints around the tollgate of Howland's bridge that the prosecution claimed were Avery's. On Saturday morning the prosecution opened the last day of testimony with Harvey Harnden, who swore to the discovery of the half sheet of paper in Iram Smith's store; then Staples read a discourse from several tracts on midwifery to demonstrate that the fetus taken from Sarah's womb might have been conceived at the Thompson camp meeting. The defense spent the rest of the day reinforcing its case—and poking holes in the prosecution's. Sarah Honey was called to recount how Sarah had once been tempted to commit suicide; Sarah Slade testified that, while the cord found around the corpse's neck was not available in the weaving room, it was to be found in the factory on a higher floor. William Hamilton swore that he had heard the shriek of a stricken woman on the night of the twentieth at about eight forty-five—much too late for Avery to have traveled from the scene and arrived at Gifford's ferry less than an hour later (Drury 1833, 44). Joseph Merrill was recalled to vouch for Avery's habit of making "excursions," and Abraham Merrill took the stand again to reinforce the image of Sarah's bad reputation in the Methodist church (Drury 1833, 44–45). John Orswell's testimony was challenged by William Pearce and Deputy Sheriff William Paul, both of whom swore that the *King Philip*'s engineer was uncertain about identifying Avery when he was ushered into his presence on Christmas day (Drury 1833, 46–47).

The defense's final thrust proved to be dangerously ineffectual. Calling Rev. Holway and Nicholas Peck to the stand, Bullock established that Avery had been told of the supply of cheap coal on the island and had expressed a desire to travel to the mines to procure a quantity for winter fuel. Oliver Brownell, who lived a mile and a half from the ferry in Portsmouth, was then brought to testify that he had seen a man—who might have been Avery—near his house on the afternoon of the twentieth (Drury 1833, 48). From Brownell's house, Avery, if indeed it was him, might have either gone on to explore to the south or traveled to the mainland to murder Sarah. The key testimony would come from the next witness, Sarah Jones. Mrs. Jones, a Methodist, lived far down the island; if she could report seeing Avery, or a man who might have been him, on the afternoon of the twentieth, she could substantially demonstrate that it would have been impossible for him to have reached Fall River in time to commit the murder. Avery's lawyers were stunned when, after carefully drawing out her story before the justices, they asked the time of day she had seen the stranger. "I am positive now," she said, "it was in the forenoon between 11 and 12" (Drury 1833, 49). The man could not have been Avery, who did not reach the island until the afternoon, and the defense had ended its case doing the prosecution's job; Avery could not be proved to have been elsewhere at the moment of the crime.

Richard Randolf suavely ignored the gaping hole that had unexpectedly appeared in the defense's armor when he made his summation. Without commenting on the problem of Avery's whereabouts on the twentieth, Randolf focused on the minister's exemplary character and contrasted it to Sarah's repulsively deformed morality. Was it reasonable, he seemed to ask, to think evil of a good man, and good of an evil woman, without certain proof? And what proof was there? Orswell's testimony, he asserted, was false. The only legitimate conclusion that could be drawn was that Sarah Cornell, driven by an insane thirst for revenge on a dutiful preacher, had hung herself (Staples 1833a, 22).

William Staples, responding for the prosecution, claimed that the evidence precluded the possibility of suicide. Sarah must have been murdered; the only real question was the identity of the perpetrator. Avery was unable to give a reasonable account of his activities on the day of the murder and had been linked circumstantially to the letters that led the girl to her death in Durfee's stack yard. The evidence was certainly strong enough to warrant binding the minister to stand trial for murder (Staples 1833a, 22). By the time Staples had finished his "ingenious and able argument" (Drury 1833, 49), it was two o'clock on Sunday morning. The court adjourned, promising to give its verdict at two on Monday afternoon.

The thirty-six hours that stretched between the court's adjournment and the reading of its verdict gave Avery and his counsel time to contemplate the degree to which the hearing had taken over the public mind. The crowds that had thronged the courtroom during the legal proceedings testified to the case's local appeal (*Republican Herald*, 29 December 1832), but the hearing was soon being reported and discussed in more distant communities. By December 27, two Providence papers had picked up the story— and both had managed to get it wrong. The *Manufacturers and Farmers Journal* reported the apprehension of "Averill"—the name on the first, mistaken warrant—for the crime, and the *Providence American* (*Republican Herald*, 29 December 1832), which got the name right, proclaimed that Avery had offered "double ferriage" in his frantic attempt to get back home on the night of the twentieth.

By Friday the twenty-eighth, the "Averill" story had reached New York (*Evening Post*, 28 December 1832), and Providence area papers were taking on the violently anti-Avery bias that many would continue throughout his court battles. "Heaven will heap its vengeful curses on the wretch. . . . He converted the temple of the most high God into a detestable brothel" (*Pawtucket Chronicle*, 28 December 1832). On the following day the story hit the Boston papers (*New England Galaxy* and *Independent Chronicle*, 29 December 1832). By this time, even secluded in Bristol, Justices Howe and Haile could feel the effects of rising public excitement, and they

interdicted any further reporting of the hearing until the proceedings were concluded (*Manufacturers and Farmers Journal*, 31 December 1832). William Staples added his personal plea that the
court's wishes be upheld (*Providence Journal*, 1 January 1833), but
although the word of the justices' prohibition was followed, the desired effect was not achieved. Left without reliable information,
minds, mouths, and newspaper columns began to fill with rumor.
In Fall River the *Weekly Recorder* (2 January 1833) was already congratulating the local committee for a job well done, as though the
minister not only had been bound over for trial, but also had been
convicted. Published in Boston as the journal of the New England
Conference of the Methodist Episcopal church, the *New England
Christian Herald* (2 January 1833, 54) cautioned its readers not to
believe everything they read in the Providence papers, which were
"replete with errors"; but even the Methodist paper was smitten by
the force of the widespread desire to find the minister guilty. Admitting that Avery's acquittal was "highly improbable," the *Christian
Herald* (2 January 1833, 54) declared that "judgment should be suspended until after the trial, and then, should the issue prove fatal
to him, the obloquy and the evil consequences rest upon himself—
not upon the order to which he *did* belong nor upon the religion of
which he was once a professor."

By January 4 the story was published in Augusta, Maine (*Kennebec Journal*, 4 January 1833), where unfounded rumors of Avery's
behavior were already circulating. On the following day, the *Virginia Herald*, in Fredericksburg, printed it. Nearer to home, new
rumors were circulated. The Providence *Republican Herald* (5 January 1833) claimed that Avery's handkerchief had been found on the
body and proven in court. In Boston the *Independent Chronicle*
(5 January 1833) asserted that engineer "Horswell" remembered
Avery because he pressed the letter on him so fervently. But by
Monday, January 7, the papers were silent, awaiting the justices'
conclusions.

Justice Howe opened his opinion with a disclaimer of any bias
in "this most exciting and strange case" (Drury 1833, 49). His purpose was to answer two questions: Was there reason to believe that
Sarah Cornell was murdered, and, if so, was there reason to believe
that Ephraim K. Avery did it?

The cause of the young woman's death was obviously strangulation, and by casting doubt on the identification of the knot at
her throat as a clove hitch, Howe advanced the possibility that her

death was self-inflicted. The bruises on her abdomen—if, in fact, they were bruises—and the grass stains on her knees suggested to him that she might have attempted abortion before her death, but were not conclusive evidence of an attack by another person. The very neatness of the death scene, with shoes and handkerchief primly arranged at the knees of the suspended corpse, reinforced Howe's belief that the death was suicide. Would a murderer, he reasoned, carry the body to the stack yard, so near a populous village, risking detection as he laboriously arranged the appearance of suicide? The reasonable murderer would have fled the scene immediately. The only rational conclusion was that Sarah Cornell had died as Elihu Hicks's original jury had believed—by her own hand.

Howe, assuming the unreasonable position that she had been murdered, questioned whether Rev. Avery could have been the attacker. Blithely ignoring the inconsistencies in the testimony, Howe firmly established the death at nine o'clock and Avery's arrival at Gifford's ferry house at half past nine (Drury 1833, 51, 53). It was clearly impossible for the minister to have traveled the eight or more miles between Durfee's stack yard and the ferry house in such a short time. Howe dismissed attempts to place Avery in Fall River on the afternoon of the twentieth as the overheated imaginings of people who recalled every stranger seen that day as "Methodist-Minister-looking folks" (Drury 1833, 52). Relying on his own experience with theology students who showed a marked tendency toward afternoon sight-seeing excursions, Howe asserted that Avery's account of his trip to the island was much more reasonable than anything the prosecution had produced.

The letters introduced in the case were, and remained, a problem. Howe thought the memory of Fall River's deputy postmaster "extraordinary, but perhaps not impossible" (Drury 1833, 53) when he linked Avery to the messages sent through his office. Howe failed to mention Orswell's testimony. However, the justice found the memory of the Methodist ministers, who accounted for every minute of Avery's time at the critical points of the last few months, unexceptional and unimpeachable.

Having disposed of the hard evidence of the case, Howe launched himself into the most remarkable—and to the prosecution the most shocking—part of his opinion. Avery, he said, was proven to be a man distinguished by the "purity of his moral, christian, and ministerial character" (Drury 1833, 55), while Sarah Cornell was "addicted to almost every vice," an "undoubted prostitute" who had profaned the Sabbath by dedicating it to the "sensual gratification of a young man" and who had been "notoriously afflicted" with a venereal disease (Drury 1833, 55). Howe, convinced of a great disparity in their characters, declared that if he were forced to believe that Avery had written the letters, arranged the meetings, and gone to Fall River on the twentieth—even then he could not believe him guilty of the seduction or the murder. "I should much more readily," he said,

> and with less outrage to my own feelings and notions of the course probable under such circumstances, have supposed him to have used to her some such language as this, and left her: "Maria, you have given me a great deal of trouble heretofore, and your late letters, which I wrote you so much surprised me, have given me a great deal more. You are pursuing me, who never did you an intentional injury, with great malignity. I did not know but it might be in your power to do me and my family an injury and bring a scandal upon my profession, when I solicited this interview and promised you aid. I have since thought more of the character of your threats, and the effect of your executing them; and, as it would only be encouraging you to extort from me again, and I could have no security that you would not, after all, do all you could to injure me, I have concluded to retract my promise and set you at defiance. If I thought you had any sense of future accountability, I would warn you of the sin of thus following up one crime with another; and I do warn you of the danger of perjury." (Drury 1833, 56).

Rebuffed and stymied by the minister's virtuous determination, the vice-ridden young woman was, in Howe's eyes, capable of taking her own life in a final, insane frenzy for revenge on the man who had expelled her from Christian society in Lowell.

After his incredible invention, which may have embarrassed the defense as much as it outraged the prosecution, Howe had little more ground to cover. The letters, he said, which had not been proven to have been the prisoner's, might have been produced by the dead woman herself as part of her scheme to press false claims on the minister. In this light, Sarah's seemingly innocent questions to Lucy Hathaway about impropriety between a girl and a respected man became the subtle beginnings of a sinister campaign against Avery's character. Only once, thought Howe, had Sarah Cornell uttered or written the truth, and that was when, in a pass-

No. 2   Fall River

Rev. Mr Bidwell

Sir I take this opportunity
to inform you that for reasons known to God
and my own soul I wish no longer to be connected
with the Methodist Society When I came to this
place I thought I should enjoy myself among them
but as I do not enjoy any Religion at all I
have not seen a well nor a happy day since I left
Thompson camp ground You will therefore please to
drop my name from Mr Greens class and I will try
to gain all the instruction I can from your public
labours I hope I shall feel different some time or other
The Methodists are my people when I enjoy any
Religion To them I was indebted under God for my
spiritual birth I once knew what it was to love
God with all my heart once felt that God was my
Father Jesus my friend and Heaven my Home but
have awfully departed and sometimes fear I shall lose
my soul forever I desire your prayers that God would
keep me from this
                        Yours   Respectfully
                              Sarah M Cornell

11. Sarah Cornell's unsent letter to Ira Bidwell renouncing her
membership in the Methodist church. From David Melvill, *A Fac-simile of
the Letters Produced at the Trial of the Rev. Ephraim Avery* (Boston:
Pendleton's Lithography, 1833).

ing fit of remorse for her scandalous life, she penned the unsent confession to Ira Bidwell that she had "awfully departed" from the paths of virtue and feared she would lose her soul forever.

Howe, surprising no one in the courtroom, concluded that there was no probable cause to suspect that Ephraim Avery had murdered Sarah Cornell. Levi Haile's opinion was an anticlimax, and he knew it. Rehearsing the evidence, he said, was unnecessary after Howe's able discourse. Having reached his conclusion independently, he could only concur with his fellow justice. Together they pronounced it their duty to discharge the prisoner.

Avery, of course, was overjoyed by the decision (Avery 1834, 19); his lawyers, while pleased, were less certain that the matter had been completely resolved, and they suggested to the minister that he offer to post bond for a future appearance before the Rhode Island Supreme Court if the prosecution might desire it. In fact, making the offer was more difficult than getting Avery to agree to it. Called away on other business, William Staples had not been in court to hear the justices' opinion. In his place he had delegated Harvey Harnden, who in his dual capacity as deputy sheriff and a member of the Fall River Committee had done much of the investigative work on which the prosecution's case was based. Harnden appears to have been barely civil when he replied to Avery that "no such recognisance could . . . be entered into, as there was . . . no process upon which to predicate it" (Harnden 1833a, 3). While Harnden stayed in court to try to get a copy of the justices' decision to read to the people of Fall River, Avery went home.

Recognizing that there was inevitably some public excitement against him, the minister believed that it would soon fade away, particularly after the publication of the hearing made its contents generally available. This serene assurance that the crowds in Bristol would respect the court's opinion was not shared by Avery's counsel. After observing "considerable excitement" at the hotel among men who expressed dissatisfaction with the justices' decision, Bullock called on Avery at his home and, over tea, suggested the propriety of the minister's removal from his house (Hallett 1833a, 159). Although Avery at first objected, claiming that the delicate health of his pregnant wife required his presence, he finally agreed to follow his lawyer's prudent suggestions and spend the night at a friend's house (Hallett 1833a, 164).

Tuesday seemed quiet enough to Avery's lawyer, and he may have found himself laughing at the apparently unnecessary precautions of the night before, but by Wednesday he had disquieting news. The people in Fall River were reported to be agitated again, and in Newport there were angry public mutterings against his client (Hallett 1833a, 161). With the memory of the mob that descended the gangplank of the *King Philip* on Christmas still fresh in his mind, Bullock suddenly found Bristol to be a dangerous neighborhood. Accordingly, he went to Avery's home, probably accompanied by Bristol's Episcopal minister, John Bristed, and urged him to leave the area, at least until the worst of the public anger subsided. Once again Avery objected, surmising that flight would appear to be an admission of guilt, but under the lawyer's dogged insistence, he relented and agreed to go (Avery 1834, 19).

Whether or not Avery was actually in any physical danger, it soon became apparent that the lawyer was right; the community was not going to be satisfied with the findings of the court. By Friday the *Pawtucket Chronicle* (11 January 1833) openly stated that the decision of the justices was inconsistent with the truth: "We believe him guilty of the enormous crimes with which he is charged," declared the editors, who wondered how Howe and Haile could possibly have freed the "Rev. Criminal." The *Rhode Island Republican* (15 January 1833) was quick to concur. Daniel Mowry preached virulently against "priestcraft" in general and Avery in particular in the pages of his *Daily Advertiser and American.* Aware that a multitude of questions remained unanswered, newspapers friendly to the minister and those convinced of his guilt called upon their readers to volunteer information that would help clear up the mystery (*Rhode Island Republican,* 15 January 1833; *New England Christian Herald,* 16 January 1833). As both instigators and reflectors of public excitement, the newspapers made clear that in the towns surrounding Bristol Avery's status was, at best, uncertain.

The real threat to Avery's continued freedom—though probably not to his physical safety, as was implied by Connecticut's *Windham Gazette* (*Fall River Weekly Recorder,* 30 January 1833)—came not from the superheated prose of the newspapers, but from Harvey Harnden and the Fall River Committee. Unhappy with the outcome of the hearing, Harnden waited from Monday, when the decision was read, until Wednesday to get a transcript of the justices' statements. He almost certainly had dispatched a letter to the committee immediately on discovering that Avery had been set free. On Tuesday, January 8, while Harnden waited on Justice Howe in Bristol, the committee called a third public meeting, this time in the vestry of the Congregational Church (Harnden 1833a, 35). Chaired by David Anthony, Sarah Cornell's employer and a prominent member of the Congregational Church, it was attended by nearly seven hundred people (Harnden 1833a, 35). The court's decision was announced, but no action was taken until Harnden could return with complete details. Although it was late on Wednesday when Harnden finally obtained the documents he sought, he traveled immediately to Fall River, where another meeting had been called, again in the Congregational Church, in expectation of his arrival. John Eddy, Jesse's brother, chaired this meeting in which another crowd of seven hundred heard Harnden read the justices' statement (Harnden 1833a, 35). The concensus of the meeting was that Howe's decision was

> a most singular production, partaking much more of the character of a plea in behalf of the accused, than of an impartial decision, based upon the authority of the testimony given in; and withal intermixed with that particular and flimsy kind of sophistry, which serves to mystify and mislead, rather than elucidate and enlighten (*Fall River Weekly Recorder*, 16 January 1833).

Unimpressed by Howe's argument, the crowd followed Harnden's report with an angry general discussion that resolved itself in a resolution that the committee should take proper measures to obtain another warrant for Avery's arrest (Harnden 1833a, 3).

A reason for the new warrant was not hard to find. Avery had, after all, been improperly held and examined outside the county in which the crime was committed (Harnden 1833a, 3). Elihu Hicks, however, had turned over his records to Bristol authorities, and it was possible that this might be taken for an admission of the competence of Howe and Haile to hear the case. To forestall any such argument by Avery's counsel, the committee augmented its position with new evidence obtained from Grindall Rawson. On November 18, Sarah had written a four-page letter to Rawson describing her meetings with Avery and asserting that he had admitted—almost—fathering her child. That letter, the committee argued, which the justices at Bristol had not seen, demanded a reassessment of the evidence (*New England Christian Herald*, 23 January 1833, 67).

Accordingly, on Thursday morning, a committee member (probably Harnden) called on Elihu Hicks and asked for a complaint to obtain a warrant against Avery. Hicks complied, and the complaint that he provided was soon taken by Harnden to Charles

Durfee, a justice of the peace and town councilman of Tiverton, who duly provided the warrant (Harnden 1833a, 3–4). With the warrant in hand, Harnden traveled to Providence, where he met with Judge Samuel Eddy, chief justice of the Rhode Island Supreme Court. Eddy explained to Harnden that his signature on the warrant would require Avery to go to Newport to post bond for his appearance, and suggested that it would be a courtesy to the minister to require him to post bond at a more convenient location by getting a Bristol County judge to sign the warrant. The result, Avery's trial before the Supreme Court of Rhode Island, would be the same, and would be obtained with less trouble. Accepting the judge's reasoning, Harnden left Providence in the company of William Staples (who had introduced him to Judge Eddy) and went to Warren, the town immediately north of Bristol. There he attempted to get Judge Samuel Randall to travel to Bristol to take Avery's recognizance. Unfortunately, Randall was too ill to make the trip. Harnden was unwilling to expend more time or energy to make life easier for Avery; in Warren he composed a letter to Nathaniel Bullock informing him that his client should appear before Randall at his earliest convenience.

On Friday Harnden personally delivered his letter to Bullock, only to meet with an unexpected obstacle. Anticipating such a turn of events and aware of the minister's flight, Bullock had withdrawn from the case; thus instead of accepting the document that honor would have forced him to forward to Avery, the lawyer directed Harnden to Randolf, then in Newport, as the minister's legal representative. This masterstroke directed pursuit away from the direction taken by Avery and dropped the mantle of legal responsibility on a lawyer who knew nothing of the minister's whereabouts. However, it was only partially successful; instead of docilely traveling the length of Rhode Island once again, the exasperated Harnden exploded. The further delay was unwarranted, he said; he considered Avery unwilling to post bond and therefore subject to arrest and confinement.

Angrily returning to Warren, Harnden sought out Nathan Luther, the high sheriff of Bristol County, and presented him with the warrant for Avery's arrest. All costs related to the apprehension of the minister, he promised Luther, would be paid by the committee. It may have been compassion or good sense, but in Harnden's unpleasant mood it was probably malice that prompted him to suggest that Luther employ the services of William Paul, the deputy sheriff at Bristol who had protected Avery on Christmas, to aid in the capture. Having accomplished all that he could, Harnden returned to Fall River (Harnden 1833a, 4).

Sheriff Luther was unable to carry out his mission. The minister had left Bristol the previous Wednesday afternoon, riding with John Burges to the house of Isaiah Stevens, a mile south of Warren, overtly to see about procuring hay (Harnden 1833a, 5). Once safely out of town, Avery transferred to a closed carriage, which he shared with Ellen Griggs, Rev. Griffin of East Cambridge, and Rev. Griffin's wife (Hallett 1833a, 119). The group spent the night in Dedham at Sumner's Tavern (Harnden 1833a, 7) and arrived in Boston the next day (Hallett 1833a, 120). Avery probably stayed at Rev. Griffin's home until Tuesday or Wednesday of the following week and then—perhaps hearing of the pursuit and believing Boston too obvious a retreat—moved to the home of Simeon Mayo in the tiny New Hampshire community of Rindge.

The choice of Mayo's house was probably based on several considerations. First, any pursuit in New Hampshire would require extradition papers both from that state and from Massachusetts, through which Avery, if returning to Rhode Island, would have to travel. By involving more court systems, the minister and his advisers must have realized that they hampered any legal arrest. If removal to a retreat in a state not contiguous with Rhode Island was a good idea, Mayo's home was a natural choice. Avery had first met the Mayos in Eastham, where they had resided during his ministry. When the family moved to Rindge in 1828 (Harnden 1833a, 36), they retained their ties with the preacher. Those ties were critical to Mrs. Mayo, who summoned Avery to her defense when she was "called up" by the local church. Avery left his post—then at Lowell—and traveled to Rindge on her behalf, arguing her case successfully before the Rindge congregation. The Mayos owed the minister a favor, and their secluded residence made it easy for them to repay him.

After four years in a little back-country community, Mrs. Mayo probably enjoyed the excitement that preparing a room for her notorious visitor provided. The windows were carefully covered to keep in the light, and a stock of all the necessities for several days' confinement was laid in (Harnden 1833a, 28). When the minister arrived, modestly disguised by an unfamiliar coat and the first shadow of a new beard, the stage was set for a perfectly safe adventure that would make the Mayos the toast of their Methodist community for months to come.

Back in Fall River, news of Avery's disappearance was not so entertaining. On Monday morning, January 14, the committee decided that its services were again needed. Nathan Luther seemed remarkably uninterested in ferreting out the minister's hiding place; thus Harvey Harnden, once again called into action, was sent by the committee to locate, arrest, and return the missing man.

Harnden first traveled to Somerset, Massachusetts, where he obtained an interview with Joseph A. Merrill, Avery's presiding elder. Merrill, who had last seen Avery on the preceding Wednesday, reported that he had given the minister a summons to an ecclesiastical trial later in the month, and rather imagined that Avery was away collecting evidence for his defense. When Harnden asked if Avery might have gone to Lowell, Merrill suggested Woodstock, Connecticut—in the opposite direction from Avery's actual path— as a better prospect (Harnden 1833a, 5).

An unconvinced Harnden returned to Bristol, where his questions elicited information that Avery had left, that he was hidden in the city, and that he had emigrated to Cuba. Without a likely lead, the sleuth decided to spend the night in town. On the following morning, John Burges admitted to Harnden that he had taken Avery to the Stevens house just outside Warren. Probably aware of the warrant out for Avery's arrest, Burges may well have been attempting to shield himself from prosecution for aiding a fugitive (Harnden 1833a, 6). Convinced that he was at last on Avery's trail, Harnden questioned the toll gatherer on the turnpike and discovered that Avery had probably left in a closed carriage drawn by two white horses. At Munroe's Tavern in Seekonk, Harnden learned that the carriage had passed that way.

With the information he had gathered, Harnden traveled the short distance to Providence, where he reported to William Staples. Together, the sheriff and the lawyer called on the governor of Rhode Island the next day, January 16, to get a requisition on Governor Lincoln of Massachusetts for Avery's return. Although Harnden had only traced the minister to the road to Providence, he was sure that Boston was his ultimate destination. Apparently the governor was convinced as well, because he issued the necessary papers, including the appointment of Erastus P. Allen as the Rhode Island agent to accept Avery, should he be apprehended, at the Massachusetts border (Harnden 1833a, 7). The pursuit was made completely legal by finding a deputy sheriff of Bristol County to perform a duty that Nathan Luther had neglected—signing a statement that Avery had been sought at his home and had fled the neighborhood.

Now armed with the legal justification to pursue the fugitive preacher, Harnden and Allen set out toward Boston. By stopping at all the taverns on the major roads leading in that direction, they were able to trace Avery's carriage into Massachusetts. After spending the night at Wrentham, on Thursday they followed Avery through Dedham and into Boston. Hoping to keep his mission a secret (to keep Avery from being warned), Harnden tried to mask his true intentions whenever possible. In Dedham he pretended to be more interested in the young women in the carriage than in the men (Harnden 1833a, 8). When he stopped at the Broomfield House in Boston he refused to sign the register; drawing owner Preston Shepard aside, he told him privately of his purpose and enlisted him in the cause (Harnden 1833a, 8).

Once settled at the Broomfield House, which would serve as his base of operations in Boston, Harnden called upon Azariah Shove, a representative from Fall River in the state legislature, and, through him, was introduced to Howard Lothop, who introduced him to the governor. Governor Lincoln agreed to provide the papers to deliver Avery to Rhode Island, and asked Harnden and Allen to call for them in an hour. While they waited Harnden indulged in a busman's holiday as he called upon "Mr. Read, the man so celebrated for finding the resort of those who would avoid the public eye" (Harnden 1833a, 8). Perhaps disappointed that Read was too busy to join him in the case, Harnden returned to the governor's office and was provided with the necessary papers. Elder Merrill's suggestion that Avery had not gone to Lowell probably convinced Harnden that the minister had, in fact, gone there, because as soon as his papers were in order, he and Allen set out for that city. Merrill's assertions, however, turned out to be correct and the journey was unprofitable. Discouraged and abandoned by Allen, who became ill, Harnden returned empty-handed to Boston on the eighteenth (Harnden 1833a, 9).

Certain that Avery could not be traced in a city as large as Boston by ordinary means, Harnden decided to attempt a minor subterfuge. Calling on Charles P. Sumner, the sheriff of Suffolk County, Harnden asked for his company (to provide the image of legal authority) on a visit to a local man whom he suspected of aiding a fugitive from justice. The man was the Methodist minister, Rev. Griffin, who had accompanied Avery in his flight from Bristol. Whether Harnden had gained information that led directly to Griffin, or whether he had decided to visit all local Methodist ministers with the same story, is unclear. However, combining bullying and threats of prosecution with an explanation of the illegality of the first warrant, Harnden got Griffin to suggest that Avery *might* have gone to Rindge, New Hampshire (Harnden 1833a, 12). The deputy sheriff was presented, upon receipt of this intelligence, with a quandary. If Avery were in New Hampshire, he would have to return to Providence to get a new requisition directed to New Hampshire's governor. But if he were to do so, the time lost might easily allow Avery to move again and be permanently hidden. Pledging Griffin not to contact Avery, Harnden returned to Governor Lincoln for advice.

Lincoln had a solution to Harnden's problems; he suggested that the sheriff go to New Hampshire, swear out a local complaint (using his Rhode Island and Massachusetts papers as its basis), and have Avery held until proper extradition papers could be forwarded from Rhode Island. Pleased with the governor's idea, Harnden returned to his hotel, sent the ailing Allen home, and prepared for the trip. Disguised in a new cap and driving a horse and sulky obtained on credit from Mr. Shepard of the Broomfield House, Harnden headed north from Boston on the evening of the nineteenth.

The journey took Harnden through Lowell, where he was advised to stop at New Ipswich, a town near Rindge, to find a trustworthy deputy (Harnden 1833a, 13–14) and a good tavern. Harnden called upon New Ipswich's deputy sheriff, Mr. Edwards, and, through him, a local lawyer. Upon explaining his position to the lawyer, Harnden was surprised to learn that New Hampshire had recently passed a law that made a requisition from the governor unnecessary in cases of extradition. Any justice of the peace could issue a warrant for the arrest of an out-of-state fugitive. Unfortunately, the lawyer to whom Harnden spoke was a justice of the peace in Hillsborough County, while Rindge lay in Cheshire. On Harnden's urging, the best he could do was provide the sheriff with a blank form to be filled out by a justice in the right county (Harnden 1833a, 14).

Needing a local accomplice who could unobtrusively scout out the situation, Harnden enlisted a local baker, who informed him of the Methodist community and of Avery's previous visit several years before. Because Avery was presumably known locally by sight, Harnden correctly concluded that the minister was probably in hiding. Traveling into Rindge on the evening of the twentieth, Harnden asked his confederates to direct him to the house of the first justice of the peace they might pass. He soon found himself in the presence of Esquire Converse, a bumbling caricature of a country magistrate who initially refused to fill out the warrant on the grounds that he was tired of being a justice (Harnden 1833a, 16). When he was finally cajoled into signing it, he reported that there was no deputy in Rindge. Harnden suggested that Deputy Sheriff Edwards be sworn to execute the warrant, only to have Converse balk at the idea of swearing in a lawman from another county. The disgruntled but persevering Harnden finally got his warrant directed to any sheriff of Cheshire he might encounter (Harnden 1833a, 17). Unwilling to spend the night in Rindge, where his presence might alert Avery's confederates, Harnden traveled to nearby Fitz William and applied for lodging at the tavern of Colonel French.

At Fitz William, Harnden took French into his confidence and asked him to recommend a trustworthy deputy and someone else to aid in the capture. French complied, and Harnden was soon introduced to Deputy Foster and Mr. Parker, both of whom agreed to join in the enterprise (Harnden 1833a, 18). During the daylight hours of Monday, the twenty-first, Harnden sent his men out to discover the minister's hiding place. While they variously and discreetly investigated the Methodist community, he took the opportunity to compose a letter to N. B. Borden, outlining his progress and expectations of an early capture. As the day drew to a close, Harnden posted his letter and left Fitz William, taking up residence in the tavern in Rindge. There Edwards, Foster, and Parker reported no success in finding the hideout, but the baker had seen suspicious behavior at the house of Simeon Mayo and was convinced that Avery was there.

With his landlord told of his intentions and added to the band, Harnden planned his attack. Foster and Harnden would enter the house, Foster to gain legal access and Harnden to do the talking and, if necessary, the fighting. The other four would station themselves around the house and make sure no one escaped. The plan worked perfectly. When Foster and Harnden burst into Mayo's home they were clearly unexpected. Harnden demanded that the minister be produced, and the startled Mayo could only stammer that he "never knew such a man as Ephraim K. Avery" (Harnden 1833a, 23), an assertion that convinced no one and certainly did not forestall the systematic search of the house. After a bit of cat-and-mouse, Harnden discovered Avery hidden in his secured bedroom. Offering his hand in the best manner of victorious pursuer, the deputy sheriff said smoothly, "Mr. Avery, how do you do?" Surprised and concerned for his safety, the minister was unable to speak, and Harnden added, "Do endeavor to overcome this agitation; you need fear no personal violence; you shall be kindly treated" (Harnden 1833a, 26).

Although it was eleven o'clock in the evening when Harnden finally caught up with the minister, he decided to begin the return journey without delay. By quarter past five the following morning, the pair had reached Ipswich, ten miles distant, where Harnden hoped to catch the stage for Boston (Harnden 1833a, 29). Settling his accounts while waiting for the stage, the sheriff was embarrassed to discover that he was short of funds. After paying most of his local bills, Harnden had to depend on his credit to obtain passage to Boston.

The stage arrived in Boston by seven o'clock on Tuesday evening, the twenty-second. Asking to be let out at the Broomfield House, Harnden got the hotel's barkeep to settle his account with the driver. Fortunately, the financially drained sheriff was soon met by Bradford Durfee, who had come up from Fall River after Nathaniel Borden received Harnden's letter from Rindge. Durfee was well supplied with money and advanced Harnden enough to pay his expenses in Boston and on the trip home (Harnden 1833a, 31).

At Broomfield House Avery became the center of attention for an increasing number of people. Most were turned back by Harnden, who admitted only those whom Avery selected (Harnden 1833a, 32). When Joseph Merrill, Avery's presiding elder, asked for the opportunity to speak privately with the preacher, Harnden refused, still fuming over the rebuffs he had suffered at the hands of Methodist clergy during the pursuit (Harnden 1833a, 32). The following morning at five o'clock, Harnden and Avery left Boston on the Newport stage. At every stop along their route the minister attracted a crowd of gawkers. Their entry into Fall River, however, whose citizens' presumably murderous ambitions had prompted Avery's flight, was relatively quiet. Harnden took a room for the preacher at the Exchange Hotel, where Avery was held from two o'clock in the afternoon of the twenty-third until Friday, the twenty-fifth, at ten o'clock in the morning, when he was transferred to the custody of the Rhode Island agent, E. P. Allen (Harnden 1833a, 33).

With the prisoner off his hands, Harnden was free to engage

in what could have become a personally profitable postscript to his adventure. During his absence in pursuit of Avery, the Rhode Island legislature had passed a bill authorizing the governor to offer a three-hundred-dollar reward for the preacher's capture and return. The resolution, considered in committee on January 18, was passed without opposition and sent to the House on January 19 (*Manufacturers and Farmers Journal*, 8 April 1833). Passed by the House, it was given to the Senate belatedly and was not considered by that body until Monday afternoon, the twenty-first. After the Senate passed it on Monday, it added to the delay by not returning the resolution to the House until Tuesday morning; thus it was not until noon on January 22 that the governor was legally empowered to offer the reward. Governor Arnold, by that time knowing that Harnden was in hot pursuit of the preacher, prudently waited a day before acting on the resolution. By that time Avery was known to be in Harnden's custody, and the reward proclamation was never issued. After leaving Avery with Allen, Harnden called on the governor to collect the money, only to be told that there was no legal basis for the payment. The sympathetic but frugal Governor Arnold could only suggest that Harnden present an itemized bill to the legislature for possible reimbursement of his expenses.

Fortified with a published account of his pursuit (Harnden 1833a), Harnden applied to the legislature for three hundred dollars. The issue was taken up on May 2—delicately, because of the proximity of Avery's trial—but no money was granted. The legislature apparently felt, as did one reporter, that Harnden "commenced the pursuit for the acquisition of the *glory* it might produce; he enacted the part of a hero, and let the trophies of the *hero* be his reward" (*Daily City Gazette*, 4 May 1833).

While the sheriff tried to find a little profit in public service, Avery was taken to Tiverton, where his examination before Justices Durfee and Grey was brief and to the point. Backed by a jury of thirteen men, the justices listened as the charges and evidence against the minister were presented. Although it was erroneously reported that the jury had some difficulty in binding Avery over for trial and had to be packed with ten additional men (*New Hampshire Patriot*, 18 February 1833; *New England Christian Herald*, 27 March 1833, 102), the court promptly declared the evidence sufficient to warrant a trial before the next session of the Rhode Island Supreme Court, to be held in Newport the following March (*Newport Mercury*, 26 January 1833).

Committed to the Newport jail, with no opportunity to post

bail, Avery was condemned to spend the remainder of the winter in what promised to be a cold and uncomfortable confinement. His cell was approximately fourteen feet square with a ceiling seven feet high. Light, insufficient for reading without a candle even in broad daylight, was admitted by one tiny window, six inches wide and ten inches high (*Sangamo Journal*, 1 June 1833). His first night in prison was predictably miserable; with no decent bed and only a pair of threadbare blankets for warmth, he could not sleep. Morning found him pacing the floor in an attempt to generate a little heat (Avery 1834, 20).

The brutal conditions under which he suffered were soon improved. Asa Kent, the Methodist minister at Newport who would labor untiringly in Avery's behalf throughout the trial, brought him a suitable bed and a stove. Richard Randolf, Avery's counsel, provided another bed, which was probably used by Sophia Avery when she brought their newborn son to share her husband's confinement (*New England Christian Herald*, 27 March 1833, 102). Even the jailer's wife, Mrs. Allen, thought of the minister's comfort and contributed a Bible, a Bible dictionary, and a few other volumes (Avery 1834, 20). The jailed preacher soon became a popular figure as his Newport supporters brought him choice offerings of food and stayed in his cell for prayer meetings. The *Pawtucket Chronicle*, always critical of Avery, was disgusted by the way the "Reverend Prisoner" had managed to convert "a dreary desolate abode of crime, into a house of prayer and feasting, not fasting" (*Pawtucket Chronicle*, 22 March 1833). However, the minister's friends could reasonably retort that he had not been proven guilty, only accused, and that killing an unconvicted man by the rigors of a winter prison was hardly justice.

In the first week of March, Albert C. Greene, the attorney general of Rhode Island, aided by the Fall River Committee that he had inherited from William Staples (Staples 1833b), presented the state's case to the grand jury. After two days of testimony, on the morning of March 8 the jury confirmed the findings of Justices Durfee and Grey. Avery remained impassive as the court clerk stumbled through the indictment for murder, but the perspiration on his upper lip revealed the impact of the clerk's words (*Mail*, 15 March 1833). After the preacher entered a plea of not guilty, his lawyer, Richard Randolf, requested a time for the trial. Asserting that the trial would take at least a week, Randolf suggested that there was not time enough remaining in the present court session to complete it (*Emporium*, 16 March 1833). The court agreed and set the trial for a special session to be held in Newport beginning on the first Monday in May. Avery was returned to his cell to await his trial, but this time with the reasonable expectation of better weather conditions to reduce the discomforts of his confined existence. Though the delay may have been tedious for the preacher, for whom tasty morsels and attentive friends could never banish the specter that haunts accused men, it proved valuable to his allies, who used the time to prepare his defense.

In the second week of Avery's examination in Bristol, the minister had been visited by his presiding elder, Joseph Merrill. Avery later wrote:

> [Merrill] never gave me, from the first, to understand any thing but his most fervent wish that the truth should come to light, however painful it might be to bear. I had no encouragement to expect any thing from him but his pity and prayers, should circumstances during the examination satisfy him that I was a guilty man (Avery 1834, 19).

While Merrill assured Avery that he could hope for no special aid from the church if he were found guilty, he certainly did not oppose the use of the church community to generate evidence for the defense. Ira Bidwell and Samuel Drake worked locally to find and recruit witnesses, as did others throughout the New England Conference. The church later claimed, probably accurately, that it was "that kind of individual and friendly aid" (New England Annual Conference 1833, 3) that any man could expect from his associates in such a situation. The new indictment, however, coming after the church had been implicated in Avery's flight, required stronger countermeasures, and the Methodists took them.

In April, the conference engaged Jeremiah Mason, tall, sixty-five years old that month, and one of New England's most celebrated lawyers, to take Avery's case (*Pawtucket Chronicle*, 19 April 1833). Mason had impressive credentials. A long-time friend of Daniel Webster, Mason had spent most of his career in New Hampshire, where he had been attorney general of the state in 1802 and United States senator from 1813 to 1817, before moving to Boston in 1832 (Franklin, Conn. 1869, 87). Recognizing the magnitude of the task he had taken on, the lawyer immediately put together a legal staff that included Richard Randolf, George Turner, Henry Cranston, Joseph Hathaway, and Joseph Blake. Combined with the manpower made available by the well-organized New England Conference, which had agents in every community in which Avery or Sarah Cornell had lived, this legal battery combed New England for evidence that would free its client.

The church organization proved to be a valuable tool—witnesses were procured by Merrill, Palmer, Drake, Stoors, Kilborn, Griffin, Demming, Taylor, Bonny, Jennison, and other ministers—but it became costly when the conference had to agree to underwrite the expenses of those it brought to testify. Asa Kent, whose house became the Methodist command post in Newport when Avery's trial began, was later given the unpleasant task of settling the church's accounts. "In regard to witnesses," he wrote:

> Some of them gave their time & pd their own expenses: Others gave their time, but had their expenses pd for them. Others again demanded for both time & expenses. Numbers made demands who did not expect to at the time, but as others were pd, they felt an equal claim—Others did not make a *positive demand*; but gave me an account of *time* & *money* spent—they thought they ought to receive *something* but would leave it with me to do what I tho't proper—Others again made a *demand* provided there should be surplus funds & & (Kent 1836).

Kent estimated that the conference and its agents paid over six thousand dollars to witnesses they provided for the defense. There could be no doubt that the conference was fully committed to Avery's support.

They were not unopposed, but it was an opposition that was running into problems. William Staples, while collecting evidence for the prosecution, learned of a doctor from East Greenwich who could testify that he had seen Avery deliver the letter to Orswell aboard the *King Philip*, but the doctor steadfastly denied any knowledge of the subject and a potentially decisive witness was lost (Staples 1833c). Grindall Rawson, Sarah's brother-in-law, found the same problem as he attempted some amateur detective work in Woodstock. "I find that many mouths that have been open," he wrote to Staples, "are now sealed up in silence" (Rawson 1833). Rawson was referring to his stymied attempts to implicate Avery in an earlier seduction. Where previously the matter had seemed easily proven, when an attempt was made to firm up sources and get agreements to testify, difficulties arose. The original source of Rawson's information balked, saying that he had made no such accusations against the minister, but that a doctor had suggested something similar to him. When asked to name the physician, he refused to answer but enigmatically replied to the question of whether or not it had been Dr. Cooley by observing that "Cooley is a strange fellow" (Rawson 1833).

Before mid-March, the prosecution was joined by Dutee J. Pearce, the former attorney general of Rhode Island, who left his seat in Congress to help prosecute the case. Pearce brought with him to Newport an interesting bit of information gleaned from a fellow traveler. He had been told that a respectable lawyer in Lowell could swear that Avery had been on "very *intimate* and *friendly* terms with Sarah Cornell" (Pearce 1833). This and a multitude of other stories would have to be investigated, and the Fall River Committee provided the government with the manpower to do so.

In fact, the committee had never stopped working. By the time of the minister's return to Rhode Island, a rumor was widely believed—as rumors later would be believed about the preacher's pirate career in the Caribbean and his broken-hearted first wife who died as the result of his abuse—that Sarah Cornell's arm had been broken, thus rendering her unable to hang herself and indicating a violent struggle. Hoping the story might be true so it would quash any attempt to prove suicide, the selectmen of Tiverton (probably Charles and John Durfee) commissioned Foster Hooper and Thomas Wilbur to do another autopsy. The body was exhumed on January 26 and the examination made. After the arm was found disappointingly intact, the opportunity was taken to investigate the bruises on the lower part of the torso that modesty had kept covered during the first examination. When Staples asked Harnden to get an autopsy report at the end of the month, he received a letter from Foster Hooper outlining the doctors' findings: no broken bones, but almost certain evidence of violence indicating rape or attempted abortion (Hooper 1833). The examination seemed not to have been a total loss.

After the Supreme Court's grand jury confirmed that there would indeed be a trial, the Fall River Committee continued to aid the prosecution. By April 8 Nathaniel Borden could report to Staples that a great deal had been done (Borden 1833). The rumor circulating about a Mr. Cook who had startling evidence was probably, Borden wrote, a hoax. Inquiries had been made into the activities of Ira M. Bidwell, and Borden was convinced that the local

Methodist preacher could satisfactorily account for his time on the night of the murder. Harvey Harnden had received letters suggesting that a visitor (Ephraim Avery in disguise) had approached Dr. Alden of Bridgewater some time before the murder, requesting information about producing an abortion. He had also been told that Avery made infamous proposals to a lady in Duxbury, but Borden doubted that it could be proved. The committee had also learned that Avery's father, Amos, lived in Richmond, Massachusetts, but had no other information about him. Borden closed his letter by mentioning that Harnden was ready to return to Lowell if an important purpose were found for the trip, and by asking Staples to check into a story of a Woodstock witness who could place Avery and Sarah Cornell together at the Thompson camp meeting.

When the trial opened the committee continued to operate as an adjunct to the government. On May 5 Harnden was in Boston seeking witnesses (Harnden 1833b), and by May 11 he had moved to Providence on a similar errand (Kingsley 1833). It might be easy to assume that the deputy sheriff was acting in his legal capacity serving summonses were it not that he reported, not to the attorney general, but to Nathaniel Borden of the Fall River Committee. The heavy involvement of the committee in the operation of the government case seemed a matter of general knowledge. When Moses Pierce wrote to Albert Greene asking that the court appearance of Lucy Hathaway be expedited because her services were needed at home to care for his ailing daughter, he called upon Borden, Harnden, and Hooper to promote his case (Pierce 1833). In the same way, Jervis Shove assumed that Borden had some influence in the order of the witnesses' appearance and the line of questioning to which they would be subjected (Shove 1833).

Thus, if there had been any doubt before, by early spring in 1833 the battle lines were clearly drawn. The Fall River Committee, representing the cotton industry in which Sarah Cornell had worked for years and the town in which she had briefly resided before her death, was committed to the minister's conviction. Opposing it, the New England Conference of the Methodist Episcopal church, which early in Avery's troubles had been cautiously detached, swung its considerable weight and resources behind its embattled member. The trial would be as much a contest of institutions as a quest for personal justice.

6. The Prosecution

Thomas Gill, reporter for the *Boston Post,* arrived in Newport at about seven o'clock on the evening of May 4. Eager to begin his assignment, he searched out the prison, ironically across the street from the Methodist meeting house, and requested an interview with Ephraim Avery. The minister was not usually easy to see, but Gill was armed with an introduction from a friend of the jailer Allen, and the visit was quickly arranged. The reporter could find no trace of a homicidal maniac lurking in the eyes of the man who civilly invited him into his cell. Two days later, Gill wrote:

> I was particularly struck with the moderation, justness, and liberality of his remarks—not one harsh, impatient or repining word escaped him. He is about 33 years of age and has been a minister 10 years: is a peculiar, but not an ill-looking man, his features being very regular and placid; his complexion dark with very black hair and heavy eyebrows, that give to his countenance rather a sombre expression, which, however, is entirely destitute of any trait that could lead one to imagine there was any malignity in his disposition (*Sangamo Journal,* 1 June 1833).

Gill was not alone in finding Avery disappointingly ordinary. The correspondent of the Providence *Literary Subaltern,* who had had the opportunity to observe the preacher for a longer time, reported:

Although I have not found in him the qualities of the great man, I have arrived at the conclusion, that he is a man of more than ordinary mind, and had been well fitted by birth and education to meet the perils incident to life. I think he would have made a hardy and a gallant soldier, had he been nurtured to arms, and of all things the pulpit should have been the last choice of a man like him. I have heard him preach, and, if he has not, in private life, more address than he has in the pulpit, I should think him but illy calculated for the victor in the female world. As a preacher he is dull, jejune and uninteresting; and, as he seems not to take any interest in his sermons, he as a matter of course, fails from imparting any thing like interest to others. I should think, in what I have seen of the man, that indolence, and a disposition to live easy, induced him to forego the labors of a

12. Colony House, Newport, Rhode Island. The lower floor of the courthouse was the site of Ephraim Avery's trial before a special session of the Rhode Island Supreme Court during May and June 1833.

farmer, to attend the duties of the pulpit (*Literary Subaltern*, 10 May 1833).

With the monster not in evidence and lethargy his greatest visible crime, Avery spent the last two months before his trial alone. His family had been sent home to Bristol (*Sangamo Journal*, 1 June 1833), partly to avoid the stresses that the trial would inevitably bring, and partly to escape the verbal barbs of malicious wags who, when the jailer was away, gathered under Avery's window to call out insults and sing offensive songs. Without his wife's support, the months of imprisonment began to tell on him. It was a haggard man, whose complexion had become "cadaverous" (*National Banner*, 22 May 1833), that was finally led to face his judges on the morning of May 6.

He was, however, neither cowed by authority nor driven into a show of bravado. Bowing to each judge as he entered (*National Banner*, 22 May 1833), Avery remained impassive as the machinery of justice began to move. His "firmness and propriety of demeaner" won him instant respect and, as his trial ground through the weeks that followed, brought him the grudging admiration of many who marked his "surprising and unparalleled fortitude and manliness" (*Literary Subaltern*, 24 May 1833).

Whatever the minister's capacities were, there was not much to tax him on that first day. Chief Justice Samuel Eddy, assisted on the bench by Associate Justices Charles Brayton and Job Durfee, did little more than call for an additional forty-eight jurors to supplement the fourteen already called and extract an oath from the newsmen present that they would not publish an account of the courtroom proceedings until the trial was completed (Hallett 1833a, 4–5). Because the new jurors were not to be local men, the court adjourned until the following day to give them time to be called and collected.

When court was called to order at nine o'clock the next morning, Tuesday, it was immediately met with another delay. Having received the sheriff's list of new jurors only a few moments before, Richard Randolf asked that the defense be given time to examine the names before jury selection began (Hildreth 1833, 6). The court agreed, and it was not until an hour later that the prisoner was finally brought into the courtroom. Dressed in a dark frock coat, a surtout, black vest and pantaloons, and shielding his eyes with a pair of green spectacles, Avery sat at his counsel's table (Trial at Large 1833, 3). Called to stand for the reading of the indictment, the minister complied, lodging his right hand in the breast of his coat and his left on the back of the chair before him (*Fall River Weekly Recorder*, 29 May 1833). He betrayed no emotion as he listened to the state's assertion that "being moved and seduced by the instigation of the devil" (Marshall and Brown 1833, 6) he had beaten, strangled, and hung Sarah Cornell, causing her instant death. Only a quiver of his jaw, as if he were biting his lips, indicated that he understood the import of what he heard (Trial at Large 1833, 4). Asked by the clerk how he pled, the minister answered firmly, "Not guilty, sir," and the jury selection process began.

Attorney General Albert C. Greene opened with a polite aside to Jeremiah Mason, hoping to make the Massachusetts lawyer hesitant to challenge the procedures of a Rhode Island lawyer in a Rhode Island court. He would, he said, follow local legal tradition by asking each prospective juror three questions (Hallett 1833a, 5): Was he related to the principals of the trial? Did he have scruples about convicting a man of a capital crime? Had he already formed an opinion of the merits of the case? If Mason was supposed to be cowed by Green's instructions, the attempt fell short; the defense lawyer immediately asked the court if the second question were actually admissible, then wrangled with Greene over the logic of asking a man who had admitted an opinion unfavorable to the prisoner if he still felt he could render an impartial verdict. The legal debate threatened to be interminable. By lunch time, only fourteen prospective jurors had been examined, and three impaneled (Hallett 1833a, 8).

When the court resumed at three o'clock that afternoon, Chief Justice Eddy announced that the judges had decided that any prospective juror who had formed an opinion, no matter in whose favor and no matter how impartial he might think he could remain, could be challenged for cause. With that ruling in place the proceedings went more rapidly but with less effect. By five o'clock the entire list of sixty jurors had been examined, and only six impaneled (Hallett 1833a, 11). The court was forced, then, to issue a summons for five new juries—sixty men—to be collected by the sheriff and delivered when the court was reconvened at three o'clock Wednesday afternoon.

The sheriff produced fifty-nine of the required sixty men, and most of Wednesday was taken up in searching out the necessary six unbiased individuals among them. By five o'clock the jury was complete, comprised of ten men from Newport, one from Portsmouth, and one from Middletown (Marshall and Brown 1833, 8). The indictment was once again read, the clerk announced Avery's plea of not guilty, and the court settled down to hear the prosecution's opening argument.

There was no argument to hear. Only a few moments before, William Staples had informed the attorney general that he could not make the opening statement as planned. Embarrassed, Greene had to report that he was unprepared and ask for a recess until the following morning. Asked to give an explanation for Staples's withdrawal, he had none to give. Dutee Pearce assured the justices that he would be ready to take his colleague's place in the morning (Hallett 1833a, 14), and the defense expressed polite surprise at such unprofessional disorganization in the government's ranks. Stung by the implied criticism that surrounded him, Staples rose and told the court that "circumstances of a personal nature" had occurred during the day, making it extremely distasteful for him to play the part in the prosecution he had planned (Trial at Large 1833, 8). Nonetheless, he said, if the court required it, after a momentary delay to send for some papers, he would proceed.

The court, however, did not require it and adjourned. Staples's sudden defection was probably caused by a squabble of seniority with Dutee Pearce who, as a former attorney general and current member of Congress, may well have seen political hay in the making (Hallett 1833a, 14). Whatever the cause, the withdrawal of the younger lawyer left Pearce squarely in the limelight when the court reconvened at nine o'clock Thursday morning.

If he did not reach oratorical heights when he addressed the jury to open the case, neither did the former attorney general disgrace himself. Apologizing for his unfamiliarity with the details of the evidence to be presented, he outlined the government position (Hildreth 1833, 8). The prosecution would prove, he said, that Sarah Cornell had not died by her own hand, and that Rev. Avery had both the motive and the opportunity to have murdered her. Admitting there was no ironclad proof—no witness to the crime— he pointed out that a man bent on murder typically "does not call his neighbor to witness it" (Hallett 1833a, 17). The circumstantial evidence, which could trace the minister to the very point of the attack, was sufficient to hang him. Concluding in Ciceronian style, he reminded the jury that he need not remind them of the public excitement over the case. Avery, he said, was a minister of a denomination with three hundred thousand members (the Methodist report of the trial compulsively corrected his figure to six hundred thousand) who were personally concerned with the forthcoming verdict (Hildreth 1833, 10), while the murdered woman was a factory girl whose comrades in labor rightfully demanded justice to her and to themselves. Feelings and prejudices inevitably ran high, but the jury would acquit itself best if it would ignore all but the logic of the testimony presented in court.

Pearce had taken forty-five minutes, and had convinced the jury foreman, Eleazer Trevett, that the government case would necessarily be a patchwork of circumstances fitted together to make unobserved crimes inescapably apparent. Recognizing the difficulties this might present to his jury, Trevett asked the court if the jurors might be given paper and pencils to note down some of the testimony. The attorney general casually remarked that he had nothing to say about it, and Chief Justice Eddy, following the tradition of his court, said that it was not usual. In a system in which the most complex trials rarely took a week, a juror's memory was supposed to be sufficient to keep the facts in order. Thus, without saying a word, the defense won an important victory that would be magnified as long days of testimony accumulated; the uncertainty of confused minds overwhelmed by a month-long flood of contradictory evidence could only work in the prisoner's favor (Hallett 1833a, 18).

The prosecution opened its testimony by calling John Durfee to testify to the condition of the body on discovery, and Williams Durfee, a retired sailor, to testify that the rope around the corpse's neck was knotted in a clove hitch—a knot used commonly on sailing ships and which, significantly, could not be pulled tight with both ends held together (Hildreth 1833, 11–12).

Seth Darling, Fall River's elderly assistant postmaster, followed them to the stand. He had been at Durfee's stack yard when the body was discovered, and his testimony substantiated that of the previous two men. More important, however, in his official capacity he had taken over for the ailing postmaster on November 19 of the previous year, and could testify that the same person who had sent a letter to Grindall Rawson that day had also sent one to Ephraim Avery (Hallett 1833a, 25). Rawson's letter was produced and identified; it was, of course, from his sister-in-law, Sarah Cornell. The prosecution was well on its way to establishing a correspondence between Avery and the mill girl that would ultimately lead them both to Durfee's stack yard.

Darling's testimony did not go unchallenged. Mason quickly got the assistant postmaster to admit that he was on the committee of vigilance that had been organized to seek out the murderer (Hallett 1833a, 25) and, in a long, rambling examination about time, finally got him to make a slip. "I did not know Mr. Avery," Darling said, "but had heard, for a year or two, he was the minister there [at Bristol]" (Hallett 1833a, 27). At the time, Avery had been at Bristol for less than six months.

The prosecution was prepared for the attack that made Darling seem both biased and inaccurate: Lemuel Briggs, the postmaster at Bristol, was called to testify that the letter to Avery from Fall River had been processed through his office. Eager to get home and already a day later than he had anticipated (Briggs 1833), Briggs did not stay on the stand long. He had forgotten to bring his books and his memory was uncertain. Over a defense objection that testimony based on documents alone was inadmissible, the prosecution obtained the court's permission to send the postmaster home for his records.

Elihu Hicks was called next to clear up the matter of the coroner's verdict that first asserted suicide and then murder. Unfortunately, the old man's memory was not up to the task. Under cross examination he fell apart, retreating into a self-serving vagueness that merged the two verdicts into one, denied the validity of the first, admitted that the jurors changed their minds, and brought a smile to the prisoner (Hallett 1833a, 28–30). It was not prejudice that prompted the Methodists' reporter at the trial to claim that "if there is any obscurity or discrepancy in the statements of this witness, in regard to the coroner's jury, it is his fault, and not that of the reporter" (Hildreth 1833, 16).

Hicks was followed by Dr. Foster Hooper, called to demonstrate the medical evidence on which the murder charge was based. Hooper's medical testimony, however, was compromised when the defense questioned him about his anti-Masonic politics and a lecture he had given in Swanzey, during which he supposedly asserted that Avery was a Mason who had been freed at the Bristol hearing solely because the presiding justices were Masons (Hallett 1833a, 33). When Hooper refused to be flustered by the attack and calmly set out to demonstrate that his remarks had not been prejudicial, the defense made its point clear to the jury.

"Go on, sir," shouted Richard Randolf, "and show your prejudices against Mr. Avery!" (Hallett 1833a, 34).

13. Dr. Foster Hooper. One of the physicians who performed the autopsies on the body of Sarah Cornell, Hooper played a prominent role in Ephraim Avery's prosecution, both as a witness and as a member of the Fall River Committee. Courtesy of the Fall River Historical Society.

"I have," the witness replied, "none to show," and the court stepped in to curb Randolf's enthusiasm.

Called next, Dr. Thomas Wilbur, an older man without Hooper's political fervor, substantiated what his colleague had said about the condition of the body they had both examined, then recounted his experiences with Sarah Cornell as his patient. Having taken hold of her wrist and looked at her tongue, the doctor came to no "very definite conclusion" about her reproductive situation, but he did gain her confidence to the extent that she confided her suspicions to him. When he reached the point of describing the interview in which she had named the father of her unborn child, the defense objected. It was purely hearsay, they contended, neither sworn testimony nor a dying utterance. The prosecution countered with the argument that they wished to demonstrate that Sarah Cornell *said* it, not that it was true, and thus Wilbur's testimony was legally competent (Hallett 1833a, 36). With this legal hair to split, the court adjourned and the first day of testimony was over.

The attorney general must have known that his position in the dispute over Wilbur's testimony was weak, and he may have suspected that the defense would play into his hands if he could avoid a court decree that Sarah Cornell's conversation was inadmissible. Consequently, when court resumed at eight o'clock Friday morning, he immediately waived the disputed question, and Randolf began his cross examination. Was it not true that Wilbur had given a medical deposition to the coroner during his deliberations? Had Wilbur not retrieved the deposition, now lost, and used it as the basis for a report published in the *Rhode Island Microcosm* in March? The doctor agreed that both statements were true. Then, said Randolf, "we have a right to offer the paper to show that the witness did not tell the same story in his deposition, and the account that was published from him, or by him" (Hallett 1833a, 38), and the defense lawyer began to question Wilbur closely about discrepancies between the newspaper account and his sworn testimony. Nothing more serious than omissions in the published version could be demonstrated.

When Randolf produced a copy of the *Microcosm* for Wilbur's inspection, the attorney general found the opening for which he had waited. The newspaper, placed in the witness's hand by the defense lawyer, should be admitted, he said, as evidence in the trial, and as such given to the jurors so that they could determine if there were in fact differences between the doctor's two statements (Hallett 1833a, 40). Painfully aware that the newspaper recounted Sarah Cornell's declaration to Wilbur that Avery was the father of her child, Mason objected, claiming that the contents of the paper were not in evidence; it was only introduced to show that there was a discrepancy in the doctor's testimony. Even to Mason the argument must have sounded illogical; to the attorney general it sounded absurd. How can the jury judge any discrepancy, he asked, if its members cannot see the document?

Now Randolf was on his feet. The object, he shouted, of the prosecution's motion was to get Sarah Cornell's statement to the jury. Having tacitly admitted that it was inadmissible, how could the attorney general stoop so low as to attempt to trick a man out of his life by a legal maneuver? Unruffled, Greene shook off the insult and steadfastly contended that the defense had introduced the paper to discredit his witness, and thus it was essential that the paper go to the jury.

Mason saved the point for the defense when he rose and, without visible sign of embarrassment, explained to the court:

> We deem it important to show that this publication was made by the consent of the witness, at a critical time, and to illustrate by it the prejudices and preoccupation of public opinion, which in this case have become so widely extended as almost to have precluded the possibility of finding a jury to try it. Our object was not to show a difference of statement, to affect the credibility of the witness, but to prove that he has published it, and leave the jury to infer from it, the feelings under which the witness testifies (Hallett 1833a, 41).

Greene commented caustically on the chameleonlike quality of the defense's argument, but the court, recognizing that to agree with the attorney general would bring inadmissible evidence before the jury, chose a gracious compromise. The jury was not to get the newspaper, but Wilbur was allowed to show how and why the published report varied from his testimony to the coroner's jury. The tempest died an ignoble death when the doctor finally testified, newspaper in hand, that after all the article was just about what he said to Coroner Hicks. By the time Dr. Wilbur was finished on the stand, postmaster Lemuel Briggs had returned from Bristol with his books. Again over Mason's objections, Briggs testified that his records showed that Avery had received two letters from Fall River, one on November 12 and one on November 19, 1832 (Hallett 1833a, 44). Satisfied that the jury must be at least suspicious of Avery's connection with the dead woman, after the postmaster's testimony the prosecution shifted its focus back to the discovery and condition of the corpse.

After William Allen, a bystander at the discovery of the body, testified briefly that he had seen the dead woman, her hair disheveled and partly covering her face, Benjamin Manchester was called to the stand. A day laborer, Manchester was a solid man and a solid witness who had much to tell. He was present at the discovery of the body, and he could testify that the rope around her neck was indeed knotted in two half hitches—or a clove hitch—much more after the fashion of a sailor than a weaver (Hallett 1833a, 45). Furthermore, he had found a fragment of comb later identified as Sarah's lying in the weeds beside a cowpath, twenty rods toward town from the body. Her hair was disarrayed, she had lost her comb far from the stack yard where she was hung, and the cord embedded in her neck was knotted in such a way that it would not tighten if both ends were held together. It seemed evident that another party was involved, and Manchester had an idea who it was. On the afternoon of December 20, he had been employed with Abner Davis blasting rocks on Andrew Robeson's land. Just as a charge was about to explode, he and Davis observed a tall man, dressed in a dark surtout and a wide-brimmed hat, sitting on a nearby wall. Although Manchester did not get a good look at the stranger's face, his size and general conformation seemed remarkably similar to Ephraim Avery's (Hildreth 1833, 23).

Finally, Manchester explained the origin of the murder weapon. He and Davis had some old bagging, taken from Robeson's calico works, on which they knelt while drilling rock. It was from the seams of these bags, left overnight on a cart in the field, that the cord used to strangle Sarah Cornell was probably taken. At least, said Manchester, he could see no difference between the cord he had extracted to tie a rag around a sore finger and the cord that was pulled from Sarah's neck (Hallett 1833a, 46). He left the stand on that somber note, and the court recessed for lunch, leaving the jury to ponder the weight of his testimony.

When the trial resumed at three o'clock that afternoon, the prosecution turned to the indelicate but necessary examination of the women who laid out the body. In sequence, Meriba Borden, Ruth Borden, Dorcas Ford, and Susannah Borden were called to the stand. Their combined testimony revealed that the corpse had had green marks on one knee (indicating that she had knelt roughly in the grass before death), had been seriously bruised over the lower abdomen, and had had mashed feces on the underclothing (indicating that she had lain on her back during or after the struggles of strangulation) (Hallett 1833a, 47–49). The testimony was embarrassing to everyone. One court reporter was sufficiently shaken by hearing such public statements by women that he misspelled two of their names, and got a third entirely wrong (Trial at Large 1833, 19–20). A second condensed the testimony in his transcript so severely that it contained nothing offensive—and very little that was informative (Hildreth 1833, 24). A third solved the problem by simply omitting that section from his published version (Marshall and Brown 1833, 27).

In the courtroom there was to be no concession to feminine modesty where it might obscure the truth. When Ruth Borden timorously mentioned that there was "a natural appearance on the clothes behind, as though mashed on by the person lying down," she was pressed to clarify just what a "natural appearance" was; "the natural discharges," she was forced to admit, "of the body" (Hallett 1833a, 48). Not all the women, however, could be intimidated into such blushingly direct language. In his cross examination, Richard Randolf hoped to demonstrate that Dorcas Ford's opinion that Sarah Cornell had been raped was inexpert and unacceptable.

"Did you give your opinion at Bristol," he began gently, "you thought she had been violated?"

"I said she had been dreadfully abused," Mrs. Ford returned, "and I think so still."

"What did you say at Bristol? Did you not say you thought she had been forced?"

"Violated" had apparently been Mrs. Ford's precise word at Bristol (Drury 1833, 34), but now she was being more careful. "I was asked if there had been an attempt to produce abortion, and I said no. My opinion is that she had been dreadfully abused."

"I wish to know," said Randolf, unsatisfied and becoming irritable, "if you swear it was an attempt to force her?"

"I think she was abused."

"Do you think she was violated? I wish you to answer that question."

"I repeat it, I think she was dreadfully abused."

Now Randolf's craft came into play.

"In what way?" he asked coolly.

"Does not the bruise indicate abuse?" was the reply.

Exasperated, Randolf begged the attorney general to put the question to his witness. Hoping to settle the problem, Greene complied.

"Did you mean that she had been forced?" he asked hopefully.
"I meant she had been abused."

It was becoming a game that no lawyer could resist. Dutee
Pearce took over, certain that precise wording would turn the trick.

"Did you believe," he asked, "there had been an attempt by any
man at violent connexion?"

Now as thoroughly irritated as the lawyers, Mrs. Ford flared
back, "I suppose her life was forced from her, and you must judge
in what way yourselves." Even Chief Justice Eddy could get no
other response; when Mrs. Ford finally left the stand, she went with
her modesty intact (Hallett 1833a, 48).

Most of the rest of the day's testimony was unexceptional.
Susannah Borden identified the papers taken from Sarah Cornell's
bandbox (Hildreth 1833, 24), Thomas Hart testified to discovering
the second half of her comb near where Manchester had found the
first (Hallett 1833a, 49), and Abner Davis substantiated the rest of
Manchester's story (Hallett 1833a, 49). A moment's excitement occurred when Richard Durfee testified that the corpse's bonnet had
been in perfect order, but her hair was wildly disarrayed, suggesting that the bonnet had been replaced after a struggle. Objecting to
the implication that her death was not a suicide, Randolf indignantly told the court that he had "never seen a case in which there
has been more anxiety to press the case, and crowd in testimony."
Greene bristled, but let this insult, as others, pass (Hallett 1833a,
51). It was not until the conclusion of the trial, after the defense
had had its opportunity to press and crowd, that Randolf's outburst could be appreciated for the jest that it became.

The day's testimony was concluded by William Hamilton, who
heard a distressed female's "squalls" near John Durfee's house at
quarter to nine on the evening of December 20; Benjamin Hambly,
who remembered Hamilton leaving his store that evening at about
twenty minutes before nine (Hildreth 1833, 25); and Eleanor
Owen, a Welsh woman that no one took seriously—probably because of her halting English—who had heard a woman cry out near
Durfee's stack yard at half past seven on the night of the murder
(Hallett 1833a, 52).

On Saturday morning the attorney general opened by calling
Ruth Borden, the last of the women who had laid out the body, to
remind the jury of the corpse's condition, then began a systematic
attempt to demonstrate that Avery had been in Fall River at the
time of the death. William Pearce, the forty-year-old ferryman at

Bristol, testified that he transported Avery to the Portsmouth side at about two o'clock on the afternoon of the twentieth, charging him double fare—sixteen cents—because there were no other passengers (Hallett 1833a, 54). Jeremiah Gifford, the ferryman on the Portsmouth side, substantiated the time of Avery's arrival on the island, and reported that he next saw the minister near half past nine that night when he came into his sink room and demanded passage back to Bristol. Complaining that it was too late and the weather was too bad, Gifford had refused to cross until the morning (Hildreth 1833, 26–27).

William Anthony, whose house was on the road from the ferry to Howland's stone bridge—the route to Fall River—followed the ferryman on the stand. He swore he had seen a tall man heading for the stone bridge on the afternoon of the twentieth (Hallett 1833a, 56). Even the transparent tricks of the cross-examining defense lawyers, who purposely used wrong dates in their questions (Hallett 1833a, 57), could not shake his testimony. Although Anthony could not describe the stranger's dress, William Carr and his brother Charles could. When they saw him near the Charity Bridge (over a small stream on the route to Howland's stone bridge) at three o'clock that afternoon, he was wearing dark clothes and a broad-brimmed hat. A handkerchief muffled the man's features from the cold, and Charles remembered remarking that he was "rather proud" as he hurried by without a greeting (Marshall and Brown 1833, 28).

At Howland's stone bridge itself, the stranger was met by Peleg Cranston, gatekeeper and, incidentally, father of Henry Y. Cranston, one of Avery's lawyers. Although he did not know the man who passed over his bridge, the elder Cranston testified that he looked like a doctor, lawyer, or minister, dressed in dark clothes with a broad-brimmed hat. The stranger had not returned by sundown when Cranston closed the gate and went home, but in the morning there was a lone set of tracks in the sand, indicating that someone had come back to the island that night (Hallett 1833a, 59).

The path of the stranger across the island seemed fairly well established, but none of the witnesses could swear absolutely that the man they had seen was the minister. Might not the stranger have been, then, another man, and might not Avery have followed the course to the south that he claimed, rather than east to the bridge and then north to Fall River? After lunch the prosecution produced Robert P. Lee, a merchant from Newport, to demonstrate

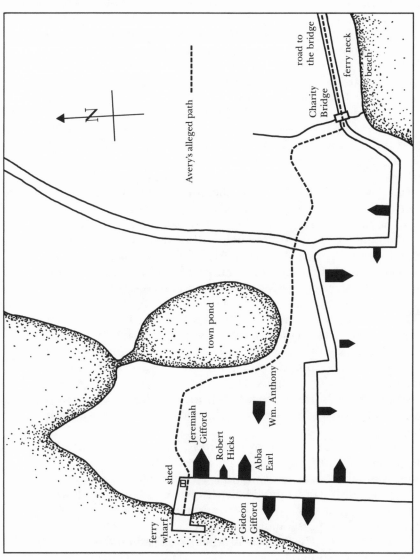

N

Avery's alleged path ---------

ferry
wharf

shed

Jeremiah
Gifford

Robert
Hicks

Abba
Earl

Gideon
Gifford

Wm. Anthony

town pond

Charity
Bridge

road to
the bridge

ferry neck

beach

14. Avery's alleged path from Gifford's ferry to Howland's stone bridge, December 20, 1832. After an
unsigned sketch in the Avery Trial Papers, in the papers of Albert Collins Greene,
Rhode Island Historical Society.

that the minister's story was a lie. On December 20 Lee had walked from Fall River to Newport, following the stage route. Had Avery returned from his sight-seeing trip as he claimed in Bristol, then Lee would surely have met him on the road. Lee saw no one (Hallett 1833a, 61).

Isaac Burdick was next called to testify that he had once walked from Fall River to Lawton's tavern at Howland's stone bridge in an hour and ten minutes—admittedly by "shagging" (Hildreth 1833, 28) down some of the hills and at the expense of wearing out his socks (Hallett 1833a, 61). George Lawton, to whose tavern Burdick had "shagged," was then called to swear that he had seen a man, closely resembling Avery, hurriedly cross the bridge and head toward Fall River at three o'clock on the afternoon of December 20 (Hallett 1833a, 61). Annis Norton substantiated Lawton's sighting; at the same time, she saw a stranger in a broad-brimmed hat leave the bridge and head north, walking "so fast that he would get to Ohio, before night" (Hallett 1833a, 61). If all were right, then the stranger had ample time to get from the bridge to the stone wall on the outskirts of town where Manchester and Davis saw him at sunset—about half past four—as they blasted rocks.

The stranger reappeared at Lawton's Hotel in Fall River (not Lawton's Tavern at Howland's stone bridge) at five forty-five. Gardner Coit, the barkeep at Lawton's, swore that a tall man, wearing a flat fur cap, stopped in that evening for a hurried, solitary dinner, then left a few minutes after six (Hallett 1833a, 63). A stranger was next seen by John Borden at quarter after nine, three miles south of town, walking casually toward the bridge (Marshall and Brown 1833, 34).

Avery, of course, arrived at Gifford's ferry, across the island, shortly after half past nine, by "ferry time." The ferryman's son, William, was called next to testify that he had taken Avery across the bay the following morning (Hallett 1833a, 64). He was followed on the stand by his sister, Jane, who testified quite certainly that Avery had told her on the morning of the twenty-first that he had been on the island "on business at brother Cook's and did not know it was so late, or he should have staid there all night" (Hallett 1833a, 65). If her testimony was true, the minister—who had not been to see either of the "brother Cook's" in Portsmouth—was caught in a lie.

With the murderer's path to and from the crime outlined, the prosecution turned to another problem. By bringing Sarah Cornell's landlady and her daughter to the stand, Greene hoped to demonstrate that she had shown no signs of suicidal depression before her death. In fact, there was every indication that she expected and looked forward to a long life. Harriet Hathaway, the landlady, testified that although Sarah was sometimes moody, on the day of her death she was noticeably more cheerful than usual. Her daughter, Lucy, whose poise and self-control in such a trying circumstance elicited extravagant praise from one court reporter (*Virginia Herald*, 22 May 1833), had more to tell. Lucy worked in the same weaving room with Sarah at Anthony's mill. On the day of her death, Sarah had been worried that she might lose her position at the mill if the overseer would not grant her an early departure—surely not the concern of a woman about to kill herself. Sarah had also bought material for a new apron, and encouraged Lucy to do likewise, that they might wear similar outfits the next week; she had further asked that her loom be repaired while she was out and had asked Lucy to wind some waste yarn for her for knitting (Hallett 1833a, 67). There was no evidence at all in her behavior that she was intent on bringing her life to a close.

By the time Miss Hathaway had finished her testimony, it was nearing seven o'clock. Court was therefore adjourned until Monday morning, with the jurors given into the charge of four officers who were to allow them to walk on the island and speak to their families—in the presence of an officer—but not to speak of the case (Hallett 1833a, 69). The day had seemingly gone well for the prosecution, yet Avery had remained cool and self-possessed, watching with dispassionate interest and several times writing questions to his lawyers as the testimony progressed (*National Banner*, 28 May 1833).

On Monday morning, after the court had replaced its ailing clerk (Eddy 1833), the prosecution began a systematic attempt to demonstrate the web of interaction that linked the minister and Sarah Cornell in the months preceding her death. Harvey Harnden was the first witness. His investigation, he testified, had conclusively proven that the letter found in Sarah Cornell's possessions, dated in Fall River on December 8—the one that set up the fatal December 20 interview—was written on a half sheet of paper whose mate, identified by microscopic analysis of fibers along the tear, was found in the supply of paper in Iram Smith's store.

Digressing momentarily because Harnden had played a major part in Avery's apprehension and examination at Bristol, the prosecution took the opportunity to have him explain his actions in Avery's capture at Rindge, and the defense questioned him about the reasons behind his refusal to accept recognizance for the minister's appearance before the Supreme Court after he had been discharged by Howe and Haile at Bristol.

"I had not the means to enter a prosecution," Harnden explained, "and did not wish to take any illegal step."

"Was it not," Mason pursued him, "because you were satisfied that there was no ground for the charge?"

Harnden answered, "No" (Hallett 1833a, 70).

William Lawless, a packet master, was next brought to the stand to testify that he had met Avery in Bristol, coming up from the ferry landing, fifteen minutes after sunrise on December 21. Avery explained to him that he had not meant to stay on the island overnight, but heavy winds had prevented his earlier return. Lawless, as a sailor, thought he had caught the minister in a gratuitous lie, for "it did not blow more than a whole sail breeze" that night (Hallett 1833a, 71).

Attorney General Greene next questioned Mrs. Zeruiah Hambly, a young Fall River matron who remembered seeing a tall man and a short woman turn down the lane leading past the home of Mrs. Owen (the woman who had heard screaming) at about seven o'clock on the evening of the twentieth. Greene then questioned Amy Durfee, who had worked with Sarah in the mill and could substantiate Lucy Hathaway's testimony about the dead woman's behavior on her last day (Hallett 1833a, 71–77). Greene tried to lead Miss Durfee into a discussion of Sarah's letter-writing habits, but objections from the defense stopped his line of questioning before it was underway.

Nancy Gladding was called to testify that she had invited the Averys to afternoon tea at her home on Thursday, December 20, only to have Avery himself change the date to Friday with no solid explanation. She was followed by Rebecca Diman, who lived above Avery in the same house and could testify that he typically wore a dark "surtout box-coat," and Sylvester Luther, who had seen Avery wearing that coat, coming up from the ferry one morning of the week of the murder (Hildreth 1833, 33).

As useful as these witnesses were to the prosecution to re-emphasize and support the testimony of the previous day, Greene could not let the jury's attention be drawn too far away from the matter of the letter written in Iram Smith's store on December 8.

Smith, who had not been notably precise in his testimony at Bristol, was no more certain with the passage of time. Because he had not "charged his mind" with the casual events of that unexceptional morning, he could not be sure of the details. The paper Harnden had presented was from his store. On the morning of the eighth, Avery did go into the shop and perhaps asked for paper. Smith had to go to a neighbor to get a wafer (to seal a letter) for a customer, but he could not be sure for whom. Avery may or may not have been at his desk—and he may or may not have been writing—when the merchant returned. There was some discussion between Avery and Ira Bidwell about writing a letter to the editor of the *Fall River Weekly Recorder*, but Smith had no idea what had ever become of it. Smith was little help to either the prosecution or the defense, perhaps because, as some of his critics suggested, his Methodist affiliations clouded his memory, and perhaps because he was an honest man who found it difficult to remember unimportant details from an average working day several months before.

After the lunch recess the prosecution digressed for a few moments by bringing two witnesses whose testimony was relevant to earlier points. George Gifford, who lived three quarters of a mile from the ferry at Portsmouth, remembered seeing a man leave the ferry on the afternoon of the twentieth and strike out east, toward the stone bridge (Marshall and Brown 1833, 43). He was followed on the stand by Walter Briggs, the fourteen-year-old son of Bristol's postmaster, who was called in an attempt to improve his father's testimony that Avery had been in correspondence with someone in Fall River. Although he contradicted his father on one point, and was no more conclusive, he handled himself well under the pressure of giving testimony. "This," wrote Chief Justice Eddy in his trial notes, "is a very intelligent Lad" (Eddy 1833).

The court's attention was drawn back to the letter of December 8 by the testimony of Jeremiah Howland, who was in Iram Smith's store that morning and clearly remembered Avery with a piece of writing paper in his hand, and that of Stephen Bartlett, the young stage driver who admitted that he saw Avery pass the post office in Fall River as the minister walked from Lawton's to the stable where Bartlett was hitching up a fresh team (Hallett 1833a, 76). Avery had been in the store where the letter originated, had been seen with paper in his hand, and had walked by the post office where it was mailed. Feeling secure on those points, the attorney general turned his attention to an earlier letter, the pink one Sarah

Cornell had received from Providence on November 27, and which requested a meeting in Bristol either on December 18 or 20.

John Orswell, engineer on the steamboat *King Philip*, came to the stand and testified that one morning during the Methodist four days meeting at Providence in November—the steamboat's schedule made it inevitably the twenty-seventh—a man had come aboard and pressed Orswell to deliver a letter to Sarah Cornell at Mr. Cole's in Fall River. To the best of the engineer's recollection, that man was Ephraim Avery, whom he had identified in Bristol on the following Christmas day (Hallett 1833a, 76–77). Elija Cole and his young daughter substantiated part of Orswell's story; Cole had received the letter from Orswell, and his daughter had given it to Sarah Cornell (Marshall and Brown 1833, 47–48). Attorney General Greene now proposed to place the three letters found in Sarah's trunk—including the yellow one postmarked in Warren on November 13—into evidence. The defense objected, and the court, recognizing a lengthy debate developing, put off the question until the following morning (Hildreth 1833, 37).

There was, however, time left in the afternoon, and the prosecution decided to use it to demonstrate the temporal origin of Sarah Cornell's pregnancy. The prosecution's first witness was J. J. Paine, the young man who had driven Sarah to the Thompson camp meeting. Cross examination directed at discovering impropriety in the woman's conduct or reputation gave Greene the opportunity to make his point perfectly clear.

"I will put a question to you which you are not bound to answer," he said. "Is there any fact within your knowledge, from which you have any reason to know who was the father of her child?"

"There is not," Paine replied.

"Do you know of any illicit intercourse between Sarah M. Cornell, and yourself or any other man?"

Paine replied stiffly, "I do not" (Hallett 1833a, 79).

The next witness was Lucretia—called Nancy—Rawson, Sarah's sister, who, because she did the wash, could testify that her sister had been regularly "unwell as females are" during her stay at Rawson's tailor shop, and that the last occurrence had been exactly one week and one day before the Thompson camp meeting (Hallett 1833a, 79). Her testimony was substantiated by that of Ruth Lawton, a tailor who had shared a bed with Sarah when she was apprenticed at the Rawsons' (Marshall and Brown 1833, 49). When

court adjourned that evening, Albert Greene must have felt satisfied; his witnesses' testimony had been orderly, clear, and precise,
and he could look forward to a positive resolution of the question
of letters the next day.

Greene started out the next morning, Tuesday, May 14, by
offering to read the pink letter into evidence. The defense, which
only the afternoon before had commented on how "dangerous" it
was to base legal deliberations "upon a knowledge of handwriting"
(Hallett 1833a, 75), objected on the grounds that the letter had not
been proven to be in Avery's handwriting. Dutee Pearce replied that
the prosecution did not seek to prove the letter's authorship, but
only that it had passed through Avery's hands and into Sarah Cornell's. Greene added that the letter's contents refuted the contention of suicide because they showed that Miss Cornell had had an
appointment with some party—the author of the letter—on the
evening of her death. Mason's final objection that the most that
could possibly be proved was that the letter had passed, sealed,
through Avery's hands—thus making it evidence as much against
Orswell as against the minister—was unavailing; the court ruled
that the letter might be read to the jury, who must judge for themselves the significance of its content (Hallett 1833a, 81).

Pearce read the letter, then Greene offered the white letter of
December 8. Mason objected again. The case of this letter, the defense claimed, was entirely distinct from that of the pink one; there
was absolutely no evidence to connect it to the prisoner. Greene
contended that the letter, like the pink one, showed that the dead
woman had an appointment on the twentieth, and thus was more
likely the victim of murder than of suicide. Further, he asked how
the court could deny that he had provided evidence more than sufficient to trace the letter to Avery's hand.

The court, however, was not ready to deny or accept and reserved the decision until the afternoon. The rest of the morning
was taken up with the preparatory evidence of John Boyd, who recounted Avery's description of his walk through Portsmouth on the
twentieth—down the coast past the coal mines, then east to the
Union Meeting House, then north by the main road back to Gifford's ferry house (Marshall and Brown 1833, 50–51).

After lunch the court admitted the letter of December 8 into
evidence, and Pearce read it to the jury: "I will be here on the 20 if
pleasant at the place named at 6 o'clock if not pleasant the next
Monday eve" (Hallett 1833a, 83).

Once again, Greene used the opportunity presented by victory to admit another of the letters from Sarah's trunk—this time, the yellow one from Warren. Immediate, and justified, defense objection that the letter had not been in any way tied to the prisoner prompted Greene to withdraw it (Hildreth 1833, 42). His point had been made, and it was not necessary to jeopardize possible later admission of the yellow letter into evidence.

Returning to the question of Avery's whereabouts on December 20, the attorney general called Abner Tallman to the stand. Tallman had driven the main road from Newport to his house in Portsmouth on the afternoon of the twentieth, leaving a little after sunset and arriving home at eight o'clock. If Avery had been walking up the road, Tallman would have seen him, but he did not. Neither did Abby Earl, who lived just north of Gifford's house in Portsmouth, and who had been keeping watch from her window on the afternoon of the twentieth (Hallett 1833a, 83). Avery seemed to have neither gone from nor returned to the ferry, the prosecution could claim, in the way he had said.

Greene next called Margaret Hambly, the bargirl at Lawton's in Fall River, who had made a laughingstock of herself at the Bristol examination by several times picking out the wrong man as the person she had seen having dinner on the night of the murder. She was a weak witness, but at least she could remind the jury that someone looking like Avery had been in Fall River. No one, looking like him or not, had been seen trudging up the main road into Portsmouth, sight-seeing in the dark.

After the bargirl, the prosecution switched its attention to the night of October 20, when Avery was supposed to have had his first lengthy interview with Sarah after learning, the night before, of her pregnancy. Bailey Borden and his wife, Mary, were called to testify that they had seen a tall man, wearing dark clothes and a broad-brimmed hat, in the company of a short woman in the streets of Fall River that evening. Borden was unsure who they were, but his wife, who had seen Sarah before, was certain that the woman was Miss Cornell. At least, the woman she had seen was the same one whose burial on the Durfee farm Mary had attended in December (Marshall and Brown 1833, 52). The Bordens were followed by Lucy Spink, who was at the prayer meeting Avery supervised in Fall River that evening, and who saw him leave early to meet a short woman outside and disappear into the darkness (Hallett 1833a, 85).

Grindall Rawson was then called, for the unexceptional purpose of testifying to Sarah's residence at his tailor shop and her trip
to the Thompson camp meeting. Even his most potentially inflam-
matory statement was carefully worded: Before Sarah left his home
in October, she informed Rawson and his wife "what her situation
might be, in consequence of what she knew had taken place at the
camp meeting" (Hallett 1833a, 86). It must have been a shock,
then, to both Rawson and the prosecution lawyers when the cross
examination led the witness to discuss Sarah's plans after the camp
meeting. Prodded by Randolf's questions, Rawson told the jury
that, on the advice of a lawyer, she had decided to go to Rhode Island and, once she was certain of her condition, contact Avery.

"Mr. Rawson," Randolf replied to that information, "as you
have introduced Mr. Avery's name unasked, you will now be good
enough to state all she ever told you relating to him" (Hildreth
1833, 44).

After all the heated opposition to the jury hearing what Sarah
had told Dr. Wilbur—for it was essentially what she had told Rawson—Rawson could not believe the defense lawyer's instructions.

"Do you wish to know," he asked, "the whole she said?"

"Yes," was the reply, "the whole."

The witness then recounted the story of Avery's seduction and
rape of his sister-in-law, accomplished as a result of her desire to
retrieve letters she feared might keep her from rejoining the Methodist church (Hallett 1833a, 86).

Following the cross examination, the attorney general asked if
Sarah had had friends or relations in Bristol—she did not—to reinforce the idea that any letters she might have sent there would
inevitably have been directed to Avery, then ended with a question
about her moral character. Rawson replied that he had never, before the camp meeting, known or suspected his sister-in-law to have
engaged in illicit intercourse (Hallett 1833a, 87). When he stepped
from the stand, Rawson must have realized that the cross examination he had undergone represented the defense's attempt to reduce
the importance of Sarah Cornell's accusation of Avery—of which
the jury certainly knew though it had not been legally admitted as
evidence—by eliciting it as if it were not damaging to Avery's case.
Still, Mason had only made the best of an unfortunate situation,
and the prosecution was pleased.

Benjamin Saunders, one of Rawson's apprentices, was called
next to testify that he had taken several of Sarah's letters, addressed

to someone in Bristol, to the post office in the weeks before the camp meeting (Hallett 1833a, 87). To whom but the minister might they have been sent? He was followed by Nancy Bidwell, wife of Fall River's Methodist minister, in whose house Avery had spent the night of October 20. When she testified that Avery returned late from the prayer meeting (where Lucy Spink had seen him leave early), the prosecution hoped the jury would have no trouble imagining what kept him so long (Hallett 1833a, 87).

The final witness of the day was Sarah Jones, whose testimony was sought to shed more light on the defense's methods of eliciting facts than on Avery's activities on December 20. Mrs. Jones, who lived near the coal mines in Portsmouth, had seen a stranger near her house on the morning of the twentieth. She told Rev. Drake about the sighting when he canvassed the neighborhood for witnesses to Avery's excursion, and was immediately taken up as a defense witness. The problem with her testimony was that she had seen a man before Avery reached the island. Since her first interview with Avery's lawyer (then Nathaniel Bullock), Mrs. Jones testified, she had been under constant pressure to change her recollection to having seen a man in the afternoon. Further, she said, Avery had asked her in their first interview to describe the roads around the coal mines, and to keep their discussion secret (Hallett 1833a, 87). Why, the prosecution did not need to ask, did Avery need her information if he had in fact been in the neighborhood only a few days before?

Under cross examination, Mrs. Jones was adamant about Methodist attempts to change her testimony.

> I never told Mr. Drake that it was in the afternoon that I saw the man. Mr. Drake came to me and told me so, and asked why it was not as easy for me to think it was in the afternoon as in the forenoon. I told him because it was not so. He asked me what reason I had for thinking so? I told him because I knew the forenoon from the afternoon (Hallett 1833a, 88).

The clarity of the case for Methodist subversion of justice that she presented, however, was clouded when Randolf got her to admit that she had left Portsmouth early in 1833, moved to Fall River, and, since the beginning of May, had been employed in the Bridge Factory operated by Nathaniel Borden, a member of the Fall River Committee (Hallett 1833a, 88). Mrs. Jones's claim that she had been hired by the superintendent without Mr. Borden's knowledge (Marshall and Brown 1833, 56) was hardly convincing evidence that her testimony had not been bought. Still, the prosecution could hope that the jury would see her position in the mill as a benevolent gesture toward a woman whose heroic defense of the truth had cost her place in the Methodist community of Portsmouth. The issues raised by her testimony had not been cleanly resolved, but on the whole the prosecution must have been pleased with the impression she made; if there was even a suspicion that her story was accurate, then every witness that the defense would bring would be potentially compromised.

On Wednesday Greene brought his last witnesses. Philip Bennett, a stout young man who had taken up a commission (worth three dollars) from Dr. Hooper, reported that he had traveled from the stack yard to Gifford's ferry house in one hour and twenty-nine minutes (Hallett 1833a, 89). George Davol, in whose house the prayer meeting of October 20 had been held, testified that Avery had officiated there. Grindall Rawson was then called again to identify Sarah's handwriting, preparatory to introducing the scrap of penciled paper found in her bandbox. Along with the scrap, Greene chose to offer the yellow letter from Warren one last time. Though it was not connected to Rawson's testimony—it was obviously not in Sarah's handwriting—he hoped it would be admitted because it was clearly, by its context, part of the correspondence that had already been admitted. The ensuing debate resulted in a draw: The penciled note was admitted ("If I am missing enquire of Rev. Mr Avery") as evidence that Sarah had not gone to her death in a suicidal frame of mind (Hallett 1833a, 90–91), but the yellow letter, in which Avery presumably replied to Sarah's letter of the twelfth informing him of her certainty of pregnancy, was rejected as neither having been proven as Avery's nor having had any bearing on Sarah's mood—suicidal or otherwise—in December.

After a squabble over how much of the admitted letters could be used to indicate Avery's relationship with the dead woman, the court took its lunch recess. When it met again at three o'clock, there was little left for the prosecution to do. Joseph Lesure, a postal clerk at Fall River, was called to testify that he had seen Avery pass the post office on December 8, had heard something drop into the letter box, and had retrieved a letter addressed to Sarah Cornell. After pointed questions from Mason about why Lesure had not remembered this remarkable information at Bristol (he said he had, but had not been asked about it so said nothing), he was allowed to step down. The last prosecution witness was Seth Darling, recalled to swear that the Fall River post office had processed a letter bound for Bristol on November 19 (Hallett 1833a, 93). On that ambiguous note, at a quarter to five, the floor was turned over to the defense.

7. The Defense

Newport was already shouldering the burden of a second influx of tourists—those coming to hear Jeremiah Mason's summation, which they thought could not be far off (*National Banner*, 30 May 1833)—when Richard Randolf stood and faced the jury. In a lengthy discourse that took the rest of Wednesday afternoon and evening and most of Thursday morning, he told the jury that the defense would rest on a web of evidence incomparably more compelling than the prosecution's. The defense would show, he said, that the condition of the body was not inconsistent with suicide and that Sarah Cornell had been so deranged—as demonstrated by her "lewdness" and "strangeness of conduct" (Hallett 1833a, 96)—that suicide was the most reasonable explanation of her death. The defense would also show that she harbored a grudge against Rev. Avery, who had expelled her from his church, that Avery had an unblemished reputation, and that it was impossible for him to have been the father of her child. Avery's implication in the correspondence found in the dead woman's luggage would be totally discredited, as would the testimony of several state witnesses who thought they saw someone looking like the minister heading for Fall River on the afternoon of December 20. Just where the minister had been that afternoon, Randolf admitted, was impossible to prove; however, the defense would show that his own account of his movements was as credible as any other.

Of course, Randolf continued, many of the defense witnesses were Methodists, and some jurors might believe them to be prejudiced. But, after all, were not many of them respectable ministers of the gospel, and "if we go into a transaction, which happened among the Methodists, where shall we find our witnesses but among the Methodists?" (Hallett 1833a, 97). The possible prejudices of the prosecution witnesses were not, at least for a defense lawyer, so easily dismissed. Speaking of the witnesses he proposed to discredit, and certain the jury would not apply his argument equally to the Methodist camp, Randolf said:

> I do not suppose these witnesses guilty of willful perjury. A cross-examination shows that their conscience still pinches them a little. But a few of them have yet got to the pitch of saying flatly, that Avery was the man. They qualify it a little; they *think* he was the man. The influence under which they testify, is obvious. They want to satisfy the community in which they live. They believe there has been committed an atrocious murder, which ought to be punished, and are weak enough to think that the respectable part of the public are desirous of having the defendant convicted, even upon false testimony. This is the working of weak minds, under that high state of excitement that has existed at Fall River, where meetings have been held, and money raised, and time spent, and evidence searched for, with a zeal which, if directed against you or me, supposing us so unfortunate as from some unlucky circumstance to have fallen under suspicion, would leave us very little chance of escape. Suspicious circumstances and willing witnesses will hang any man (Hildreth 1833, 54–55).

How much the local hysteria, comparable in Randolf's eyes to that which produced the Salem witch trials, influenced the testimony of any particular man, was a subject worthy of the jury's speculation. However, they ought to remember that much of the medical evidence brought by the prosecution was produced by a young and inexperienced man—Foster Hooper—who did the autopsy in the excitement of the first days of Rev. Avery's hearing at Bristol. "An examination made under such circumstances," said Randolf, "cannot be relied upon" (Hildreth 1833, 56).

The defense opening was concluded when Randolf read from several volumes of medical jurisprudence on the physical evidence of suicide by hanging and the difficulty of distinguishing bruises from the marks of postmortem blood settling and decomposition. Attorney General Greene was ready with passages from these works that described the difficulty in distinguishing suicide from murder by hanging. With that, the defense brought its first witness.

Jeremiah Mason's initial objective was to discredit the medical testimony on which the charge of murder (and the preconditioning assumption of seduction) was based. To this purpose he called Dr. Nathaniel Miller, a respected surgeon for forty years, to the stand. Miller began his testimony as a critique of the assertions and conclusions drawn by Drs. Wilbur and Hooper for the prosecution. When no objection seemed forthcoming to stop this improper line of testimony, Chief Justice Eddy broke in and voiced his opinion that it was "very incorrect, but if the gentlemen have agreed upon it among themselves, the witness may go on" (Hallett 1833a, 99). Greene immediately objected, and the doctor was told to refrain from analysis of the previous witnesses' testimony. Equally helpful to both sides, the chief justice advised Mason to "put your questions in this form: the appearances being so and so, what do they indicate?" (Hallett 1833a, 99).

Requiring only occasional reminders to keep his comments factual, Miller testified that the marks described on the body might as easily be explained by the natural settling of the blood after death—suggillation—as by blows received before it. The test of washing, which Wilbur and Hooper had employed, he thought an uncertain technique to identify bruises, and an autopsy performed thirty-six days after death would be suspect. On the subject of Sarah Cornell's pregnancy, it was his opinion, supported by several medical texts, that the eight-inch fetus removed from her body was too large to have been conceived only three months and twenty days before her death (at the Thompson camp meeting in August). Testimony that she had menstruated immediately before the meeting could be ignored because, he said, "it is not very uncommon for females to have some show of periodical occurrences after gestation commences" (Hallett 1833a, 100).

Finally, he offered his professional opinion that nothing in the condition or the position of the body as found was inconsistent with a verdict of suicide. Besides, a person who was first strangled, then suspended, would show two rope marks on the neck, while the body apparently had only one.

Under cross examination, the doctor retreated from none of

his opinions, but agreed that there was some room for variation in the conventional wisdom of his profession. The marks on the body might have been the product of violence. The size of a fetus at different stages of development was much disputed by authorities and probably varied greatly within a normal range. An autopsy performed after thirty-six days of death in the winter might be more accurate than one performed after thirty-six summer days. The single mark on the corpse's neck was not consistent with suspension because it was horizontal—without the inevitable upturn at the knot. The peculiar knot and the short stretch of rope between the victim and the pole made the proposed suicide a little unusual (Hallett 1833a, 101–3). Greene's cross examination, aided by suggestions from Foster Hooper (Hallett 1833a, 102), had convincingly demonstrated that medical opinion and fact were not identical; it seemed to rest on which authority one decided to believe. Mason's final question to the doctor—"Should you place less confidence in a man who examined a body in a high state of excitement, than under other circumstances?" (Hallett 1833a, 104)—was not allowed by the court, but it had its effect. The jury could not help but wonder if the testimony of Foster Hooper, a young, fiery member of the Fall River Committee and an obvious agent for the prosecution, could rank with that of the venerable patriarch of medicine who was descending from the stand.

Miller was followed by Drs. Usher Parsons, Jabez Holmes, William Turner, and Theophilus C. Dunn. All of them swore to essentially the same opinions as Miller and were cross examined in the same way. As the hours wore on and the same medical arguments were asserted and rejected, the spectators grew restive. One reporter complained that the proceedings had become much less interesting than usual and concluded that the testimony proved that "there are medical books, just as there are law books, that prove both sides of the same question, with equal exactness" (*Phoenix Gazette*, 23 May 1833). Neither he nor the other spectators had to endure the dull medical debate for much longer. Once the issue had been sufficiently muddied to preclude any certainty in the jurors' minds about the physical condition of the body, Mason's first job was done, and he could move on to a consideration of Sarah Cornell's life history that would make the assumption that her insanity had led to self-destruction unavoidable.

On Friday morning, after Dr. Dunn had completed his testimony, the defense called Dr. William Graves to the stand. If there were groans and eyes rolled heavenward by spectators weary of doctors, such demonstrations soon ceased. Graves practiced in Lowell and had treated Sarah Cornell for nothing less dramatic than a very severe case of "lues veneira" (Marshall and Brown 1833, 72). Her manner, he said, made him think her "a little crazy." Cautioned by the court to state facts and not impressions, the doctor continued that she reported her disease to have been caused by a young man who deserted her, and she expressed outrage at Rev. Avery for turning her out of the church when he discovered her condition. In later visits, the inconstant suitor became three as she inquired about the medical treatment of two other young men, both of whom she apparently thought of as possible sources of her discomfort (Hallett 1833a, 110).

Examining the doctor's qualifications (the court had suspected that he was nothing more than an "apothecary") convinced Judge Eddy that Graves's opinions would qualify as those of an expert. Asked to express them, the doctor said:

> I hardly know how to answer. The truth is my mind was not made up. I was almost inclined to think she was insane. Her language was so different from what I ever heard from a female. I hardly know what to think. I should not be willing to give it as my opinion she was deranged (Hallett 1833a, 111).

Graves's conclusion—or lack of it—did not appeal to Mason, who questioned him until the doctor was willing to admit that he "began to incline to suspect she was partially insane." It was hardly an iron-clad statement, but by this time the entire court must have known it was the best that could be gotten from a medical expert. Cross examination produced names of the three young men Sarah had claimed as possible causes of her affliction (none was brought to court to testify) and revealed the interesting fact that Graves had at one time been the Averys' family physician.

Next on the stand was Dr. Noah Martin, who claimed to have treated and cured Sarah Cornell for chronic gonorrhea at his offices in Somersworth, New Hampshire. Like Dr. Graves, he reported that there were "appearances and oddities" in her behavior that made him consider her not quite normal (Hallett 1833a, 112). The doctors were followed by two young women—Asaneth Bowen and Mary Ann Lary—who had no scruples about declaring Sarah Cornell deranged. Miss Bowen had seen Sarah go into a "public room" (privy) in the factory at Waltham, carrying a piece of cord, apparently bent on suicide. Miss Lary had not seen such an attempt, but had heard Sarah complain that her courage failed her when she had tried to do herself in. Under cross examination, both girls admitted that they were Methodists and had been sought out to testify by Methodist ministers (information that was deleted from the Methodist account of the trial) (Hallett 1833a, 113–14).

It was perhaps because the next two witnesses were Baptists, and so could not be accused of a religious prejudice against the dead woman, that they were called. The defense certainly could not have placed much hope for swaying the jury by their unlikely, inconsistent, and sometimes ridiculous story. Ezra and Ruhana Parker were tavern keepers in Thompson, Connecticut. According to Ezra, most charitably described as an eccentric and colorful old man, Sarah came to his tavern late in the afternoon of the last day of March—or was it the first of April?—seven or eight years earlier. She appeared to be so pregnant that Parker feared she would go into labor that very night. Asking asylum until the stage for Providence left, she settled her bulk near the fire. It was almost seven o'clock that evening, while Sarah still "sot" with the Parkers, that Charles and William Taylor entered, looking for an evening's entertainment. According to Ezra, "The devil, says William Taylor, Maria, be you here? Yes, says she, and you can't help yourself, William Taylor!" (Hallett 1833a, 114). In the exchange that followed, Sarah swore her unborn child on Taylor and demanded payment for a bond releasing him from further responsibility. Warming to his story, Parker reported that, upon receiving her money, Sarah exclaimed triumphantly, "William Taylor, you must get up earlier than ever you did yet, to make a garden of me to bear seed to you" (Hallett 1833a, 115). The meaning of her outburst became clear when Ezra's wife took the stand and reported that, when Sarah retired that evening, she unwrapped a blanket from her middle and lost all appearance of pregnancy. When she left the tavern in the morning, she was stylishly trim.

The Parkers were contradictory about the details of their story, and Attorney General Greene soon demonstrated their shortcomings to the jury. According to Mrs. Parker, Sarah had removed her disguise long before Taylor handed her the money in the morning. When questioned, the old woman could not think of a reason why the man would pay after the trick had been exposed. Ezra's story that the money had been paid the evening before was more credible, but it failed to explain why Sarah would choose to expose her deception at the tavern. The simple resolution to the Parkers' inconsistencies was to call the Taylor brothers to the stand. Not surprisingly, that was impossible; William Taylor was dead and his brother Charles had disappeared "somewhere in the state of New York" (Hallett 1833a, 115).

However amused by their cracker-barrel speech, the court was not much enlightened by the Parkers. The comedy stopped abruptly, however, when Brooks Shattuck, who had been the overseer in a Lowell weaving room where Sarah Cornell had been employed, took the stand. A grim young man, he recounted discharging Miss Cornell after hearing of her bad character and receiving her confession that she had engaged in intercourse with "as many as two" men at Lowell (Hallett 1833a, 115). After Shattuck, Nathan Howard testified; as Sarah's class leader in the Methodist Church at Lowell, it had been his duty to prefer charges against her for fornication. After her conviction she confirmed his low opinion of her character, admitting the validity of the charges and expressing a desire to destroy herself. Her forward conversation came as no surprise; Howard noticed a new "flash" in her eye and a peculiarity in her walk. "She appeared," he said, "as though she was not rational" (Hallett 1833a, 116).

It was too good an opportunity to pass up, and Mason asked him to elaborate on his answer. How did she appear irrational? When Howard replied that her eyes had looked fiery and reddened, Mason coached him helpfully.

"Was there any appearance of wildness?" the lawyer asked.

"Yes, sir," Howard dutifully replied (Hallett 1833a, 116). There was no objection from the prosecution.

The next two witnesses were women to whom Sarah had made confessions of her sins in an attempt to get them to sign the certificate that would allow her conditional readmission to the Methodist church. Mary Anne Barnes reported that under interrogation Sarah had admitted to improper conduct with one, then two, then four men. Lucy Davol recounted much the same conversation with Sarah, adding that the distraught girl had admitted to suicidal desires. The day's testimony was ended with Lydia Pervere, who could recount Sarah's aversion to Avery, her admission of improper conduct, and her disordered state of mind. One day, Lydia said, Sarah had come into the factory dressed entirely in white. If that were not sufficient evidence of derangement, she had flung her arms around Lydia's neck, screamed and cried, and carried on until Lydia was

disgusted (Hallett 1833a, 118). It was a bizarre picture that the jury
was left to contemplate when court adjourned until the following
morning.

On Saturday morning, the eighteenth, the defense began with
Ellen Griggs, a young married woman who had heard Sarah Cornell, when in Lowell seeking signatures on her certificate of forgiveness, threaten revenge on Avery if it cost her life. Asked by
Greene if she told Avery of the threat, she recalled telling him in
the carriage that had carried him from Bristol to Boston after the
hearing before justices Haile and Howe. After a careful cross examination about the trip, during which the witness several times
broke into nervous laughter when she could not remember the details requested, Greene asked her, "Can you give me any reason
why you should recollect so well, what you heard her say three
years ago, and not recollect what took place so recently?" (Hallett
1833a, 120). She had an answer, supplied by the defense attorneys;
she was becoming partially deaf, an affliction that was not quite so
bad years before in Lowell.

Sarah Worthing was next on the stand. She recounted the fa-
miliar story of confession and suicide, but added a new note. Sarah
Cornell, she said, had admitted strained relations with her sister
over Grindall Rawson, who had told Sarah that she was far more
attractive than her sister, his wife Lucretia. After Lucy Howe had
added her recollection of Sarah's hysterical Lowell confessions, the
defense returned to the interesting story of adultery within the
family circle. Elizabeth Shumway was called to testify that in 1825
or 1826 at Slatersville, she had known Sarah Cornell, who had been
overtly suicidal and had explained her depression as the product of
an unhappy courtship—her sister had won Grindall Rawson from
her "by art and strategem" (Hallett 1833a, 122). However, Sarah
had gone on smugly, her sister had become jealous, as well she
might, for Sarah and Rawson had since been "as intimate as husband and wife" and she had become his favorite (Hildreth 1833,
66). As proof of the relationship, Miss Shumway offered a poem
that Rawson had written to Sarah on the blank flyleaf of a testa-
ment. Though she had no copy of it, the witness managed to recite
all twenty-eight lines, "with most approved emphasis" (*Virginia Herald*, 29 May 1833), a remarkable feat of memory all the more impressive because of the execrable quality of the poetry. Rawson had
written lines such as: "Maria when you these lines peruse, / I pray
the errors do excuse: / A poet I do not pretend to be, / Therefore

excuses are for me" (Marshall and Brown 1833, 34). Spectators who heard Miss Shumway recite might have considered indicting Rawson for crimes against the English language, but there was nothing in his poem to indicate anything other than a friendly interest in his young sister-in-law.

The next witness was Miriam Libby, who had known Sarah at Dover, where she had expressed desires to kill herself and to seek revenge on Avery. Following her was Caroline Tibbits, also from Dover, who had much the same story. The morning's testimony was concluded by Mary Warren, Ann Cottel, and Sarah Honey, all of whom had known Sarah in Great Falls, where she apparently expressed intentions of suicide and revenge to anyone who would listen (Hallett 1833a, 124–26).

The afternoon's first witness was the Reverend John Dow, who in 1830 had been the Methodist minister at Dover. When Sarah Cornell applied to him for admission to the church, he wrote to Avery and was informed of her bad character. As a result, she was barred from membership (Hildreth 1833, 68). Timothy Paul, with whom Sarah had boarded in Somersworth, was next called to swear to her confessions of sexual transgressions with three men in Lowell (Hallett 1833a, 126). He was followed by Thaddeus Bruce, a dour, fifty-year-old Congregationalist, who reported firing Sarah from his weaving room in Jewett City because of her generally disreputable character. Bruce's wife, Zilpah, the next witness, elaborated on her husband's theme. Sarah, she said, had looked suspiciously thick-waisted in 1822 and 1823 at Jewett City, only to disappear and later reappear at Slatersville, much reduced in girth. When asked about the girl's "character for chastity," Zilpah cautiously replied, "Her character was not good, she was tattling."

"But what," persisted the lawyer, "was her character for chastity?"

"She was a young woman unstable in her ways," said Mrs. Bruce, beginning to appear nervous.

It was Chief Justice Eddy who fathomed the problem. "Don't you know," he asked, "what chastity means?"

Mrs. Bruce admitted that she did not, Randolf put the question in more colloquial terms, and the court learned that Sarah's chastity was as bad as her reputation for tattling (Hallett 1833a, 127).

The rest of the afternoon was occupied with a litany of second-hand observations of Sarah's deviance and suicidal tendencies. Philena Holmes remembered her from Slatersville in 1826, when she confessed that her sister's marriage had made it impossible for her to go home, and that she was tempted to drown herself in the river (Hallett 1833a, 127). William Holmes, who had known her there two years before, came closest to offering a substantiated report of her lack of character. As her class leader in the Methodist church, it was his duty to bring charges against her when her "lewdness" was called to his attention. Unfortunately, the church records could not amplify his report, for no written records of the expulsion were kept. "We did not take that trouble," was his disdainful explanation (Hallett 1833a, 128).

Susan Walton repeated the story of the riverine suicide attempt and added that Sarah had once called the Methodists a "set of damned fools" (Hallett 1833a, 128). Hers, however, was not the crowning testimony of the day; she was followed by Rebecca Fuller, a young married woman in whose house Sarah Cornell had boarded during her stay at Waltham. During her short stay (abbreviated, according to Mrs. Fuller, when Sarah fled to avoid bad reports from Lowell), Sarah had taken Rebecca into her confidence, showing her a letter she had composed to Rev. Avery in which she admitted to the charges brought against her (Hildreth 1833, 70). Though the letter was lost, Mrs. Fuller remembered its content and wording in great detail. She also remembered Sarah's spoken declaration about Mr. Avery: "I hate him above all flesh living" (Hallett 1833a, 128).

After a desultory cross examination in which Mrs. Fuller admitted that she had seen the letter only once, court was adjourned until nine o'clock Monday morning. Warning the jury not to talk to anyone on Sunday, Chief Justice Eddy drew a wail from one middle-aged juror: "What, can't we speak to our children?" (*Eastern Argus*, 27 May 1833). Quickly, before Greene could speak, Mason intervened for the jurors, and the judge revised his instructions to allow visits with their families in the presence of court officers (Hallett 1833a, 129). The lawyer may have secured the good will of a dozen people, but outside there were whisperings of a gathering storm. Though the courtroom had remained decorous through the day's proceedings, the many Methodist clergymen in attendance found their treatment by the "rabble" increasingly offensive (*Virginia Herald*, 29 May 1833). There were no actual attacks, but the hostility in the air was palpable.

Veiled hostility was not all that kept the "rabble" occupied. Unable to gain access to the crowded courtroom and unable to get reliable reports from those who did, the more imaginative began to

generate rumors. Both Noah Barker and Edwin Wilbur were suspected of being incompetent jurors. Other jurors were suspected
of having avoided military duty by claiming "conscientious scruples" against bearing arms; what that might have to do with their
ability to try a case was unclear to the anonymous "Freeholder" who
reported the rumors to Attorney General Greene (*Freeholder*, 20
May 1833), but he thought it was worth investigating. It was also
widely believed that Avery had been indisputably proven to have
been in Fall River on the night of the murder and that the gatekeeper on Howland's bridge had positively identified him (*Literary
Subaltern*, 31 May 1833). By the end of the month, as if to create a
reasonable equity in inaccuracy, it was also rumored that a woman
had testified that Sarah Cornell had admitted to her before the
Thompson camp meeting that she was "in a state of domestic solicitude," and that the father was from Hebron, Connecticut (*Literary
Subaltern*, 31 May 1833).

When court resumed on Monday morning, the defense called
Samuel Richmond and Charles Hodges, both merchants from Providence, to testify to Sarah's shoplifting ten years before. Greene
objected, claiming their evidence had no bearing on the case, but
was countered by Mason who said he wished to show not that she
had committed suicide, but that she was of such a character that she
might (Hallett 1833a, 130). Mason won the point.

The rest of the day was taken up by a seemingly interminable
parade of witnesses who, collectively, could trace Avery's every
movement at the Thompson camp meeting. Jonathan Cady had arrived with him at the camp grounds on Tuesday evening (Hildreth
1833, 71). Sophia Elliot, John W. Elliot, and Chloe Elliot testified
that he had taken lodging at young Mr. Elliot's house and had never
during the meeting appeared at old Mr. Elliot's (Marshall and
Brown 1833, 97–99). Elias C. Scott remembered seeing Avery in
the critical evening hours of both Wednesday and Thursday (when
the seduction was supposed to have occurred) and recounted Avery's
comments that Miss Cornell, an altogether bad young woman, was
on the grounds (Hallett 1833a, 133). Phineas Crandall had likewise
seen Avery on Thursday evening and had shared a room with him
that night (Hildreth 1833, 73). Abraham D. Merrill was the morning's last witness, and he testified that Avery had been in plain sight
at seven twenty-five on Thursday evening, that his character was
good, and that Miss Cornell's reputation was rather less than admirable (Marshall and Brown 1833, 103).

Merrill was called back for cross examination at the opening of the afternoon session. Had he not, Dutee Pearce wanted to know, once said that Avery had a bad temper? The elderly minister thought he might have characterized his subordinate as a "man of warm temperament." Were the suspicious females removed from the Thompson camp ground? Yes. Was Sarah Cornell among them? No. Pearce left it to the jury to determine how a woman specifically identified as a moral threat could have been excluded from the roundup of unsavory characters (Hallett 1833a, 136). Had Merrill been aware of any charges against Avery before the present case? The answer was yes—a suit for defamation of character (the reference being to the action brought by Thomas Norris, in which Avery was convicted). Mason objected to the line of questioning unless court records were forthcoming; Attorney General Greene, having made his point, thought it was probably not necessary to go on.

Mason, however, could not let the matter drop. Resuming the examination, he asked Merrill if the prosecution had damaged Avery's reputation. It was Greene's turn to object, requiring that the outcome of the trial be presented to the jury, not just Merrill's interpretation. Mason tried another approach: Did the Methodists have their own examination of the charges? Yes. The outcome? He was acquitted. Did that injure his reputation? Greene was on his feet, undoubtedly livid.

"I object to that question!" he shouted as the witness replied, "Not in the least." Too late to stop the answer, he turned to Merrill. "What was the result of the suit at common law for slander?"

"I object," said Mason.

"Then I object to the other," Greene flung back.

Chief Justice Eddy solved the problem by throwing out the whole line of questioning (Hallett 1833a, 136). They had, however, managed to wake up the spectators, who were rewarded by much more entertaining witnesses for the remainder of the afternoon.

Henry Mayo followed Rev. Merrill on the stand. Middle aged, married, and clerical, Mayo still retained an irrepressible nature that made him observant of the ladies and prone to levity. After the inevitable assertion that he had seen Avery at sundown on Thursday at the Thompson camp meeting, Mayo proceeded to describe his observations of Sarah Cornell. "I noticed the manner in which she walked," he said, "and that her clothes did not appear to be large enough. Principally the opening of her clothes attracted my attention" (Hallett 1833a, 137). There, he had told his wife, was a young woman who ought to be married to save her credit, implying that she appeared to be pregnant. Betsy Mayo disagreed and rebuked her husband for his comment as she testified when he left the stand. It was not the only criticism he was to draw for his witticisms about the dead girl. The attorney general attemped to discredit his testimony by pointing out that he had said, after the examination at Bristol, that Avery ought to go free, guilty or not. No, said Mayo, that was not the case. Taunted by an acquaintance about Avery, he had responded ironically that "if universal doctrine were true and brother Avery was guilty of killing the girl, I did not see why he might not be acquitted, because, if death was instrumental in converting souls, according to his doctrine, then if Mr. Avery did kill the girl, he had been instrumental in her conversion" (Hallett 1833a, 138).

After Betsy Mayo testified to her husband's remark about Sarah's "credit," her reaction to it, and her steadfast belief in the good character of the dead girl (whom she had known at Lowell before marrying), young Samuel Parker was called to recount his observation of Avery at the preachers' tent throughout Thursday evening at Thompson (Hallett 1833a, 139). Mercifully, he was not too long on the stand, and was replaced by the infinitely more interesting Patty Bacon.

Something of an expert on pregnancy, having undergone nine of her own (Hildreth 1833, 76), Mrs. Bacon had seen Sarah Cornell changing clothes in the Muddy Brook tent at Thompson on Thursday morning. She began to express her opinion, but was interrupted by the attorney general.

"We don't want your opinion," he said. "State what you saw."

Mrs. Bacon was taken aback. This was clearly not what she had been led to expect. What had she seen? "Her countenance," she said. "Her appearance."

It was also not what Randolf had expected; his witness, who was to swear that Sarah Cornell's breasts were enlarged by pregnancy, needed prompting. "What else was there?" he asked.

"Nothing more, sir."

Randolf could not be satisfied by her retreat. "Did you see her bosom?"

"I did."

Silence.

Now Chief Justice Eddy thought he might help. "What do you mean by the countenance?" he asked.

"I mean her countenance looked as though she was in a state of pregnancy."

It was still not enough for the defense. "What," Randolf cried, "was the appearance of her bosom?"

All he got for his trouble was an assertion that her countenance was "sickly," like that of a pregnant woman.

"Describe it," he commanded.

"A sickly countenance," she responded; "pale."

"Describe her bosom!" the exasperated lawyer shouted.

"I noticed nothing but her countenance," his witness replied, now firmly entrenched in a position she would not easily give up.

Randolf realized that a frontal attack could not succeed; he decided on a flanking maneuver instead.

"Describe her eyes," he requested.

"Her eyes did not look well."

"Describe her appearance. Can't you use your own words, and tell the jury how it was?" Perhaps pleading could get the job done.

"I can describe nothing more than I have. Her countenance was sickly and she did not look well. That is all I saw."

The exchange threatened to go on all day. After three more ineffectual attempts by the lawyer, Chief Justice Eddy broke in. "Is it worthwhile to press her any further?" he asked.

Randolf was desperate; he could see Mrs. Bacon leaving the stand never having given the testimony she was brought to give, and making the defense seem remarkably foolish in the process. Throwing decorum to the wind, he made one final effort.

"Was there," he asked, "any unusual prominence?"

"Oh! Mr. Randolf," shouted the attorney general, "don't!" Then the chief justice gracefully suggested that questioning be directed along other paths.

Finally it was Greene, in his cross examination, that spurred Mrs. Bacon into the assertion that Randolf had sweated blood to procure.

"Do you feel authorized," the attorney general scornfully asked Mrs. Bacon, "to draw the conclusion from a pale countenance and dull eyes, and not seeming well, that such [pregnancy] was her situation?"

"I have told you all I have got to say," was the reply. Then, as if a light had dawned, Mrs. Bacon thought of a way to say it delicately. "Her bosoms appeared rather full," she added, satisfied that she had at last done her duty.

The attorney general, however, was not willing to let her get away easily. "Do you know," he asked, "at what time that appearance takes place in a female in that situation?"

Mrs. Bacon was shocked; the man was trying to badger her into a discussion immensely more intimate and repugnant than that she had avoided with Randolf. Clearly it was time to recant, to try to reach the protection of her abandoned defenses.

"I have said all I have got to say," she said. "I don't know that her bosoms were fuller than usual."

"Then her bosoms were not full?"

"I have said all I have got to say," the witness repeated with such conviction that she was soon allowed to step down.

It is small wonder that Almira Waters, a younger woman called to substantiate Patty Bacon's story, scurried for cover as soon as she reached the stand. She had seen nothing out of the ordinary in Muddy Brook tent, she said, and would never have thought anything at all if Mrs. Bacon had not mentioned it (Hallett 1833a, 139–40).

The last witness of the day was Polly Horton, who had seen Sarah Cornell pat a young man's shoulder at Thompson when he asked her where she would like her trunks delivered. After Mrs. Bacon's monumental defense of propriety, old Mrs. Horton's demonstration of shoulder patting—executed on a willing gentleman of the court—was anticlimactic. The court adjourned until the morning.

Tuesday's witnesses were hard pressed to equal the theatrical impact of their predecessors on Monday afternoon. Milton Daggett, master of the Weston tent at the Thompson camp meeting, testified that he had seen Avery at his tent at half past seven on Thursday, and saw him walk from the preachers' tent just after the evening horn blew (Hallett 1833a, 140). Satisfied that they had proven Avery's location at the critical period of the proposed seduction, the defense brought two relatively ineffectual witnesses— Abby Hathaway, who had heard of Sarah's bad character, and Josiah H. Ormsby, who remembered the shoplifting episode in Providence—to remind the jury of the dead girl's moral stature. Then they turned to the problem of building an alibi for Avery that would clear him of suspicion of having sent Sarah the letter that John Orswell received on the *King Philip* in Providence on the morning of November 27, 1832. It was to produce a day of detailed, confusing testimony.

Nathaniel Chadwick, the mail-stage driver from Bristol to Providence, was first called to testify that he had carried Avery to Providence on Monday, November 26, to attend the four days meeting (Hildreth 1833, 78). He was followed by Pardon Jillson, at whose house Avery had lodged. Jillson had seen Avery at sunrise on the twenty-seventh, then again from ten minutes after eight to half past the hour, when the minister left for Joseph Fuller's house. Greene's cross examination demonstrated that Jillson was less precise in his memory of the time of events on other mornings, but failed to discredit him (Hallett 1833a, 144). Samuel Boyd, the next witness, had seen Avery walking from Jillson's at about sunrise and had observed him again—at nine o'clock—at the Methodist prayer meeting. Once again, Greene's questions focused on the peculiar clarity of the witness's memory of time on that morning (Hallett 1833a, 145). The Reverend Jotham Horton then testified that he had seen Avery at the Methodist meeting at five minutes after nine, and that he himself had been late because of an errand that took him to the wharf, where the packet boats were docked. Neither on his trip to nor from the packet did he see a man like Avery on the streets (Marshall and Brown 1833, 113). Once again, Greene's tedious and time-consuming cross examination hammered at the witness's certain timetable for unremarkable events six months before the trial. Aside from a small mistake about distances, which he corrected after the court's lunch break, Horton remained firm in his story (Hallett 1833a, 147–48).

The afternoon's first new witness was the Reverend Joseph Ireson, who remembered seeing Avery leave Jillson's for Fuller's at about twenty minutes before nine. He was followed by Abraham Holway, with whom Avery talked at Fuller's, who remembered Avery's visit as lasting from about twenty minutes to nine (it must have been, Holway asserted, because Avery stayed twenty minutes and left at nine) to nine o'clock (it must have been nine because Avery was leaving to go to a nine o'clock meeting) (Hallett 1833a, 150). Holway also remembered talking to Avery on an earlier occasion about an excursion to see the coal mines and revolutionary fortifications on Rhode Island. Joseph Fuller then swore that Avery had indeed been at his house until nine o'clock that morning, and Samuel Fuller reported that he had seen the minister come into the prayer meeting at about five minutes after the hour, then stayed in his company for the remainder of the day, until four o'clock in the afternoon (Marshall and Brown 1833, 116–17).

The last witness of the day was elderly William Pearce, who had been at Avery's house on Christmas day and had been present at Orswell's interview with the minister. Although not certain of the precise wording of Orswell's conclusions, Pearce testified that the engineer had expressed uncertainty about Avery's identity as the man who had passed him the letter at Providence (Hildreth 1833, 83).

On Wednesday morning the defense finished with the Providence episode by calling Elias Smith, a young man who attended to his father's ferry in Providence, to testify that Avery had not passed the ferry on the morning of November 27 (Hallett 1833a, 156). With no witnesses to call who could shed light on the one remaining question—Avery's excursion on December 20—the defense next turned to rebuttal and began the systematic destruction of the government's case and witnesses.

William Henry D'Wolf, of Bristol, was called to testify to the mildness of the weather on December 20, making Avery's decision to tour the island more plausible, and to inform the court that he had received a six-cent letter on November 19, thus clearing Avery of having received Sarah Cornell's letter, as the government had implied. Actually, said D'Wolf, he did not remember receiving it precisely on the nineteenth, and he did not presently have it; it had been a bill from the Fall River Iron Works, and he had thrown away the postmarked wrapper (Hallett 1833a, 157). James P. Dimond next came to the stand and asserted that D'Wolf had indeed bought iron hoops from the Fall River Iron Works, and that by November 16 he had not yet received the bill (Hildreth 1833, 84).

The defense then called Susan Moore and her elderly mother, Susan Smith, to swear that Avery had had a handkerchief wrapped around his hand when he walked into Bristol on the morning of December 21, but was carrying no package (Hildreth 1833, 84). When Mrs. Moore stepped down, people in the gallery must have groaned, for moving up to be sworn in was Nathaniel Bullock, Avery's first lawyer. With lawyers on the bench, in the witness box, and doing the questioning, the prospects for interesting, or even intelligible, testimony were slight. It turned out, however, better than most expected. Almost immediately, Bullock drew a sharp rebuke from the bench for testifying to an inference he had drawn.

"Mr. Bullock," said Chief Justice Eddy, "you are a lawyer, and there is no excuse for you to testify to what you know is not legal evidence."

"I will endeavor to avoid it," Bullock replied, and managed

through the rest of a lengthy examination to do just that (Hallett 1833a, 158–62).

Bullock's first task was to discredit Sarah Jones, whose testimony that she had seen a man on the island on the forenoon of December 20 was not particularly damaging, but whose insistence that the Methodists and their lawyers had tried to convince her to commit perjury cast a threatening shadow over the defense's case. Mrs. Jones, he said, had first claimed she saw a man in the afternoon, when Avery said he was on the island. After looking at Avery and questioning him about the peculiar paint on her gate, she was convinced that he could have been the man. Although she did, in fact, draw a rough map for Bullock's benefit, Avery was not present when it was sketched on the floor and never saw it (Hallett 1833a, 158–59).

His second task was to explain Avery's flight after his Bristol hearing. Though his discourse was long-winded, its content was simple: He had advised Avery to leave town because public excitement against him was intense and apparently growing. Cross examination yielded little except a momentary flurry when Greene confused the witness and got him to state three times that Sarah Jones had first told him she had seen the man on the island in the forenoon (not, as he had testified, in the afternoon) (Hallett 1833a, 160).

The Reverend John Bristed, an Episcopal clergyman, came next to the stand, intent on pronouncing that his advice to Avery to leave Bristol had not been motivated by a desire to see him evade justice.

"Having made up my mind as a lawyer," the minister said, "that there were no grounds whatever . . ."

"We do not want you to argue the case," interposed the chief justice; "state the facts."

Bristed was allowed only to testify that he had advised Avery to leave town. It was not enough to soothe his conscience.

"I understood," he complained, "that I was to be permitted to state what induced me to give that advice."

"We only want the fact," insisted Eddy.

Asked to step down, the minister was still not through, muttering "I only wished to state that I did not intend to advise him to escape from justice" as he walked back to his seat.

"I think that there are some besides lawyers," observed the chief justice, eyeing the retreating minister, "who do not know how to testify," and the next witness was called (Hallett 1833a, 162).

The next witness, William Simmons, and Mary Davis who followed him, swore that Sarah Jones's story was inaccurate. Simmons had heard Sarah admit that she had seen the stranger in the afternoon, and Mary had been present at Avery's house when she was first interviewed by Bullock. The young woman's account substantially agreed with the lawyer's testimony (Hildreth 1833, 86–87).

The rest of the afternoon was filled with witnesses whose testimony contradicted a variety of prosecution positions. Peter Gladding remembered putting varnish on Avery's skinned knuckles a week before Sarah Cornell's death, making the minister's bandaged hand somewhat less sinister. Clarissa Munro, who lived in Bristol, saw Avery trudging home early on the morning of December 21 carrying neither a handkerchief nor a bundle. Andrew Brownell remembered seeing Sarah Jones's father, Stephen Brownell, coming home from the mill late in the afternoon of the twentieth; if he was correct, then Mrs. Jones must have been watching for her father in the afternoon, not the morning, when she saw the stranger. Sally Swan and Jane Sprague both testified that Annis Norton, who had seen a man heading toward Fall River on the afternoon of the murder, had described him as having heavy whiskers—unlike Avery—and had voiced a determination to get the minister convicted. Finally, David Davol reported that it was probably he who had made the tracks returning to the island at Howland's bridge on the night of the twentieth, and gatekeeper Peleg Cranston had told him that he knew Avery and that the minister had not passed over his bridge on that day (Hallett 1833a, 164–67).

On Thursday morning the attack on Peleg Cranston's testimony continued. The Reverend Daniel Webb and Benjamin Tilley swore that while crossing the bridge on January 19 they had engaged in conversation with the gatekeeper, who told them he thought Avery had not passed his bridge on the twentieth of the previous month (Hallett 1833a, 167–68). Gideon Gray added that Cranston told him that the mysterious stranger who had crossed the bridge that day had been wearing a spencer under his surtout—unlike Avery (Hildreth 1833, 90).

Randolf next called Fanny Reynolds, intending to show that Mary D. Borden, who claimed to have identified Sarah Cornell walking with a tall man in the streets of Fall River on the evening of October 20, had, in fact, not known Miss Cornell at the time. The attorney general objected, and Dutee Pearce explained; Mrs. Borden apparently said she was never acquainted with Sarah Cornell but could recognize her. Because the state of "being acquainted" was difficult to define, it was necessary for Mrs. Borden to have the opportunity to clarify her meaning before any attempt was made to contradict her. The prosecution won the objection, and Fanny Reynolds was asked to step down, but not before lawyers for both sides had assured the justices of their opinion that the court was being totally fair (although Mason suggested that the ruling was futile because he could circumvent it by calling Mrs. Borden back to the stand) (Hallett 1833a, 168–69).

The defense next called four Methodist ministers, all of whom unsurprisingly gave Avery good references. Nicholas Peck, who remembered Avery's father, Amos, when he was stationed on Rhode Island during the Revolution, added that Avery had asked him about procuring island coal in November (Marshall and Brown 1833, 133). Lydia LeBarron then gave Avery an "irreproachable" character and mentioned that back in East Greenwich, Connecticut, the minister had been addicted to "rambling" over the countryside (Hallett 1833a, 170).

Isaac Alden, a young man from New Bedford who sold clocks, was then called. He had been in Fall River on the afternoon of December 20, taking tea at Lawton's, where he had seen the other man who had called and could be sure that he was not Avery. Though it was only half past eleven when the cross examination of Alden was completed, the defense asked to adjourn for lunch. Avery's lawyers needed time, they said, to arrange their afternoon testimony (Hallett 1833a, 170).

When the court resumed at half past two, Reuben Smith, another Providence ferryman who had not seen Avery on the morning of November 27, and Luther Chase, a middle-aged man who had seen the minister heading for the stables by himself, after the prayer meeting on October 20 in the Annawan block at Fall River, were the first witnesses called (Marshall and Brown 1833, 133–34). They were followed by nine men from Warren and Bristol whose composite testimony was that it had been pleasant, cold but still, on the afternoon of December 20 (Hildreth 1833, 92).

Having disposed of the weather, the defense turned to discrediting Jane Gifford, the ferryman's daughter, who seemed to have caught Avery in a lie about his trip onto the island. John E. Cook, one of the "brother Cook's" of Portsmouth whom Avery had not been to see on the twentieth, was called to swear that Miss Gifford's "character for truth and veracity" was not good. He was in

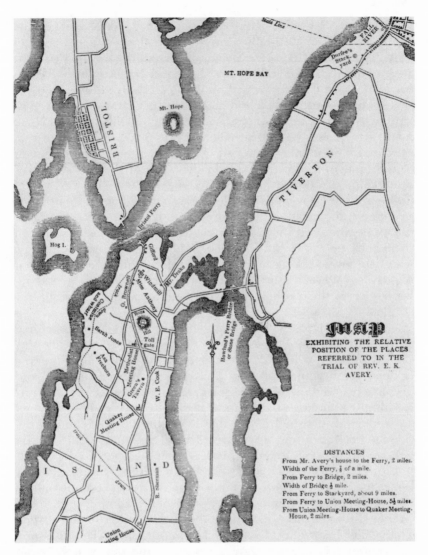

15. Bristol–Fall River area, 1832. From Ephraim K. Avery, *Vindication of the Result of the Trial* . . . (Boston: David Ela, 1834); courtesy of the Library Company of Philadelphia.

a particular position to know, he said, because he had been on the committee of the Methodist church that had investigated charges that she was a liar before expelling her from the meeting (Hallett 1833a, 172). He was followed by Levi and Nancy Sherman, husband and wife, who confirmed his opinion (Hildreth 1833, 93).

If Avery had not lied and had spent that afternoon on the island, why had he not been seen? According to Oliver Brownell, he might have been. Both Brownell and his wife, Sally, testified that they had seen a tall stranger in George Brownell's (the father of Sarah Jones) meadow one day in the week of December 20. Although they could not be certain about the date—it was a mild day—another Brownell, the elderly Sarah, could be sure; she saw a stranger in the meadow on the twentieth. Unfortunately, she could not remember the time, nor what he wore, nor his description (Hallett 1833a, 173), but someone had been there. Amy Anthony, who had been walking home between eight and nine o'clock that night, also had seen him slowly trudging up the west road, making his way from the south part of the island toward the Bristol ferry (Hallett 1833a, 174).

After court closed that evening, Chief Justice Eddy was handed a copy of that day's *Boston Morning Post* (*Daily City Gazette*, 28 May 1833). Disdainful of the pledge exacted at the beginning of the trial to delay publication until after the verdict had been reached, and perhaps fearful that the expense of keeping a reporter at the court for almost a month would be lost if the story were allowed to get any older unpublished, *Post* publisher Charles G. Greene had decided to begin printing his reporter's transcript of the trial. The risk Greene ran was not great; the trial was almost over, so the expulsion of his reporter, Thomas Gill, would hurt very little, and any legal sanction the judge might try to impose would certainly fall on the man in the courtroom, not the publisher in another state. Thus Greene outfoxed his competitors and the *Post's* circulation surged while Chief Justice Eddy pondered his most appropriate response, and Thomas Gill, when shown a copy of the newspaper, began to wonder what unpleasantness the future might hold. Nothing, however, was said of the matter when court reconvened Friday morning.

The defense began by calling Patience and Mary G. Anthony to testify that their sister, Amy, had indeed been walking home on the evening of the twentieth and had mentioned to them that she had passed a man on the road (Marshall and Brown 1833, 137–

39). They were followed by Elizabeth Hall, wife of George Hall, at whose house the Anthony girls had spent the evening of the twentieth. Mrs. Hall recalled that Amy had started for home on that evening some time past eight o'clock (Hallett 1833a, 176). Amy was then called to explain an earlier remark that she had not had a conversation with anyone about her testimony; she said that was correct. She had been asked if her sisters' description of her experience was accurate and she had replied yes—hardly a conversation (Hildreth 1833, 95).

After Robert Hicks had sworn that someone had come to his door looking for the ferry house on the evening of December 20, and Crawford Easterbrooks had testified that Avery had had a broken or sprained ankle in August (accounting for his lameness and slow progress on his trip to the Rhode Island mines), the defense turned its attention back to Mary Borden. Mrs. Borden declared that she had never said she could not recognize Sarah Cornell; she only said that she was not acquainted with her. Fanny Reynolds then returned to the stand and told a different story. Mrs. Borden, she said, had told her that she had never seen the hung girl before. Nancy Perkins was called to add that Mrs. Borden had admitted to her that she did not recognize the dead woman, and the defense moved on to other matters (Hallett 1833a, 177–79).

Sophia Avery's lame niece, Betsey E. Hills, who had lived with the minister's family for seven of the last eleven years, next hobbled to the stand, supported by two crutches. Mr. Avery, she reported, was prone to take long rambles and was a "remarkable kind, affectionate man" to his family. Sarah Cornell, on the other hand, was a designing wench who had come to the Averys' house at Lowell pretending penitence in order to gain reentry into the church.

Under cross examination, Miss Hills was asked how she could tell that Sarah Cornell's repentence was pretended.

"I can't tell," she replied, "only she shed tears."

"Are tears," she was asked, "a sign of real or pretended repentence; you said pretending?"

There was a pause as the witness considered what she might say.

"Can you answer the question?"

"I did not see her shed tears," replied Miss Hills, thinking it better to follow another line. "After she left there, we heard of her conduct, that we should not think she was penitent" (Hallett 1833a, 178–79).

After admitting that Avery had studied medicine before becoming a preacher, she was allowed to step down. Being questioned by an aggressive lawyer in front of a hostile crowd was a harrowing experience that she was not strong enough to withstand again. Returning to her room at Miss Perry's boardinghouse to await possible recall, she was prey to the stress of anticipation. Within a week she had succumbed to "distressing nausea, puking & complaint in her head" and had been certified by Dr. William Turner (who already had testified for the defense) as incapable of taking the stand (Turner 1833).

The defense next concerned itself with the supposition that Avery had met with Sarah Cornell after prayer meeting on the cloudy night of October 20. To dispute the dead woman's written assertion that she had conversed with the minister that evening for an hour, John E. Greene was called; it was to his house that Mrs. Ira Bidwell had come looking for the missing Avery that night. Greene testified that Mrs. Bidwell had come to his house no later than twenty-five minutes after nine; she therefore would have been home—and would have found Avery there—no later than half past nine, too soon for him to have spent an hour anywhere (Hallett 1833a, 179).

The rest of the morning, and much of the afternoon, was taken up by the examination of Levi Haile and then John Howe concerning their examination of Avery at Bristol. The defense was set on demonstrating the inadequacies of the case presented before these justices, and the prosecution was equally intent on showing their incompetence. Both at least partially succeeded. Mason managed to play up the gaffs of witnesses like Margaret Hambly while Greene got John Howe to admit that Avery's written statement was unsigned, not in Avery's hand, and not presented to the court by the minister himself, but by his lawyer, Mr. Blake.

"I am certainly surprised," said the attorney general, who obviously was not surprised at all, "that I do not find the original paper, signed by Mr. Avery. I confess I never saw a voluntary examination taken in that form before. There are some magistrates, it seems, besides Coroner Hicks, who can make mistakes" (Hallett 1833a, 181).

Following the magistrates, the defense brought to the stand another Providence ferryman, Waldron Potter, who testified that his ferry was not running on the morning of November 27; in fact, it had been closed since October (Hildreth 1833, 99). Its next witness was Eldridge Gerry Pratt, a young traveling merchant with a remarkable story. He had been in Iram Smith's store, he said, on the day that Harvey Harnden had been there to find the half sheet that matched the paper of the note Sarah Cornell received on December 8. Three-quarters of an hour before the deputy sheriff arrived, a stranger in a cap and cloak had entered the store, dramatically rolled his eyes at Pratt, whispered something to Smith, and passed suspiciously close to the ream of paper from which Harnden was soon to draw his evidence (Hallett 1833a, 182). New life had just been breathed into the theory that a conspiracy existed against the unfortunate Avery.

The defense followed Pratt with an attempt to introduce into evidence the first coroner's verdict of suicide to discredit Williams Durfee, who had signed the document and then sworn that the death was a homicide. Judge Eddy was irritated that a document of which everyone was already apprised should be presented. The paper could not impeach Durfee, he said, and was "no evidence in this issue at all" (Hallett 1833a, 183); the defense was invited to move on to more useful endeavors.

Wishing to enhance the idea of a plot against Avery, Mason recalled Lucy Hathaway, whom he hoped to induce to state that she had been told of the pregnancy by Sarah Cornell. Lucy remained, however, an unsatisfactory witness, disclaiming any knowledge of the pregnancy and assuring the court that Sarah Cornell had remained uniformly vague in speaking of the troubles that might befall a "poor weak girl" (Hallett 1833a, 183). When she left the stand, the day's testimony was over.

After waiting all day Friday for the judicial axe to fall, Thomas Gill, the reporter whose newspaper had broken the pledge of silence, went to Attorney General Greene with a request; he hoped that Greene would transmit two documents to Chief Justice Eddy. One was Gill's disclaimer of responsibility for the breach of trust, and the other was a letter from his editor, Charles G. Greene, agreeing to the court's publication ban (Gill 1833; C. Greene 1833). The attorney general agreed and at the opening of court handed the documents to Eddy. It seemed clear that Gill had not been party to his editor's duplicity, and the justice told the much-relieved reporter that he would not be held personally accountable for his employer's actions. Eddy added, however, that since Charles Greene had clearly broken his word, his employee could no longer be accepted at court, and Gill was asked to retire before the trial proceeded (Hildreth 1833, 101).

The punishment was light and gentlemanly, and it immediately created a stampede. When the day's testimony was over, Benjamin Hallett rushed his notes to Boston to be published in pamphlet form and in the pages of the *Boston Daily Advocate* as quickly as possible. Soon trial transcripts appeared in the New York papers (*Pawtucket Chronicle*, 31 May 1833), and even within Judge Eddy's jurisdiction in Providence (*Republican Herald*, 29 May 1833). It would have been hopeless for the justices to have attempted restraint, and on the thirtieth of the month they admitted defeat and rescinded their ban.

Papers that had honored the pledge, at the expense of losing circulation, could then enter the competition with a clean conscience and a scathing disgust for their less scrupulous fellows. Speaking of the New York papers that had violated the ban on the grounds that the *Boston Post* had already done so, the *Pawtucket Chronicle* commented: "Oh this is modesty. 'I can't steal them ere apples' said the boy, 'it would be wrong oh yes—I can't steal, but since you have stole 'em, I should like to eat one, to see how they taste'" (*Pawtucket Chronicle*, 31 May 1833). It was a rare publication that, like the *New England Christian Herald*, refused to consider itself freed from the pledge and waited until the verdict was in before beginning publication of the trial transcript.

While the publication ban collapsed, however, the trial went on. Saturday's first witness was Dr. Walter Channing, professor of midwifery and medical jurisprudence at Harvard University. In a grueling three-hour stay on the stand, Dr. Channing testified that an eight-inch fetus could not be only three months and twenty days old, that marks on Sarah Cornell's neck were consistent with suicide, that the bruises on the corpse's abdomen could have been the product of nothing more than the settling of blood after death, and that an autopsy done thirty-six days after death could produce only questionable results (Hallett 1833b, 195–205). Cross examination could not shake him from his opinion of the late autopsy, but it managed to elicit the information that some authorities believed a fetus could be eight inches long at four months, that the bruises just might possibly have been bruises, and that the condition of the body was as consistent with murder as with suicide. It was the kind of medical testimony that the court had come to expect: long, detailed, and inconclusive.

After the doctor stepped down, the defense finished the morning session with two witnesses. Seth Darling was recalled and questioned closely about his recollection that a letter to E. K. Avery passed through Fall River's post office on November 19. Following the aged postmaster, Louisa Whitney, a factory girl who had previously testified to Avery's whereabouts at the Thompson camp meeting, was asked to demonstrate a "harness knot" to the jury. Making one first around a cane and then around her own neck (Hallett 1833a, 184), she skillfully produced two clove hitches. With that subtle bit of drama, the defense's rebuttal was complete.

8. The Verdict

When court reopened Saturday afternoon, May 25, the prosecution had the floor, beginning with Samuel Randall, postmaster of Warren, who could testify that the letter dated November 13 and found in Sarah's possessions did in fact bear the Warren postmark. The next three witnesses—Benjamin Greene, Joseph Fish, and Nathaniel Munroe—were called to assert that Amy Anthony had told them she had seen no one on the road in Portsmouth on the evening of December 20 (Hallett 1833a, 184–85). Most of the rest of the afternoon was taken up by a parade of ten witnesses, ranging from Diana Dennis, an elderly Quaker, to Joseph Childs, a retired chief justice of the Rhode Island Court of Common Pleas, who all agreed that Jane Gifford, the ferryman's daughter, was honest and reputable.

As the afternoon drew to a close, Attorney General Greene called one last witness, Content Parry, who was to testify that she had lent a sealing wafer to Iram Smith on the morning of December 8—the same one on the letter that set up the meeting that preceded Sarah Cornell's death. When the direction of questioning became apparent, Mason immediately objected. The trial, he said, had reached the period of rebuttal, and the attorney general was free to try to discredit any defense witness presented. He was not, however, free to introduce new evidence. Pearce's argument that

Content Parry's testimony was a rebuttal to the defense assertion that Avery did not write the letter appeared untenable to Mason; was there not a distinction between rebuttal and cumulative evidence? Judge Brayton being absent from the bench, Chief Justice Eddy decided to reserve his opinion on the objection and adjourned the court until nine o'clock Monday morning (Hallett 1833a, 187).

On Monday Brayton was back and Eddy was ready to give his decision. After listening again to both sides, the chief justice admitted that Mason's arguments were good, "according to the rules of English law," but in his court he was inclined to hear the testimony of the witness (Hildreth 1833, 108). The prosecution was given permission to proceed. Before recalling Content Parry, they first questioned Bailey Borden, his wife, Mary, and Lucretia Jones, all of whom testified that Mary had stated she knew Sarah Cornell by sight but not personally (Hallett 1833c, 1–2). Then Mrs. Parry was returned to the stand, where she explained that she had given Iram Smith a wafer on the morning of December 8 and identified it on the letter found in Sarah Cornell's trunk (Hallett 1833c, 2–3).

The last witness of the morning was John Smith, Sarah Cornell's overseer in the weaving room in Anthony's mill, who testified that clove hitches were not used in making or repairing harnesses on his looms (Hildreth 1833, 109) and that the cord with which the woman had been strangled did not match any that he knew of in the mill.

After lunch John Durfee took the stand. Although he had not measured the stake on which the body had been hung, he had brought it to Newport to be displayed. Unfortunately, he had displayed it a little too often before being called to bring it to court, and souvenir hunters had whittled it down to a stub of its former self. Though he presented the stub, it was not very useful in reconstructing the hanging (Hallett 1833c, 4). Durfee was followed by three Fall River weavers—Lucy Hathaway, Mary Borden, and May Durfee—all of whom swore they never used clove hitches in their work, and then by Elias Parry, Content's husband, who supported her contention that she had given Iram Smith the wafer on December 8 (Hallett 1833c, 4).

Harvey Harnden was the next witness; using his notes, he recounted his studies of relative timekeeping in the area, demonstrating that Fall River time was generally fast and Bristol and Tiverton, generally slow. In his recital he included the information that Rev. Holway, at Warren, kept time seventeen minutes slow. Randolf was

quick to note the inclusion, and when he rose to contest the validity
of a measure of time taken several days after the death, he added:
"Why was the time of Mr. Holway's watch taken in Warren? What
had that to do with the case? The only reason it was done was because he was a Methodist Minister" (Hallett 1833c, 5).

Randolf had raised the idea of harassment and antagonism toward the church, and Greene was quick to deny the charge. He was
no more interested in Methodist minsters in this trial, he said, than
any other variety. Turning to the witness, Greene asked him how he
had come to take Holway's time. Harnden admitted that there was
no good reason; his curiosity about time variations had simply gotten the better of him (Hallett 1833c, 5). Leaving the subject of time,
Harnden went on to testify to the events in Bristol on Christmas,
then turned to the discovery of the half sheet of paper in Smith's
store. Eldridge Pratt, who claimed to have been in the store at the
time, was not, to his memory, actually there. The deputy sheriff
would have recognized him because they had become acquainted
the July before when Harnden confiscated goods from Pratt's store
for nonpayment of a bill (Hallett 1833c, 5–6). Enos Briggs and
Iram Smith were then called and swore that they knew Pratt, had
been in the store when Harnden found the paper, and did not remember Pratt being there (Marshall and Brown 1833, 159–60).

The next witness was Benjamin Hall, who had traveled near
the Rhode Island coal mines a week before the murder, who was
stopped by a defense objection before he could recount his impression of the accuracy of Avery's account of the countryside. After
that failure, the prosecution was faced with another one: Louisa
Whitney could not be shaken from her assertion that clove hitches
were used to mend weaving harnesses in Lowell and in Waltham.
The day ended with Zenas Thomas and John Gray, both of Bristol,
who could testify rather vaguely that they had seen Avery in the
streets of their town, at the end of November or the beginning of
December, with a reddish paper in his hand—presumably, though
of course they were not allowed to say it, a letter from Sarah Cornell (Hildreth 1833, 113).

On Tuesday morning, the twenty-eighth, the long process of
rebuttal continued. George Lawton, the first witness, was called to
support Peleg Cranston's testimony. No matter what anyone might
say about subsequent conversations, Lawton assured the court,
Cranston had told him on the Sunday following the murder of a
stranger resembling a Methodist minister who had passed over the

bridge on the afternoon of the twentieth (Hildreth 1833, 113). Then Gideon Hicks was called to swear that he had been at his father's house, near the Bristol ferry in Portsmouth, on the evening of the twentieth, and had, near ten o'clock, heard a man—presumably Avery—ask if this were the ferry house (Hallett 1833c, 7). Robert Wilcox, George Brownell, Sr., George Brownell, Jr., and Russell Anthony followed Hicks on the stand; all four had been at or near the coal mines on the twentieth, and none of them had seen a stranger wandering nearby. That they did not see anyone, the defense lawyers pronounced unremarkable. Questioning the elder George Brownell, Mason asked, "Is it impossible for anyone to have passed, and you not seen him?"

"Impossible!" Brownell replied, "oh, no. I only said I should have stood a chance to have seen a stranger if he had passed" (Hallett 1833c, 9).

To reduce the testimony of Sarah Brownell, who had seen a stranger near the mines on the twentieth, the prosecution next brought Christopher Barker, who was willing to swear that the elderly woman had admitted to him that she had seen no one. The defense immediately objected, claiming that a witness could not be contradicted unless she had first been questioned about the conversation in question. It was precisely the prosecution's point about the defense attack on Mary Borden's testimony, and as the objection had carried then, it continued to do so. The witness was withdrawn until Mrs. Brownell could be returned to the stand. Unfortunately, getting Mrs. Brownell back proved impossible. Like Betsey Hills, she had become—some thought too conveniently—too sick to return to court (Hallett 1833c, 23).

After James Taylor was called to testify to the weather on December 20—his records showed that the temperature hovered around freezing all day (Marshall and Brown 1833, 162–63)—the prosecution focused its attention on Avery's return to Bristol on the following day. Their witness, William Lawless, who had testified that he had seen Avery returning from the ferry with a roll under his arm, had returned himself to Bristol only to discover that agents of the defense were planning to challenge his story. Anxious to save both his reputation and the prosecution's point, Lawless set about finding witnesses who could back him up. Writing to Greene on May 27, he reported that he had found two (Lawless 1833), and they were promptly brought to Newport to testify. Isaiah Simmons had seen Avery both as he left Bristol on the twentieth and as he returned the following morning; in both cases the minister had been carrying a small bundle rolled in a silk handkerchief (Hallett 1833c, 10). His testimony was substantiated by that of James Sanford, a sailor, who momentarily drew the displeasure of Chief Justice Eddy when he testified expansively that the weather of the twentieth had been "cold as the devil" (Hallett 1833c, 207).

Between the appearances of Simmons and Sanford, the prosecution called Dr. William Turner, who had previously testified for the defense, but who seems to have been won over to the opposing camp. The marks on the body, the doctor swore, could not have been made inadvertently by the people who took it from the stake or prepared it for the grave. His most important observation, however, the one he had been called to make, concerned the fetus; though it was undoubtedly large—though not impossibly so—for a fetus under four months old, mere size was not the best, or even a particularly reliable, indicator of age. It was his opinion that development was of much greater significance (Hallett 1833c, 207).

After Turner testified, the prosecution was willing to let the jury assimilate his ideas for a few minutes before returning to their implications. James Sanford was called; then William Earl Cook, the second of the Cooks of Portsmouth, swore that he had not seen Avery on the day of the murder. Joseph Thomas swore to Jane Gifford's good character, and Thomas Borden, who agreed with Thomas's assertion, reported that he had not seen Avery pass his house on the west road of Portsmouth on December 20 (Hildreth 1833, 115).

Foster Hooper was called next to build on the premise established by Dr. Turner before him; the age of the fetus was best determined by its relative development. Foster testified that the tiny body was hairless and its fingernails undeveloped. The implication that it was in fact very immature could neither be accepted by the defense nor disproven; it was time, therefore, for a diversion, and Randolf employed the one he had used when Hooper first testified nearly a month before.

"Who was present," the defense lawyer asked in his cross examination, "at your conversation after the lecture you delivered at Swanzey upon masonry?"

"A number were present," replied the doctor. "I stated the report of Mr. Avery being a mason precisely as I had heard it, and gave my authors."

"Who?"

"Moses Pearce, Levi Chase and Nathaniel Borden."

"How many belong to the Fall River Committee?"

"Mr. Borden. I believe no other."

It was obvious to Greene that Randolf was preparing to brand Hooper and the entire committee as anti-Masonic witch hunters. "Has your Fall River Committee any thing to do with masonry and antimasonry in this trial?" he broke in.

"No sir," Hooper replied, "not at all. There are two masons on the Committee."

Randolf turned indignantly to the bench. "Is that a proper question?" he asked.

"It is all out of order," Eddy replied, then peevishly added to Randolf, "You introduced it."

Greene virtuously noted that he brought "nothing extraneous" to the case; Randolf sat down, admonished by the court but successful in redirecting attention away from Hooper's medical testimony; and Chief Justice Eddy adjourned the court for lunch (Hallett 1833c, 10–11).

When William Lawless had written to Greene in defense of his own testimony, he had added another bit of information; his search for witnesses had turned up Lucy Munro, "who sleeped at the house of Mr Edward Masons the night that Mr Evry had the first interview with S M Cornell" in Fall River (Lawless 1833) and who had heard him comment that he had passed a very restless night— presumably because of Sarah's declaration of her condition. Hoping to be allowed to bring in this new evidence, the prosecution began the afternoon session by calling Lucy Munro to the stand. Predictably, when the direction of her testimony became clear an objection was raised. The court sustained it and the witness was withdrawn, but only after the jury had been informed by the lawyers' debate of that to which she had been brought to swear (Hallett 1833c, 11).

Rebecca Pike, a young weaver who had worked in Lowell before coming to Fall River in May, was next called to testify that she had never seen clove hitches used to mend harnesses in either town, and that, while at Lowell, the dormitory gossip she heard was not about Sarah Cornell's bad character, but about the frequency with which Avery called for her at her residence (Marshall and Brown 1833, 164–65). When Miss Pike stepped down, the prosecution called Dr. Thomas Wilbur to describe the conversations he had had with Sarah Cornell concerning her pregnancy, and the legal wrangling began again.

Mason immediately objected to Wilbur's testimony, as he had before, on the grounds that the conversations he was about to describe were neither taken under oath nor a dying declaration. For a man who had just finished an attempt to destroy Sarah Cornell's character through the systematic recital of ten years' factory-town gossip, his position was, in the eyes of Dutee Pearce, remarkable. The issue was, Pearce complained to the court:

> whether the defendant's counsel should be permitted to trace this girl through every cotton-mill in New-England, to collect every syllable she had uttered, not only against the prisoner, but against the'whole Methodist Society, until within two or three months of her death, and then to preclude us from repelling the inferences they draw by showing an entire different state of her feelings, preceding her decease.

Warming to his subject, Pearce accused the "gentleman from abroad"—Mr. Mason—of protracting the trial by converting it into a trial of the deceased instead of the defendant. Pearce said:

> They have attempted to prove her vindictive feelings towards the prisoner by her own declarations—we offer her own declaration to the witness just before her death, to show that when he told her she ought to require a larger sum of the prisoner for the inquiry he had done her, she thought it would be asking him too much, because he was poor, and that she was anxious to preserve him from public exposure. Does this not repel the idea of vindictive feelings on her part? Was not what is law for the defendant, also law for the Government? They infer insanity from her own declarations and acts, and we propose to repel it by her own acts and declarations (Hallett 1833c, 13).

Greene closed the motion that Pearce had begun, assuring the court that they only intended to show that Sarah Cornell was neither vengeful toward Avery nor suicidal—she had rejected oil of tansy as a method of inducing abortion when Wilbur told her of its possible fatal effects. They had no intention of using the testimony to charge him with fathering her child.

Mason was unruffled by the increasingly open hostility of his opponents. The question remained, he replied, whether or not Wilbur's testimony would be legal evidence. To show character by her declarations was one thing; to charge the defendant of the crime for which he was on trial was another. The court finally ruled that Wilbur could testify to the conversations, but not to those parts in which she might have directly accused Avery of fathering her child. The doctor dutifully took the stand and briefly recounted his conversations with the young woman, making precisely those points Greene had said he would make (Hildreth 1833, 117).

The next witness was William D. Fales, a stage driver on the Newport-to-Bristol run, who could testify that Gifford's clock—a wooden-wheeled one, not proverbially accurate—at the ferry house was often as much as a half hour slower than Newport time. His testimony was not particularly damaging to the defense because Harvey Harnden had already testified to essentially the same point, but Pearce's last question to the young man proved embarrassing.

"Who did you tell first," the lawyer asked, "that Mr. Gifford's clock was generally slow?"

"I told it to Mr. Randolf," was the reply. "He asked me."

Randolf knew what was coming next and called out, "I know you did."

"Yes," said the witness, "and you told me not to say anything about it."

The defense had just been caught suppressing evidence, however minor the point. It was perhaps not illegal, but the prosecution obviously hoped to make the jurors suspicious. Randolf needed another diversion.

"So I did," said the lawyer, then added accusingly, "and who did you tell it to?"

"To Mr. Bartlett," Fales replied.

When the witness left the stand the defense could only hope that the jury would remember him as a bad boy telling tales out of school and ignore the implications of his experience.

Ira Bidwell, the last witness of the day, was called to prove Avery's handwriting prior to the testimony of a handwriting expert, who could then link the letters Sarah Cornell had received with the minister. Mason objected once again, this time because Bidwell had received letters but had not seen Avery write them and therefore could not swear that the handwriting was his. Another long debate seemed inevitable and it was already seven o'clock in the evening. Hoping for more stamina in the morning, Chief Justice Eddy called an end to the proceedings until the next day (Hallett 1833c, 14–15).

On Wednesday morning Bidwell was recalled to the stand and the expected legal argument took place. Though much of the witness's time on the stand was taken up with a minute examination of

16. Unsigned letter to Sarah Cornell, Fall River, December 8, 1832. This hastily scribbled note, which the prosecution tried to attribute to Ephraim Avery, set up the meeting at which Sarah Cornell died. From David Melvill, *A Fac-simile of the Letters Produced at the Trial of the Rev. Ephraim Avery* (Boston: Pendleton's Lithography, 1833).

his dealings with both Avery and Sarah Cornell, the prosecution's major success was its ultimate demonstration that Bidwell was indeed competent to identify Avery's writing. Mason, of course, tried to stop it, but the court allowed Greene to present Bidwell with Avery's letter to the Reverend George Storrs in which he retracted his signature on Sarah Cornell's certificate of forgiveness. Flushed with success when the letter was admitted to be in Avery's handwriting, the attorney general went on to attempt to introduce, once again, the Warren letter of November 13. Mason's objection this time was successful, a setback for the prosecution but not a serious one. With a proven sample of Avery's handwriting, one showing such dramatic peculiarities as "appeare," "sens," "haveing," "tine" for "time," and "Connell" for "Cornell," Greene could hope that the jury would see the similarities between the orthography of that letter and the unsigned ones that had been found in Sarah's trunk (Hallett 1833c, 18).

The letters accepted by the court, however—the note of December 8 and the pink letter delivered by Orswell—were not in exactly the same handwriting as the one proven to be Avery's. In attempting to explain this, the prosecution brought Isaac Fiske, a teacher of penmanship, to the stand. After the expected debate over his stature as an expert, Fiske was allowed to examine the two letters (Greene tried to slip in the Warren letter but was stopped) and pronounced them to be in an "assimilated," that is, a disguised hand (Hallett 1833c, 21–23).

When Fiske was through, the prosecution had little else to present. James Sherman was called to report that Luther Chace, who had testified to Avery's movements after the Fall River prayer meeting on October 20, had told him that he was not sure of his facts (Hallett 1833a, 23). With Betsey Hills and Sarah Brownell both too sick to return to court for further questioning, Dutee Pearce read from several medical authorities on the difficulty of determining the age of a fetus by its length, and the attorney general once again rested his case.

The defense began its second rebuttal with Cyrus Whipple, a surveyor who had been hired to measure distances in Providence to show the impossibility of Avery having walked from Pardon Jillson's house to the wharf and back to the Methodist meeting house in the short time he had available. Greene piously commented that though the matter was new evidence, not a rebuttal, he would not object, and the defense called its next witness (Hallett

1833c, 24): an aged Newport sailor and weaver named Ezekiel Luther who had always fixed his broken harnesses with a clove hitch (Hildreth 1833, 124).

The final witness of the day, John Page, proved to be yet another embarrassment for the defense. Page had heard John Orswell describe the man who had given him the letter on the *King Philip* and had concluded that it must have been a Unitarian minister, Mr. Arnold, whom Page had seen on the boat a few days before. Asked if Orswell agreed that the man Page described had delivered the letter, the witness replied: "He described the man very perfectly that I have described, and I agreed that was the man I saw on board the Boat. I said I knew him myself. He did not say whether the man on board the Boat with me, was the one who gave him the letter. I agreed with him."

This did not make perfect sense to Chief Justice Eddy, who was prompted to interject, "Who did you agree with? You have stated twice differently since you stood there."

"He described the man, and I agreed with *myself*, that was the man we saw in the Boat."

Attorney General Greene now stepped in. "In what respect does the description Orswell gave you of the man who handed him the letter, differ from Mr. Avery? Can you tell?"

"No, I can't," was the reply. "The description he gave of the man, answers the description of Mr. Avery very well; very well indeed. Mr. Orswell said he had carried a letter and then he described the man as I have said. Then says I, I shall know him too. Now do you understand me?"

"Did he agree with you," asked Greene, who wanted a final clarification, "that the man you described, was the one who gave the letter?"

"No. That man he described we were both satisfied was the man delivered him the letter."

With that remarkable bit of information, the court recessed for the night (Hallett 1833c, 25).

Thursday, May 30, was the last day of testimony. Hoping to emphasize that Avery's flight after the Bristol hearing was prompted only by a legitimate fear for his safety, the defense brought six witnesses to the stand, all of whom could testify to the threatening impression left by the mob that descended on Bristol on Christmas morning. One of them, Samuel Thompson, could also report that James Sanford, the sailor who testified to Avery's bundle, was "a poor miserable creature" who "wrangles in the streets and tells things there is no truth in" (Hallett 1833c, 26). John G. Harding was called to support Thompson's opinion of Sanford, and the defense moved to its next point.

Completely unsuccessful in impeaching John Orswell's testimony on the previous day, Mason called Jonathan Browning to swear that Orswell had contradicted his court testimony in private conversation. Greene objected that the engineer had not been questioned about any conversation with Browning, and the court agreed. Mason withdrew his witness and declined taking advantage of Greene's offer to bring Orswell back to court for a full examination.

He was, however, ready to requestion William Lawless, who was brought to the stand and asked if he had told Peter Gladding that he had seen Avery on the morning of December 21 wearing a green pea jacket. Lawless responded that he had said a box coat, perhaps green, but not a pea jacket. Gladding was then sworn in, and he testified that Lawless had in fact specifically mentioned a pea jacket (which Avery did not own). Under cross examination, Gladding first swore that he told none but his family about the conversation, then admitted that he had also told Avery's lawyers, Blake and Bullock.

"Is this the way you answer a question under oath," asked the chief justice. "You have twice stated you could not recollect who you had conversed with, and now you name two persons" (Hallett 1833c, 28).

It took the attorney general very little time to suggest to the jury that this was not a particularly reliable witness. He was less successful in shaking the testimony of young Mary Freeborn, who had seen Avery come up from the ferry wearing a box coat and carrying no bundle (Hallett 1833c, 28), but when George Pearce was called to shore up Gladding's unconvincing testimony, Greene was once again able to force the witness to demonstrate flaws in his memory (Hallett 1833c, 29–30).

Before Pearce was called, the defense brought out the one final witness who might indirectly support Avery's account of his wanderings on Rhode Island. The minister had reported that he had seen a man with a gun, and Anna Cooke testified that she had seen Robert Wilcox that afternoon carrying a gun under his arm. If she had seen Wilcox, so might have the minister.

After stage driver Stephen Bartlett recounted Avery's travel arrangements to reach Fall River in October, another attempt was made on Jane Gifford's character. John S. Brownell was called to swear that her reputation for honesty was exceedingly poor. After contradicting himself several times, he was haughtily dismissed by the attorney general. Angered, as he left the stand he called out, "You will put it down as a naught, I suppose!"

"I should think so," replied Greene.

"Rather a blank, we think," Pearce added (Hallett 1833c, 31).

Such gentlemanly disdain, however, did not satisfy Jeremiah Gifford, who had become increasingly agitated as he listened to the young man attack his daughter's character. Leaping to his feet when Brownell started to leave the stand, the ferryman shouted, "I wish they would ask this witness what Jane Gifford has done, to make these people try to ruin her!"

"You must keep still, Mr. Gifford," the attorney general soothed. "I will take care of that."

"I can't keep still," Gifford shouted back. "She is my *darter.* I must speak!"

"Then you had better go out."

It was good advice, and Gifford complied, muttering, "Well, I will go out; I can't stand it here" as he left. Unfortunately for the composure of John Brownell, the brawny ferryman reached the courthouse door at the same time he did. The indignant father glared, raised a powerful fist to strike, and then was dissuaded by a friend.

"Well, well, I won't hurt him," Gifford said, lowering his arm and stalking away (Hallett 1833b, 43).

Brownell escaped with his face intact, and the courtroom's attention was once more focused on the witness stand. There was little there to hold their attention; Luther Chace, whose testimony had been contradicted by James Sherman, was called to assert that Sherman was wrong and left the stand without incident, then Chief Justice Eddy recessed the court for lunch (Hildreth 1833, 128–29).

That afternoon the prosecution called Anna Cooke back to the stand and asked her if she had ever told Albert G. Cooke or John Burrington that she had not seen a man with a gun on December 20. When she replied that she had not, both Burrington and Cooke were called to swear that she had. They were followed by Robert Wilcox, who swore that he had not carried a gun that day, and

Andrew Brownell, Mary Wilcox, and Elizabeth Brownell, all of whom could testify that indeed Robert had had no gun (Hallett 1833c, 32–33).

Testimony ended with a whimper, as Anna Cooke was brought back to the stand to admit that she had, after all, told Albert Cooke she knew nothing about a gun—but it was just, she explained, an attempt to avoid being called to the trial (Hallett 1833c, 34). When the old woman stepped away, two hundred and thirty-nine witnesses had been called in an examination lasting twenty-one court days. It was six o'clock, but if the exhausted jury expected a night's rest before listening to the lawyers' summations, they were quickly disappointed. Randolf spent the next half hour arguing that the medical evidence demonstrated suicide rather than murder, setting the stage for Mason's appeal, which would begin in the morning.

When Jeremiah Mason began his comments Friday morning, it quickly became apparent what his attack would be. Congratulating jurors on their stamina through weeks of detailed and contradictory testimony, the lawyer lamented that "such a degree of popular prejudice has been excited, and still exists " (Hallett 1833b, 5) that a fair and impartial hearing for the prisoner had become almost impossible. The atmosphere surrounding the case forcibly brought to mind the witchcraft trials of Salem, where popular delusion led men otherwise "distinguished for their piety, learning and intelligence" to hound the innocent to death. How else could one account for the peculiar language of many prosecution witnesses, who qualified their testimony with "I think," "I believe," and "it is my impression"? Under the zeal of a community that wills itself to believe, "what was at first a slight impression—a mere gossamer of the imagination, will be found strengthened and worked up into firm conviction and full faith" (Hallett 1833b, 7).

The source of this popular prejudice against Avery, Mason said, was not the antireligious who wished to degrade the priesthood, or even those other denominations competing with the Methodists for converts in New England. No, the source was the community of Fall River, which called boisterous public meetings for the purpose, not of dispassionately seeking the murderer, but of convicting Avery of the crime. In this persecution the town was aided by a willing press that poured out "newspapers, pamphlets, and handbills, with vulgar caricatures—all inflaming the public mind with bold statements of the defendant's guilt" (Hallett 1833b, 9).

Under such pressure, jurors were cautioned to be particularly careful; their conclusions should come from the evidence, rather than before it. And what evidence was there to be had? It was all circumstantial, and hence particularly dangerous in a trial, particularly in a capital case in which public passions had been so inflamed. The jury, Mason warned, would have to consider not if Avery might have committed the crime given the available evidence, but if it was a moral certainty that he did—that is, if the evidence had drawn a web of circumstance so tightly around him that it was fundamentally impossible to believe him innocent.

That the government had failed to weave so tight a web, Mason was quite sure. In fact, he said, they have not even satisfactorily demonstrated that there was a crime. Did not the original coroner's jury reach a verdict of suicide? Was not the examination of the body made by persons interested in the prosecution? Did not the changed verdict of murder depend on the discovery, under unclear circumstances, of the penciled note calling attention to Avery? The evidence that might have supported the conclusion of murder, or denied it completely, was so sloppily collected by the government and placed in such obviously biased hands that a sound conclusion could not possibly be drawn from it. In any case, there was nothing in the condition of the body that made the verdict of murder inevitable.

Could Sarah Cornell have hung herself? Could she have created the image of Rev. Avery's guilt by a cleverly forged set of letters left to be discovered in her trunk? Mason found it exceedingly strange that though all her other letters were destroyed, those that dealt with her supposed negotiations with the prisoner were carefully preserved. Why was it, he asked, that in the last months of her life she flashed mysterious papers before her acquaintances? Was it to excite suspicion? Her behavior was certainly thought provoking.

But could she have committed suicide? To answer that question, her character must be known, even though "it is a painful duty to perform—to describe a woman, to describe the dead, in a light as revolting as duty to the defendant requires." Mason said:

> That there is a charm, a refinement, a delicacy in the female sex, superior to man, no civilized community has ever doubted. It is female character, when pure and unstained, which contributes to the embellishment and refinement of society in the highest degree, but in the same proportion as woman, when chaste and pure, excels the other sex, by just so much, when profligate, does she sink below them; and if you were to seek for some of the vil-

est monsters in wickedness and depravity, you would find them
in the female form (Hallett 1833b, 25).

It took the lawyer the rest of the morning to outline the dead
woman's career in "wickedness and depravity" through the manufacturing centers of New England. How could anyone doubt, he
wondered, having learned of her "habitual sensual indulgences"
and "strange abstractions of mind" (Hallett 1833b, 27), that she was
capable of violent hostilities and self-destructive passions? "Suicide
is so common a termination of their career," Mason said, "that it
may almost be called the natural death of the prostitute. Excited by
violent and unrestrained passions, driven to extreme distress and
often desperation, self destruction is the ready resort of the profli-
gate" (Hallett 1833b, 27).

The clock was ticking slowly to twelve when Mason concluded;
if there was any reasonable doubt that the woman had been murdered—if the possibility of suicide was real—then the jury's deliberations were at an end. "The crime must be proved," said the
lawyer, "before you can inquire who was the criminal" (Hallett
1833b, 28).

When the lunch recess ended at three o'clock, Mason turned to
the evidence against his client, as was his duty if the jury were not
convinced that the death was suicidal. Given that the woman was
murdered, might Rev. Avery have done it? The first question was
one of motive. The government attempted to show that he was the
father of her unborn child conceived at the Thompson camp meeting, but it was an allegation without proof. Avery's character and
the evidence of his companions, who were in his company at the
very moment the seduction was supposed to have occurred, combined to render the government story both "improbable" and absolutely "disproved" (Hallett 1833b, 30). And what of the young
woman herself? What does her behavior at the camp meeting suggest? Mason said:

> Rawson's shop, in which she worked, was frequented by fashion-
> able young men. One of them is produced here as a witness. You
> find this young man taking no ordinary liberty with a young
> woman to whom he had not been introduced—carrying her to
> the Camp Meeting. You find the intimate terms upon which the
> parties appeared to be on the Camp ground. She steps up to him
> and in answer to his inquiries about the trunk, pats him on the
> breast!

"The shoulders," Attorney General Greene corrected.

Shrugging off the comment, Mason continued, "This might not go for much, aside from the general conduct and character of the deceased. But there is no probability that there are three months of her life, in which you might not collect evidence of her unchastity. Why should her usual practices have been suspended for three months, in Thompson?" (Hallett 1833b, 32–33).

The government case that Avery had had an interview with Sarah Cornell on the evening of October 20 Mason found likewise wanting, and their evidence that he was in Fall River on the day of the death hopelessly inadequate. Detailing the vagueness of the testimony of each government witness who had seen a stranger in or around Fall River that day, Mason ended with the unfortunate Margaret Hambly. "A witness so perfectly discredited in all her bearing," Mason said, "it seems inhuman to use in a capital trial." Gesturing toward Fall River, the lawyer could not help but wonder "why did that highly-excited village, bring down this girl to swear away the life of the defendant, when she is so entirely divested of all credit?" (Hallett 1833b, 38). Could it be that she was the poor best they had to offer?

Of course, Avery had been away from home on December 20. Defense witnesses' testimony to his predilection for long and solitary rambles and his interest in obtaining a supply of island coal, gave a good explanation, particularly when coupled with the accounts of all those who saw a stranger on the island that afternoon and evening. The peculiar account of Mrs. Jones about her dealings with defense lawyers who wanted her to change her testimony could be entirely discounted. Having apparently taken offense at something at the boardinghouse where defense witnesses were staying, she determined to "enlist under another flag" and seek to create a prejudice against the prisoner. How could such an inconsistent woman be believed, particularly in the face of the testimony of Mr. Bullock who contradicted her? "If I felt at liberty to do so," Mason concluded, "I would recommend this witness to the kind offices of the attorney general. She richly deserves it. It is a case of sheer, deliberate *perjury*, basely perpetrated against the life of a man. It is a base transaction, and charity itself cannot excuse it (Hallett 1833b, 41).

After an only slightly more charitable analysis of Jane Gifford's character and testimony, Mason asked the court for a short recess; it was twenty minutes past five and he was exhausted. The attorney general suggested that a half-hour break might be sufficient for his opponent to regain his strength, but Mason rejected such liberality. Twenty minutes were all he wanted, and it was what the court gave him (Hallett 1833b, 43).

When Mason resumed his argument he took up the question of the letters admitted into evidence. The pink letter delivered by Orswell, he said, had not been traced to the prisoner. That Orswell swore Avery handed him the paper was hardly credible. That Orswell *thought* it was Avery, Mason had no doubt; the engineer was subject to the same inflammation of passion as the rest of Fall River. However, evidence that his identification had grown considerably more certain as the months passed after the Bristol hearing, combined with the recollections of Avery's companions in Providence—who swore he had not sufficient time to go to the wharf and deliver the letter—was sufficient to discredit him.

The case of the white letter from Fall River was similar. Iram Smith's testimony was far too vague to be conclusive, and the inaccuracies of Content Parry's (she had mistaken the eighth, which was a Saturday, for a Friday) invalidated hers. The pathetic attempt to bolster the government's position with the assurances of a professor of penmanship, Isaac Fiske, Mason found incredible. "If the Government mean to rely on such testimony as this to convict the defendant, I cannot help it; but it seems to me so utterly worthless, so lame an attempt, that it was an insult to common understandings to impose it on the jury" (Hallett 1833b, 49). Likewise, he regarded the testimony of Harvey Harnden too tainted by interest and the possibility of tampering to be believed.

After dismissing Avery's flight to New Hampshire as the reasonable response of a man fearing for his safety in the face of local hysteria, Mason concluded his summation with an analysis of the prisoner's character. Was it reasonable, he asked, to believe such a horrible crime of a man of Avery's unblemished character? Men take many small steps on the road to depravity; they do not leap directly from the heights of virtue. Where were signs of Avery's decline? He was a Methodist minister, a member of "a new sect, of most exact discipline in the church, and of most persevering labours in its ministry," that was founded by "one of the most shrewd, sagacious and discreet men that ever existed" (Hallett 1833b, 54). Had he slipped, his brothers would have seen it, but they did not. Good character and holy work were not, of course, a shield for the guilty, but Mason hoped the jury would give them solemn consideration when reviewing the evidence.

It was eight o'clock and Mason had finally finished. As Chief Justice Eddy adjourned court until morning, the exhausted lawyer had reason to be pleased with himself. He had kept the idea of a conspiracy against Avery and the Methodist church in front of the jury. He had painted a picture of the dead woman's suicidal insanity with a dramatic flair that exceeded his reputation as an orator, and he had cast a pall of doubt over the prosecution testimony by focusing attention on the narrow-minded dedication of the Fall River Committee to his client's conviction. He had glossed over weaknesses in his own case with calm assurance, and he had effectively assassinated the characters of threatening prosecution witnesses. His job done, he prepared to depart for Boston, leaving Richard Randolf to take care of the trial's closing formalities (Hallett 1833b, 75).

On Saturday morning, though he was on the road to Boston, Mason's words were still very much in the courtroom at Newport. Attorney General Greene's summation took much of its form and direction from the arguments of the preceding day. Beginning as Mason had begun, with an assertion that the case's "great and unusual interest" had made it difficult to try, Greene felt constrained to disclaim any responsibility for the association that was drawn between the trial of a Methodist minister and the reputation of the Methodist church. Minister or not, Avery was bound to be tried with the same impartiality as any other man, and the outcome of his trial was to reflect his character alone. Any invidious reference to the Methodist church that had entered the courtroom was not the product of government testimony. "Let it, then, be distinctly understood," said Greene, "that this trial attaches no charge, no suspicion, to any body or class of men, other than just so far as they may individually or collectively have improperly identified themselves with the defense" (Hallett 1833b, 56). Greene added, as innocent of sectarian feeling as the government case was, so too was it free of political overtones. The matter was purely one of an individual's responsibility for taking a life.

The attorney general next considered the actions of Fall River in the prosecution. This was, he said, no witch hunt. Why should the citizens of Fall River be censured for actions applauded in other communities? A murder was committed, and the community organized itself to seek out the perpetrator, creating a committee of its most respectable members, including an experienced lawyer, to conduct the affair. Through prudent and decisive action they sought to discover the murderer, not, as the defense had suggested, to hound a hapless minister to the gallows. If the people of Fall River deserved condemnation for their actions, particularly in a country that had no armed police force to apprehend criminals, Greene said, "then I confess I do not understand the duty of a citizen" (Hallett 1833b, 53).

The publications that the defense had pointed to as contributing to public prejudice Greene regretted as deeply as anyone. It was, however, his duty to point out that they began not at the insistence of Avery's critics, but at that of his friends. Staples's account of the hearing at Bristol was only published after Luke Drury's transcript was offered to the public, and only to correct the errors in it. The other publication widely available was Harnden's account of the flight and capture, and it studiously avoided making any comment about the minister's guilt or innocence. Unfortunate as they were, none of the publications had any bearing on the trial. If jurors still worried about the possibility of unconscious bias, Greene reminded them that the prisoner's case had been argued before them by a "gentleman from a neighboring state, of forty years eminent practice in the law, whose reputation came here long before he did, and has for so many years placed him at the head of his profession" (Hallett 1833b, 59). If the government could convince them, in the face of Mason's eloquence and the flood of defense witnesses, the jury had little to fear in a guilty verdict based on a "combination and force of circumstances" that removed all reasonable doubt that Avery had committed the crime.

That Sarah Cornell had sinned was, of course, without doubt. Greene pointed out, however, that her periods of transgression were precisely those in which she was in contact with Avery. Where, then, might lie the cause? Whatever the source of her fall, it was certain that her character was not stable. "Her life," the attorney general admitted, "was one of transgression and remorse—of sensual indulgence, and religious enthusiasm—of piety and passion" (Hallett 1833b, 63). But was that cause to believe she killed herself in a fit of revenge against the prisoner? The evidence showed no great wrong done to her by Avery in his official capacity with the church, and her own declarations made it clear that she bore only a solicitous concern for his well-being. Her actions on the day of her death and her refusal to take oil of tansy pointed to a woman fully intending to live out her natural life.

The correspondence found in her belongings was consistent with this interpretation of her motives. If she were meeting Avery in hopes of his "settling" the matter, she must have realized that he might want her to leave the area for her confinement. What was more natural than for her to leave a note in her unlocked bandbox directing the inquirer to Avery, who would know where to ship her belongings? The incriminating letters were safely locked in her trunk, the key to which she carried with her.

Even ignoring the dead woman's motives, was the condition of the body consistent with a verdict of suicide? Reviewing the evidence of the body's condition and the knot found at its neck, Greene concluded that suicide was impossible to accept. No woman could possibly have hung herself in the way Sarah Cornell was found, and no woman could have inflicted on herself bruises such as those found on the body. That the defense had tried to swear away the bruises by theoretical medical testimony was, Greene supposed, to be expected, but he preferred to accept the word of the experienced matrons who saw the body over the pronouncements of physicians who could only testify to what *might* have been seen (Hallett 1833b, 74). Greene asserted that the conclusion that Sarah Cornell met a violent death at the hands of another was indisputable. When court reconvened after lunch, he would seek to demonstrate that those hands must have belonged to Ephraim Avery.

Returning to his argument at half past two when the court reconvened, Greene dismissed Coroner Hicks's first verdict (suicide) as highly irregular, noted the corresponding incompetence of Howe and Haile at Bristol, and then dismissed the topic. The jury needed only to see that past irregularities in favor of and detrimental to the prisoner had no place in their deliberations. The issue was whether or not the last month's testimony had convinced them of Avery's guilt.

If proven, Avery's authorship of the two letters found in Sarah Cornell's trunk would go far in establishing his guilt because they set up the meeting at which she died. Though the defense had tried to deny it, evidence that the minister had written them was overwhelming. The pink letter from Providence, in a feigned handwriting but nonetheless retaining some of the distinctive peculiarities of the minister's style, was linked to the prisoner by

Orswell's testimony, no matter how many attempts were made to discredit the honest engineer. That a number of Methodist ministers were called to account for Avery's every moment on the morning the letter was delivered to the *King Philip* was immaterial; how likely were they, six months later, to remember events of an unremarkable morning down to the last minute?

The letter of December 8 was likewise clearly linked to the minister by the testimonies of Iram Smith, Content Parry, Harvey Harnden, and Joseph Lesure. Remembering Mason's harsh treatment of Sarah Jones, Greene described Eldridge Pratt's dramatic and discredited testimony as "rank, corrupt and deliberate *perjury*" designed to suggest that Colonel Harnden had plotted to contrive false evidence against the defendant (Hallett 1833b, 83).

That the subject that prompted the letters had also generated a meeting on the night of October 20 was also certain. Avery had disappeared after his prayer meeting long enough to worry Mrs. Bidwell, and Sarah Cornell had been seen in the company of a tall man. Once again, the defense had tried to counter the evidence with the amazing memories of witnesses who were sure that Avery had not been gone long enough for a secret interview, and with a concerted attack on Mary Borden that was extended long after the misinterpretation on which it was founded had been satisfactorily resolved. Both attempts, in Greene's opinion, had failed.

In the same way, the defense attempt to prove that the minister could not have been the father of Sarah Cornell's unborn child—and thus had no motive for murdering her—was ineffectual. Medical testimony on the age of the fetus at death had proven nothing because medical opinion varied widely, and the accounts of Avery's friends at the Thompson camp meeting were unbelievable because of their very precision. The evidence that Sarah Cornell had been pregnant when she reached the camp ground was supported by the flimsiest of evidence, a "Reverend gentleman" who was convinced of her pregnancy "because the young woman's clothes were open behind! just as the worthy old lady was, because she had a pale face and a dull eye, though she had to look over the tent to make that discovery!" (Hallett 1833b, 87).

If it was reasonable to believe that Avery might have been the father of the unborn child and might have written the unsigned letters in Sarah Cornell's trunk, was it reasonable to believe that he had committed the murder? On the afternoon of the twentieth the minister did go to the island, and Greene proceeded to list the sequence of witnesses who had seen a stranger resembling him, sometimes wearing a cap that he could have carried in a bundle under his arm, crossing the island and entering Fall River. The alternate account of his time, the defense story of a sight-seeing trip to the coal mines, was unsupported by evidence. Amy Anthony's story that she met a man on the road that evening was typical of what the defense had to offer. Under cross examination she admitted that she did not have the faintest idea of the man's description; in any case, Avery's own account of his trip mentioned nothing of passing a woman on the road (Hallett 1833b, 92).

Was it not indicative of the true nature of the minister's journey that he chose to lie about it at ferryman Gifford's house? And was it not indicative of the nature of defense testimony that an attempt was made to clear him by attacking the otherwise blameless reputation of the young girl to whom he lied? "I confess," said Greene,

> Nothing has given me more unpleasant feelings during this trial than the attempt to impeach the character of that young woman. I regret it the more, because the members of the religious society, who had united in expelling her from their church, now unite in destroying her character for veracity, while all the neighbors beside, fully sustain her good character (Hallett 1833b, 93).

It was a good point to leave clear in the jurors' minds. Just as Mason had questioned the validity of prosecution testimony because of the Fall River Committee's biases, so Greene could hope to point out possible collusion of the Methodists. If their wonderful facility in remembering precise timetables could be doubted, then Avery's being the father of the child and the author of the letters seemed apparent. How far was it from that point to murder? Greene concluded:

> I do not know, gentlemen, that there is any thing more, which is material, for me to add. We have shown that the prisoner's own account of himself is so utterly improbable, and is contradicted by so many facts, that it is impossible for you to believe it. We have shown that he did not pass from the Ferry, in the direction he says he did, to the Coal Mines, and that he did go to Fall River, on an appointment to meet the deceased at the fatal stack yard. There we leave him with her, at the time the homicide was committed, and we call upon him, as the last man with her, to account for her death! (Hallett 1833b, 93).

When the attorney general finished it was almost half past six. Chief Justice Eddy's charge to the jury followed immediately and was mercifully short. Cautioning them to use the penciled note found in the bandbox and the letter of December 8 only as evidence to rebut the assertion of suicide, the judge sent the jurors to begin their deliberations. "I was going to say," he added, "that you should take care to divest yourselves of all prejudice, but I have no right to infer that you have any prejudices, which such a caution might seem to imply" (Hallett 1833c, 37).

Before they were ushered out, one juror asked if the papers produced during the trial would be given to them for examination. No, said Eddy, such was not the practice in criminal cases. Armed with only the indictment, the jury withdrew under the close supervision of an officer who was directed to have the courthouse bell rung when they reached a verdict. Until that time court was in recess (Hallett 1833c, 38).

No one expected an early verdict, but, nonetheless, every church bell that rang on Sunday morning was greeted with a chorus of inquiries if it were *the* bell. Just before noon the courthouse bell began to peal, and before it had ceased a throng had surrounded the building, waiting for the doors to open. When they did, the crowd poured in, packing the courtroom so densely that it was only with great difficulty that a path was cleared to allow the justices to reach the bench. Once the judges were seated, Avery was brought in, escorted only by Rev. Palmer. He was followed by the silent jury, their faces haggard and severe.

The proceedings were halted at that point because Richard Randolf was not yet in court. A courier was sent to find him, and for fifteen minutes an unnatural quiet filled the room. When the lawyer was finally brought in and had taken his place, the court clerk called on Avery to stand before the jury. This the prisoner did with the same admirable composure that he had displayed throughout the trial.

Turning to the jury, the clerk asked, "Have you agreed on a verdict?"

Foreman Eleazer Trevett replied, "We have."

"Gentlemen of the Jury, who shall speak for you?"

Eleven men answered, "Our Foreman."

"Prisoner look on the Foreman; Foreman look on the Prisoner. What say you Mr. Foreman, is the prisoner guilty or not guilty?"

"Not guilty," said Trevett (Hallett 1833c, 38).

There was no outburst in the courtroom. Avery stood for a moment, then bowed to the jury and took his seat. His elbows resting on the table before him, he covered his face with one hand while a deep flush spread over his forehead and temples. By the time Randolf had asked for and received his discharge from the court, the minister had regained his composure (*Boston Atlas*, 4 June 1833). Rev. Palmer was the first to clasp his hand (*Ohio Republican*, 15 June 1833); then a cluster of well-wishers gathered around him, and he accepted their congratulations while the silent crowd began to disperse. Then, in the company of a deputy sheriff, Palmer, and Randolf, Avery walked from the room (Hallett 1833c, 39).

9. Public Justice

Freed by the court and immediately taken into the protective custody of his friends, Ephraim Avery was escorted from Newport's court-house to the home of Asa Kent and, shortly afterward, to a waiting sloop, which in three hours had transported him up the bay to Bristol, well in advance of the news of his acquittal. As the sloop neared its dock, Avery was recognized by members of his congregation who had just finished their Sunday services. The last reports from Newport having indicated that ten jurors were convinced of the minister's guilt, the Methodists were amazed to see Avery appear before them (*Providence Journal*, 6 June 1833). Bowing to the startled gathering, he stepped ashore and, surrounded by a growing crowd of well-wishers, moved toward his house. His homecoming was as unexpected by his wife as his neighbors, and when he stepped through the doorway she quite dramatically swooned (*Providence Journal*, 6 June 1833).

There was little time, however, for the minister to bask in the congratulations of his friends or partake of the simple pleasures of his domestic circle. The trial had freed him in the eyes of the law, but had done little to quell the public indignation that he faced. His effectiveness as a preacher was in serious jeopardy, as was the reputation of the New England Conference that had supported him through five months of hearings, imprisonment, and trial. Though

Jeremiah Mason had won the trial, he had not proven Avery's innocence, and the church was aware that much had to be done before it could expect communal exoneration that would match his acquittal.

Fortunately, the New England Methodists were holding their annual meeting that very week in Boston, where their assembled ministers would have the opportunity to consider Avery's case unconstrained by the rules of a criminal court. Witnesses and arguments that had been excluded at Newport could be brought, theories presented, and conclusions drawn that were outside the acceptable operations of the public trial just concluded. If, with the

17. New England Conference Group, Boston's Bromfield Street Chapel, 1833. Though Ephraim Avery is not identifable, several ministers who figured prominently in his history are. Timothy Merritt stands in the pulpit, while George Pickering sits behind him. At the base of the pulpit stairs stands Wilbur Fisk, behind the seated Bishop Elija Hedding. On the right of the altar, his arm resting over the railing, is Asa Kent. In the center of the pews, Joseph A. Merrill sits looking back at the artist.
Standing in the aisle, his arms folded, is Edward T. Taylor, while immediately in front of him sits Phineas Crandall. Abraham D. Merrill sits showing the artist his profile at the extreme right of the picture. From James Mudge, *History of the New England Conference of the Methodist Episcopal Church 1796–1910* (Boston: The Conference, 1910).

freedom of inquiry they enjoyed, the Methodists were left with even a suspicion of Avery's guilt, he could be summarily expelled from their society. If, on the other hand, they were convinced of his innocence, their fuller deliberations might prove persuasive to the public as well.

By June 6 Avery was in Boston, awaiting his church trial before a select panel of seven ministers. Asa Kent and Joseph A. Merrill, both of whom had been active in the defense at Newport, were joined on the committee by John Lindsey, David Kilburn, Isaac Bonney, and Orange Scott. Their chairman was Wilbur Fisk, recently appointed president of Wesleyan University and one of the conference's most respected intellects (New England Annual Conference 1833, 12). Only forty years old in 1833, Fisk had already established himself as a leading figure in the church. In 1828 he had turned down an episcopacy in the newly formed Canadian Methodist Episcopal church, and a few years after the Avery excitement he would turn down a similar offer in his own church, citing ill health and spiritual obligations at the university for his decision (Simpson 1882, 363). Though he was sadly afflicted by a pulmonary disorder that would soon end his life, his unaffected humility, intellectual acumen, and renowned tact in handling delicate situations made him the best choice to head the conference's attempt to resolve the Avery question. Even Aristides, the conference's most implacable journalistic foe, was compelled to admit Fisk's moral and intellectual stature (*Republican Herald*, 25 September 1833).

It appears that the committee, rather than seeking new witnesses and information, chose to spend its days of deliberation pondering the testimony given at Newport, the task made easier by the celerity with which transcripts of the trial moved from the pages of newspapers into pamphlet form. During the first week of June, both B. F. Hallett's version (for the *Boston Advocate*) and that of Richard Hildreth (for the New England Conference) had appeared on the streets (*Eastern Argus*, 3 June 1833; *New England Christian Herald*, 5 June 1833, 143), and the two unsigned reports published in New York were not far behind.

On June 11 the committee issued its report, which was hardly a model of impartiality. The prosecution's evidence was dismissed wholesale, generated as it was under a public "excitement" in which "shadows become embodied into substantial forms, dreams are changed into realities, and vague impressions become known and vivid conceptions" (New England Annual Conference 1833, 4). On the other hand, defense testimony, even the absurd story told by the Parkers, was unquestioned. Brother ministers were particularly to be believed because the committee knew them to be men of "unimpeachable integrity" (New England Annual Conference 1833, 7). By the simple expedient of believing Avery's friends and disbelieving his enemies, the committee thus concluded there was not a shred of evidence that he had either impregnated or murdered Sarah Cornell.

The ceremony in which Avery heard himself acquitted of both murder and improper "connexion" was solemn and impressive. The Reverend George Pickering, at sixty-four the oldest delegate to the meetings, was asked to take the chair momentarily from Bishop Elija Hedding (*Painesville Telegraph*, 28 June 1833) while the committee verdict was read. Asked if he had any response to make, Avery modestly replied that he had nothing prepared to say but wished to "return his sincere thanks to his brethren in the ministry, and his Christian friends, for the aid they had rendered him, in the time of his extreme peril" (*Newport Mercury*, 15 June 1833). Following the minister's short remarks, the committee report was unanimously accepted, and a motion was raised that thanks should be offered to God for his "overruling providence." Pickering then led his assembled brethren in prayer (*Newport Mercury*, 15 June 1833).

With that scene concluded, Bishop Hedding regained his chair and the meeting went on to consider the more mundane aspects of Avery's experience. It was suggested that Avery be given an assignment for the following year that would not tax his powers; accordingly, he was reassigned to Bristol with Charles K. True, who would take over the actual operation of the church (Whittaker 1912, 149). In this decision the conference acceded to the wishes of a group of Avery's parishioners, who had sent a statement to the meeting that they would "consider themselves unhandsomely treated" if Mr. Avery were not returned to them (*Republican Herald*, 8 June 1833). Their gracious gesture took the conference off what could have been an uncomfortable hook. Obviously unpopular throughout much of New England, Avery would not be easily accepted in other stations; at least in Bristol he would be among people already used to him—and hopefully among friends. With True to carry the burden of the work, Avery could retire into relative obscurity until the excitement against him could abate.

The question of lost revenues was not easily solved. Avery had applied to the conference for $248 to make up for losses incurred

during the last six months, but like all those who made similar ap-
plications, he was required to accept much less—in his case, $23.15
(Whittaker 1912, 146). Faced with the enormous cost of the trial,
the conference was in serious financial difficulty. Agents were
therefore dispatched to other Methodist conferences to solicit do-
nations. Many agents were successful, but at least one, sent to Washington, was met with a less than enthusiastic welcome (*Newport
Mercury*, 20 July 1833). In the general monetary gloom that pervaded the meeting, a momentary ray of light showed when David
Ela, the Boston printer who would later publish Avery's personal
Vindication, offered $75—and copies for each minister of the con-
ference at 2.5¢ each—for the right to publish the committee's report (Whittaker 1912, 137–38).

The day after his church acquittal, Avery preached to a packed
house at the First Methodist Church on Bennet Street at the request of its members (*Republican Herald*, 15 June 1833). His text
was from Psalms 21:19: "Oh how great is thy goodness, which thou
has laid up for them that fear thee; which thou hast wrought for
them that trust in thee before the sons of man." During the sermon, which lasted almost an hour, Avery was visibly affected when
his words related to his experiences of the past six months (*Manufacturers and Farmers Journal*, 17 June 1833). Delivered extempo-
raneously in the usual Methodist fashion, his performance was well
received by a uniformly orderly crowd (*Newport Mercury*, 15 June
1833).

The Methodists had reason to be optimistic. Avery's return to
the pulpit had been a success, and the press was taking a generally
positive approach to his acquittal—sometimes so positive that it
spurred the *Fall River Weekly Recorder* (26 June 1833) to complain
that the hard work of the Fall River Committee "is all set down by
some of our benevolent friends, as the offspring of excitement and
infatuation." The *New England Christian Herald* (12 June 1833, 147)
printed extracts from eight newspapers praising the court's verdict
and easily could have found more. Even the overtly hostile *Republican Herald* (5 June 1833) in Providence, which called upon Avery to
present more convincing evidence of his innocence before he could
expect a "favorable reception in society," admitted that it had no
quarrel with the jury's decision.

Their moment of self-congratulation, however, was short; unexpectedly, publication of the committee's report on Avery stirred
up resentment. The *Literary Subaltern*, which on May 24 had sup-

ported the Methodist right to defend Avery during the trial, on June 14 pronounced the report worthless and predicted that "until he shall have accounted for his absence on the night of the 20th of December, a vast majority of the people of New England—indeed all who are acquainted with the history of the 'Fall River murder,' will be strongly impressed with an opinion unfavorable to his innocence." The *New England Galaxy* (15 June 1833) branded the Methodist operation as "whitewashing" and predicted that it would not reduce public indignation against the minister, and the *New Hampshire Patriot* (1 July 1833) declared that a conviction of Avery's entire innocence was "not our opinion, nor is it the opinion of the public generally." It was not long before many New England Methodists could agree with Philadelphian Sumner Lincoln Fairfield who observed that, "Granting the verdict honest and the conviction of Avery's innocence unequivocal, it was certainly unwise at once to reinstate him as a Christian minister, and apparently to command the world to proclaim him a guiltless martyr" (*North American Magazine*, August 1833). The *New England Christian Herald*, which on June 12 had applauded the public opinion that seemed to support Avery's release, had by June 26 discovered that there were still some "miserable incendiary spirits" that were not convinced. By July 10, when it was apparent that the minister did not enjoy much popular favor, it was prompted to ask, almost hysterically, "Are the low, profane, and obscene ebulitions heard in Rum cellars, Soda shops,—and in holes, and at the corners of our streets,—the known haunts of the dissipated and dissolute—the voice of public opinion?" (*New England Christian Herald*, 10 July 1833).

That those outbursts did have some popular support had already been made clear. On Thursday, July 13, fresh from his happy return to the pulpit, Avery walked to Kilby Street in Boston to transact personal business at the local shops. A crowd of hostile men began to congregate in his wake as more and more passersby recognized him. Fearing violence, a Methodist shopkeeper conducted Avery into his store and shut out the growing mob. By the time Sheriff Park arrived, between four and five hundred men had surrounded the store, waiting for Avery to appear. Although the Methodist establishment hopefully construed the crowd's motivation as simple curiosity (*New England Christian Herald*, 19 June 1833, 151), the sheriff felt it prudent to stay with the minister until a carriage could be procured to take him to his residence (*Newport Mercury*, 28 June 1833). It is unlikely that Avery again walked unattended in Boston.

By the first Sunday in July, Avery was back home in Bristol, where he preached to a large congregation, performed three baptisms, and administered the Lord's Supper. Charles K. True reported that the minister's return had gone smoothly and that reports of church discord were untrue; not a single member of the flock had applied to leave the church because of Avery (*New England Christian Herald*, 17 July 1833, 167). True's assertion, however, was false; the Bristol congregation was suffering a serious division over Avery's case that would soon lead to its fragmentation (Upham 1891, 84).

Avery's troubled congregation was not the only indication that the journalistic attacks on him had some popular support. At Fall River Ira Bidwell angrily rejected a suggestion that he take as his sermon text Hosea 5:3: "I know Ephraim, and Israel is not hid from me; for now O Ephraim, thou committest whoredom and Israel is defiled" (*Rhode Island Republican*, 3 July 1833). At Providence a coffin bearing Avery's name was found floating in the river (*Niles' Register*, 22 June 1833). When it was learned, in the first week of July, that Avery planned to preach at Providence's Methodist chapel on Ship Street, the editor of the *Literary Subaltern* (5 July 1833) urged him not to appear because of the danger of riot. At both Providence and Newport effigies of the minister were hung (*Literary Subaltern*, 19 July 1833), one in Providence gaining momentary distinction as it was dragged through the streets by a tandem team of dogs, followed by a howling mob of boys (*Daily City Gazette*, 5 July 1833). The minister was not even safe from public censure in his own Bristol, where his image was hung and burned twice on the last Sunday of July (*Pawtucket Chronicle*, 2 August 1833).

In Fall River three images of the unpopular preacher were hung during the week preceding August 14. Another, strung up on July 4, was left suspended until the end of August, when it was taken down and dragged through the streets, "followed by hundreds of spectators, hollering and shouting" (Brayton n.d., 38). One enterprising Fall River artist produced a huge oil painting on which a life-sized Avery was depicted in the process of hanging Sarah Cornell's limp body on the hay stack; when the village's selectmen prudently refused him a permit to collect an admission fee to see his work, he displayed it free of charge (*Fall River Weekly Recorder*, 14 August 1833).

Avery and his friends were being pilloried in song as well. One composition, probably produced between February and May 1833, opened:

A Rev Mr Avery sure
A teacher of the Gospel pure
Stands charged with murder to the test
Seduction too in part confessed

It left no doubt as to the minister's guilt when Sarah Cornell's ghost sang:

Ye maidens all both old and young
Trust not to men's false flattering tongue
To know a man pray know his life
How few there are deserve a wife

Tho' doomed I am to an awfull end
I crave the prayers of every friend
That my poor spirit may be blest
And with my God in heaven rest

(THOMPSON 1958, 155–57)

Another, heard in the streets of Newport as early as May 5, advised:

Ye people all a warning take,
    Remember Avery's plot:—
Enough to make your hearts to ache;
    Don't let it be forgot.

He killed the mother—then the child;
    What a wicked man was he!
The devil helped him all the while:
    How wicked he must be

(*SANGAMO JOURNAL*, 2 JUNE 1833)

By the time Catharine Williams had recorded this second song in the later months of the year, Avery's "plot" had become his "knot," the clove hitch that could serve justice as efficiently as it had the murderous minister:

Hang him, hang him on a tree
    Tie around him Avery's knot
Forever let him hanged be
    And never be forgot

(WILLIAMS 1833, 150)

It was almost inevitable that the journalists would try their hand at increasing the public store of verse. The decision of Justices Howe and Haile to release Avery was thus satirically memorialized almost two months after the trial at Newport:

My friend, Johnny Howe—
Thy reasoning, I vow,
Is the cutest I've yet seen recorded—
The Laurel Wreath won,
Thou'lt blaze like the sun,
And long shall thy name be recorded. . . .

Thus—against E.K.A.
Facts, lengthening that way,
Were shorn of their strength by contraction,
But, 'gainst S.M.C.
Facts short, chance to be,
Were lengthened by logical action
(*RHODE ISLAND REPUBLICAN*, 24 JULY 1833)

Had all the attacks on Avery been confined to journalistic name calling and moments of symbolic—and thus harmless—violence, the minister's friends might have been well advised to refrain from comment and wait for the excitement to die a natural death. It became quickly apparent, however, that there was a dangerous side to the storm of controversy unleashed in the newspapers, threatening because it called into question the validity of Avery's trial.

By the end of June, a widely reprinted story appeared in the New England newspapers claiming that there lived in Providence a particularly base woman named Maria Snow Cornell (*Rhode Island Republican*, 26 June 1833). It was her crimes, the story suggested, that were attributed to Sarah Maria Cornell in the trial at Newport, where more than one witness had related stories about "Maria" or "Maria S. Cornell." Although not believed by all (*Ohio Republican*, 13 July 1833), the story did much to reduce the image of Sarah Cornell's depravity—and to call into question the bulk of the testimony on which the defense's assertion of suicide was based.

It was, of course, impossible in the light of her pregnancy to dismiss all evidence against the dead woman's character, but it was relatively easy to account for it in terms unflattering to both Avery and his church. Tracing her career, the *New-Hampshire Sentinel* (20 June 1833) commented that the desertion of her father

> in a great degree broke up the family, scattered them in different directions and drove them for shelter into different benevolent families in Norwich and its vicinity. The want of parental care, which the unhappy event occasioned, may have contributed to form the character and habits of Maria.

Growing up in a period of intense religious activity, and without parental control over her "naturally ardent temperament," Sarah underwent an early religious conversion, only to wander from "the plain and simple precepts of the gospel into the mazy regions of fanaticism" (*Norwich Courier*, 19 June 1833)—that is, she joined the Methodist church, which valued emotion more than intellect. Guided only by a "vivid and perverted imagination," it was to be expected that she would suffer a fall and sacrifice her chastity,

> and not improbably in the first instance, on the altar of a heated and misguided zeal. There is a degree in religious fanaticism, at which virtue loses its beauty and at this point Maria is supposed to have arrived before the foundation of her virtue gave way. The reins of moral and religious restraint being loosened, and the mirror of the imagination having ceased to reflect the deformity of vice, nothing was left to regulate her connexions and associations in the world, but the impetuosity of her passions (*New-Hampshire Sentinel*, 20 June 1833).

Underscoring the assertion that it was her home life and unfortunate religious affiliation that resulted in Sarah Cornell's fall, Noel Allen Tripp, editor of the *Fall River Weekly Recorder*, chose the end of June to note that the common belief that factory labor led to "the depression of the mind and the degradation of morals" was beginning to "give place to more just and correct sentiments." Quoting from the *New York Observer*, he concluded that as long as New England factories were "conducted as they are now, instead of being as those of England are represented to be, schools of vice as well as destroyers of health, I am persuaded that they are and may always be, schools of virtue and piety" (*Fall River Weekly Recorder*, 26 June 1833). Thus the factories could be exonerated, the Methodist church implicated, and a major portion of Avery's defense badly shaken.

If the public reassessment of Sarah Cornell's character and the cause of its deficiencies were not sufficient worry, the Methodists were faced with other attacks. Beginning on June 12, the Newport *Rhode Island Republican* began to publish a series of articles extremely critical of Avery, under the name of Proteus. Rather than being the typical vague pronouncement of dissatisfaction with Avery and the church, these articles made specific charges. There was incontrovertible proof, Proteus said, that Avery's "silent counsel" had illegally manipulated the jury selection process in order to pack the jury with men favorable to the minister (*Rhode Island Republican*, 26 June 1833). George Turner, who had been one of the minister's "silent" lawyers, immediately denied that he had had any part in such improper behavior, and Proteus agreed that it was not him (*Rhode Island Republican*, 3 July 1833), but the charge still stood. Nor were the lawyers alone to be criticized; Proteus also claimed that Methodist ministers had tampered with prosecution witnesses—particularly Gardiner Coit—and had been heard to conspiratorially exclaim, "We have got him clear in spite of them!!!" (*Rhode Island Republican*, 10 July 1833).

Two and a half weeks after Proteus began his comments in Newport, Aristides initiated a similar series of articles in Providence's *Republican Herald*, stimulated by the "bold and daring manifesto" of the New England Conference that acquitted Avery "even of suspicion" (Aristides 1833, 6). Though at the outset they were no more than an evaluation of the testimony given at Avery's trial, Aristides' articles managed to ask embarrassing questions. Why, for instance, Aristides wanted to know, did Avery, if he knew Sarah Cornell to be a virtual whore, not inform Ira Bidwell of her character when he discovered her in the Fall River congregation (Aristides 1833, 10)?

The challenge to the validity of Avery's acquittal had to be met, but the Methodists had little with which to fight. Any thoughts they might have entertained of instituting a libel suit against Proteus and Aristides were effectively squashed by the publication, probably by Benjamin F. Hallett, of an anonymous pamphlet recounting the effect of John Maffitt's libel suit against Joseph T. Buckingham eleven years before (Hallett 1833d). In 1822 Buckingham, then editor of the *New England Galaxy*, had capped a long series of articles ridiculing Maffitt's literary and religious pretentions with the publication of charges that the preacher was guilty of lying, betraying a confidence, ridiculing persons coming to the altar, denying Christianity, and behaving lasciviously. Outraged, Maffitt responded with a libel suit, which he could expect to win if he could prove malicious intent—something abundantly indicated by Buckingham's earlier articles—and damage to his reputation.

Under the existing libel laws, the truth was no defense against libel charges, and Maffitt could be sure that the accuracy of Buckingham's charges, legally irrelevant, would never be considered in court. However, the relevance of truth to libel was the precise issue Buckingham wished to debate, and the reason he had baited Maffitt into bringing suit (*New England Galaxy*, 12 July 1822). With Benjamin F. Hallett as his lawyer, the publisher won his point at the outset of the trial when the judge agreed that the truth was not libelous (Commonwealth v. Buckingham 1823). The result was disastrous for Maffitt; he and his counsel could only watch helplessly as testimony in court turned the questionable allegations of an impulsive and sarcastic newsman into incontrovertible fact. The not-guilty verdict that cleared Buckingham and set legal precedent was equally a pronouncement on Maffitt's moral deportment that was extremely embarrassing to the Methodist church. The subsequent ecclesiastical trial that cleared Maffitt of any wrongdoing (True and Greene 1823) only made matters worse. Its analysis of the evidence was obviously biased, and it made an unfortunate argument clearing Maffitt of the charge of having kissed his hand to some pretty girls from the altar based on a consideration of how far the report of that kiss could possibly have been heard (True and Greene 1823, 18). Accurately branded as an "ineffably silly" production (Hallett 1823, 23), the conference's attempt to exonerate its preacher was a humiliating failure.

Having grown wiser through Maffitt's experience with the courts, the New England Conference probably did not need Hallett's gentle reminder that the libel laws did not offer a foolproof response to the accusations of Proteus and Aristides. The Methodists had no desire to enter into another lengthy legal action that might prove embarrassing and would certainly be costly. What they sought instead was some new information that could swing public opinion in their favor. Unfortunately, all they had were mystical assertions of Avery's innocence, like the deathbed declaration of Elisha Williams of New York, "than whom no man possessed a more acute, comprehensive and powerful intellect, whose particular gift is was to find light amid darkness which other eyes could not penetrate" (*Spirit of the Age*, 18 July 1833). It was weak fare, falling as far short of the mark as a young clergyman's breathless declaration to Jeremiah Mason during the trial that an angel had informed him of brother Avery's purity (Clark 1917, 359). Unless solid new evidence surfaced that would break the chain of circumstance linking Avery to Sarah Cornell, the conference's position was in danger of degenerating into painfully obvious bias and ineffable silliness.

The evidence that the conference desperately needed came in the unlikely form of a thirty-one-year-old shoemaker from East Greenwich, Rhode Island, named Nathan Spencer. Soon after completion of Avery's trial, Spencer casually mentioned to a friend that he had traveled to Providence late in November, and along the road had been handed a letter by a stranger who asked that it be taken to the steam packet. Though not a Methodist, the shoemaker usually attended Methodist meeting, and his story came to the attention of the church. Asked if he could fix the date of his journey, Spencer looked through his receipts and found the one he had obtained from Sheldon and Mason on that trip; it was dated November 27. Here then was the man, remarkably similar in dress and conformation to Avery, who had actually handed the letter to engineer Orswell on the *King Philip*. Unfortunately, he could offer little information about the letter's source—a youngish man in a cloak who had given it to him outside Pautuxet—but he remembered the letter itself quite well. It was reddish, he recalled, and was addressed to a woman named Cornell (in fact, it was addressed to Sarah M. Connell) whom he thought might be related to Benjamin Cornell of East Greenwich, and he was able to identify it when the clerk of the Supreme Court showed him the pink letter introduced at Avery's trial (Avery 1834, 44–45).

Spencer's deposition was taken on July 6 before Nathan Whiting, justice of the peace in East Greenwich. Combined with the statements of his brothers, Richard and Thomas, who could swear to his trip to Providence and his conversation about a possible daughter of Benjamin Cornell in Fall River, it was offered to the press the following week. The *New England Christian Herald* (17 July 1833) reported receipt of the deposition and then printed it (24 July 1833), noting that while many would probably see it as a Methodist scheme, honest men would recognize that it was not.

As the *Herald* predicted, reactions were mixed. Some thought the deposition destroyed Orswell's testimony, broke the link between Avery and the fatal interview, and revitalized the theory of a conspiracy against the minister (*Boston Atlas*, 11 July 1833; *Emporium*, 6 August 1833). Others were more careful, admitting only that Avery's position was "greatly strengthened" if Spencer could be believed (Sewell 1833), and others were distinctly hostile.

In Newport, Proteus went immediately to George C. Mason, clerk of the Supreme Court, to find out if Spencer had been as positive in his identification of the letter as his deposition suggested. Mason said no, that Spencer had declared that the color was not right and had told him he'd paid nothing for delivery of the letter, while Orswell had testified that he was paid twelve and a half cents

(*Rhode Island Republican*, 24 July 1833). The deposition, Proteus concluded, was a rotten fabric of lies that only proved that "dying men will catch at straws." In fact, "if the Spencer affadavit should not have the intended effect we should not be surprised if some miserable fanatic should come forward and swear that he murdered Miss Cornell—and he would verily believe that he was doing God services in offering himself up a martyr for his priest" (*Rhode Island Republican*, 24 July 1833).

Aristides in Providence was no kinder; he also found "some things very suspicious" about Spencer's statement (Aristides 1833, 23). How could Spencer claim, he asked, that throughout seven months of intense public excitement, "while the history of this 'pink letter' was in the mouth of every man, woman, and child," he never thought that his delivery of a letter, addressed to a woman named Cornell, might be of significance? Could it be that both his brothers and the stranger that Spencer said was with him on the wagon when he received the letter were all as blind as he to the implications of his experience? "Four such men," said Aristides, "must be an anomaly in human nature" (Aristides 1833, 25).

Neither was the Fall River Committee willing to accept Spencer at face value. Taking a cue from Aristides, who commented that Spencer had never been subjected to cross examination (Aristides 1833, 22–23), on August 22 Harvey Harnden was dispatched with John Orswell to confront the shoemaker in East Greenwich. At the meeting Orswell declared that Spencer was neither tall nor heavy enough, nor were his hands white enough, for him to have been the man that delivered the letter. More important, Spencer, never having been there, admitted knowing nothing of Fall River.

"Then you cannot have given me the letter which I carried on the 27th November," replied Orswell, "for the gentleman who gave it me, heard my objection, among others, that I had something else to do at Fall River, besides running about to deliver letters. He stated that it would not be much trouble to me, in this case, nor much out of my way, as the family with whom the girl boarded, lived near Capt. Borden" (Aristides 1833, 99).

A little over two weeks later, Harnden stepped aboard the *King Philip* as it lay at its wharf in Providence and took Captain Thomas Borden's statement that Orswell had indeed asked him about the location of the house and told him the stranger said it was near the captain's residence (Aristides 1833, 99). Both an account of Orswell's visit to Spencer and a copy of Captain Borden's statement were then sent to Aristides in Providence to be included as an appendix to his collected articles when they were published in pamphlet form in early September.

With Spencer's deposition unsuccessful in quelling the agitation against him, Avery was rumored in early August to have left Bristol and sought refuge among the Methodists of Germantown, outside of Philadelphia (*Newport Mercury*, 17 August 1833). The Philadelphia *Pennsylvanian* reported that he was living a secluded life with a respectable Germantown family, and he was supposed to have visited a camp meeting near Darby, Pennsylvania, but to have kept himself concealed in a tent (*Raleigh Register*, 27 August 1833). "Whatever excitement may exist in Rhode Island against him," wrote the sanctimonious *Pennsylvanian*, "he must be satisfied he is now in a neighborhood where coolness, compassion, justice, and public decorum, prevail to an extraordinary degree. He may rely on the fearless independence and justice of a Philadelphia public" (*Mail*, 16 August 1833).

In fact, Avery appears to have stayed in Bristol, perhaps fading from public observances in favor of Charles True, but sometimes showing himself—nervous, shaken, and blanched—to perform his religious duties (*Literary Subaltern*, 16 August 1833). By the time the *Pennsylvanian*'s retraction of its report of his trip had reached New England (*Literary Subaltern*, 16 August 1833), however, the minister had actually left town.

On the morning of August 15, showing the effects of the tension under which he had been living since his acquittal, Avery left Bristol, traveling first to Wilbraham, Massachusetts (*New England Christian Herald*, 21 August 1833, 87). Though he may have felt his health required his escape, even momentarily, from the center of controversy, his trip was much more than recreational. At Wilbraham he met with Joseph Merrill and Wilbur Fisk who, with Timothy Merritt, were to work with him on a publication that would present his—and the church's—side of the story. Both Merrill and Merritt had had previous experience with argumentative publications, and Fisk was the conference's most respected intellect. They were a promising team.

Avery, probably at the conference's urging, had been occupied with his manuscript since his return to Bristol (*Literary Subaltern*, 28 June 1833) and had apparently made some progress. On July 10 Charles True had reported that "more light will, I trust, before long, be given" (*New England Christian Herald*, 17 July 1833, 167).

The following month, however, had seen such a proliferation of charges that Avery was overwhelmed. Proteus had claimed that an elderly Methodist minister had seen Avery and Sarah Cornell together at Thompson and had admitted it to others, but had become silent when his revelations were inadvertently made public (*Rhode Island Republican*, 31 July 1833). Proteus also had claimed that the Reverend Daniel Webb, who had testified against Peleg Cranston, was both dishonest and guilty of tampering with government witnesses (*Rhode Island Republican*, 7 August 1833). Aristides, in Providence, echoed the charges against Webb, claimed that Emor Angell had seen Avery give Orswell the pink letter, and added new assertions of Methodist witness tampering (Aristides 1833, 26–29, 38–39, 44–45) besides continuing his caustic evaluation of defense testimony at the trial. It was beyond Avery's powers to answer every attack, particularly since many focused on the church and its activities during the trial, of which the accused minister could only have had secondary knowledge. Fisk and Merrill seem to have counseled him that it was best to let the opposition expend the full force of its argument before responding—a hasty publication might give their enemies the opportunity to bring up new, unanswered arguments— and consequently the publication of his *Vindication* was delayed (Avery 1834, 5).

Waiting until a definitive defense could be produced before publishing, however, did not preclude other attempts by Avery to sway public opinion. Once again probably acting on the advice of Fisk and Merritt, Avery left Wilbraham for central Connecticut where he was to be given the opportunity to speak at Methodist meeting houses in Hartford and Middletown. Removed from centers of agitation against him, Connecticut was his childhood home and looked like the ideal place for Avery to find what he and his supporters both needed—a sympathetic audience. Unfortunately, he and his advisers had underestimated the depth and breadth of the hostility against him. In both Hartford and Middletown the minister was booed and hissed as he tried to speak (*Literary Subaltern*, 7 September 1833), and on his return to Bristol he discovered that the public agitation was becoming dangerous. Taking passage on a steamship of the Hartford line, he was recognized by his fellow passengers and threatened with bodily harm. The harried captain of the ship restored order and kept Avery from being tossed overboard only by promising to set the unwelcome preacher ashore at the first opportunity (*Newport Mercury*, 7 September

1833). The angry shouts of the people on board attracted attention on shore, and when Avery disembarked he found a crowd waiting for him that made his passage to the local Methodist parsonage hazardous and uncomfortable.

Bristol offered little encouragement when the unhappy preacher finally reached home. Charles True preached most of the sermons (Upham 1891, 82), and when Avery did offer a service it was sparsely attended. The press, which was still misreporting his presumed trip to Pennsylvania as an emigration that demonstrated the "triumph of public virtue" (*Literary Subaltern*, 7 September 1833), remained unfriendly and soon became outraged when it learned of his return (*Literary Subaltern*, 13 September 1833). In Newport theatergoers thronged to a play entitled *The Factory Girl, Or, The Fall River Murder* (*Literary Subaltern*, 13 September 1833), which presented the minister in an unflattering light. Conscious that he could count on hostile demonstrations should he venture beyond the tenuous security of his neighborhood, Avery must have often pondered the mob that had surrounded his house on Christmas and the turmoil on the Hartford line steamboat. The possibility of genuine physical assault seemed to be increasing rather than diminishing. Prudence demanded a withdrawal, at least of his family. Consequently, on September 9 Avery packed up his wife and family and took them away (*Newport Mercury*, 14 September 1833).

On the twenty-ninth of the month, Avery preached in the Methodist church at Richmond, Berkshire County, Massachusetts, the community in which his parents lived, where a collection was taken up for his benefit (*Newport Mercury*, 12 October 1833). Early in October, he had established a residence in Caanan, Columbia County, New York, just across the state line from Richmond (*Fall River Weekly Recorder*, 9 October 1833). The removal of his family to the Massachusetts/New York border made sense. Close enough to his parents for daily support, Avery had moved symbolically out of New England, but kept near enough so that it would not seem a precipitous retreat.

Throughout his difficulties after the trial, Avery had found consistent support and encouragement among the ministers of the New York Conference. They not only had offered to bear part of the expense of his defense, but also had suggested that other northern conferences should be contacted for similar contributions (Whittaker 1912, 135). In July, when he certainly needed it the most, Avery had been heartened to receive a letter from Timothy

Merritt, visiting the New York Conference, who asserted that "we are all br. A's friends here" (Merritt 1833). Even better, a public assertion of support appeared on September 10 in an article calling him "an innocent, amiable, and good, but much injured and bitterly persecuted man" that was published in the Cazenovia, New York, *Republican Monitor* (*Republican Herald*, 25 September 1833). It was unsurprising, then, that the minister should take momentary refuge among the sympathetic Methodists of upstate New York.

While Avery was at least passively accepted in Caanan, he was not so popular one hundred miles to the south. Late in August, the Richmond Hill, a mildly disreputable theater housed in Aaron Burr's old country seat on the outskirts of New York City, opened a new play entitled *Sarah Maria Cornell, Or, The Fall River Murder* (Odell 1928, 688). Theatrically undistinguished, the play was performed by a company that had but one star, Matilda Twibill, reportedly the most beautiful woman on the New York stage, who had blighted her career by an unfortunate marriage to an alcoholic actor, Thomas Flynn. The *New York Mirror* found the play, which overtly portrayed Avery as Sarah Cornell's seducer and murderer, in poor taste and an open libel that left its authors and players open to prosecution (*Mirror*, 21 September 1833). By the first week of October, the *Mirror* reported that the Richmond Hill theater was still attracting overflowing crowds with *The Fall River Murder*. "This is speaking volumes," wrote its editors, "for the moral sense of the community" (*Mirror*, 5 October 1833), but neither the Richmond Hill nor the public paid the slightest attention to the *Mirror's* disapprobation. New, expanded speeches were written for the character of Dr. Findout, probably a combination of Thomas Wilbur and Foster Hooper (*Post*, 10 September 1833), and the scenery reached fantastic proportions "to the great awe and consternation of all enlightened people and little boys, thereby producing a grand moral effect, highly creditable to the refined tastes of the manager, and exceedingly flattering to the good sense of the community" (*Mirror*, 19 October 1833). By the time the play closed late in October, it had become phenomenally popular and had demonstrated that Avery, no matter how well liked in the rural north, could expect no friendly greeting in the city of New York.

At about the same time the play closed in New York, Avery returned to Bristol, probably with his wife and children, stimulating the *Rhode Island Republican* (30 October 1833) into a new outburst against him. The last thing he wanted to do was rekindle the fires of local agitation that might endanger his family, and when on October 30 the *Republican* reported that he had been prohibited from further preaching he did not contradict it. Charles True had taken over the pulpit, and Avery was satisfied to retire to the privacy of his study, where he could continue work on the manuscript he hoped would ultimately clear his name. Even in the face of his silence, however, he continued to be the subject of a violent journalistic discussion that increasingly depended on the efforts of Aristides in the Providence *Republican Herald*.

Given the title of "under devil" by one of Avery's outraged supporters (*Republican Herald*, 31 July 1833), Aristides produced a steady stream of articles ridiculing the minister, his church, and his defense testimony. If his style was heavy and his claims sometimes extravagant, Aristides was still enormously popular. By early August, requests for back issues that contained his articles had exhausted the supply, and he proposed to publish his work in a pamphlet (*Republican Herald*, 10 August 1833) which, because of the rapid accumulation of material, did not appear until September.

The source of his popularity was not simply his flamboyant sarcasm—although he once asked Avery's defenders to consider "how long it would take a woman to hang herself . . . to a stake in a stack yard, with her hands confined under her cloak; and how quick she could do it, with a Methodist Clergyman's assistance," and suggested that the Methodists who thought him guilty of persecuting Mr. Avery might "just bargain with a few of your friends to swear me innocent" (*Republican Herald*, 31 July 1833). Along with his heavy-handed humor, Aristides published a continuing series of specific charges. Gideon Dennis, he wrote, had walked with Avery from the mainland onto Howland's stone bridge at nine o'clock on the night of the murder and could positively swear to it, but had refused after the Methodists threatened to destroy his character as they had Jane Gifford's (Aristides 1833, 57). If anyone doubted the story, Aristides suggested that they remember that the minister's attorneys had not hesitated to attack the reputation of gatekeeper Peleg Cranston, even though Cranston's son Henry was one of them. Aristides also believed that Dr. William Graves had been dispatched to New York City during the trial to stop a young man from Lowell who was telling incriminating stories about Avery (Aristides 1833, 63), and that Benjamin Sanders could testify to a continuing correspondence between Sarah Cornell and a minister in Bristol in the months preceding the Thompson camp meeting (Aristides 1833, 75).

Although Aristides did manage to uncover one piece of damaging gossip about Avery—that he was thought to have made indecent advances to a Miss Lippitt while stationed at Pomfret (*Republican Herald*, 4 December 1833), the primary thrust of his argument turned increasingly toward what he considered the shameless manipulation of the trial process by the Methodist church. His vague assertions of witness tampering (Aristides 1833, 44, 80) became concrete on October 23, when he published Sarah Jones's account of her experiences as a witness (*Republican Herald*, 23 October 1833). Still suffering the disdain of the Portsmouth Methodist community, who warned visitors not to believe anything she might say (Williams 1833, 154), Mrs. Jones probably contacted the *Republican Herald*—or responded to the newspaper's initiative—in a last attempt to salvage her good name. The story she recounted asserted that it was the pack of Methodists, not she, who were the liars. She was treated very well, she said, when first brought to confer with Avery and his lawyers, but when her story did not correspond with the minister's, Avery followed her to the entry of his house, laid a hand on her shoulder, and implored, "Can't you recollect it was in the afternoon? Mrs. Jones, my life is worth a thousand worlds to me; *but, say nothing about this*" (*Republican Herald*, 23 October 1833). Thus, she claimed, began the Methodist campaign to change her testimony, a campaign that ultimately involved Avery, Nathaniel Bullock, William Simmons—who was Bullock's agent— the Reverend Samuel Drake, and the entire Portsmouth congregation. Her unsatisfactory testimony at Bristol brought down upon her the general disdain of her fellow church members, and it was not until the minister had been bound over for trial in Newport, where her testimony would be vital, that the situation changed. Though her legitimate trial expenses at Bristol had been seventy-two cents, suddenly in March Avery's counsel sent her three dollars as "legal fees." The bribe was followed by a summons to appear in Newport, where she was lodged with other Methodist witnesses, among whom she saw Louisa Whitney, who testified that the clove hitch was commonly used in weaving rooms, diligently trying to learn to make the knot (*Republican Herald*, 23 October 1833). Repelled by the manifest perfidy around her, Mrs. Jones left the Methodist boardinghouse and had since been the subject of continuing Methodist persecution.

The Methodists had been aware since the Bristol hearing that their reputation was linked to Avery's, and that their every move had drawn them closer to him. They could not have been surprised, then, when the *Literary Subaltern* reported early in September that public anger seemed to be turning away from Avery in particular and toward the Methodist church in general (*Literary Subaltern*, 7 September 1833). A month earlier, the *Subaltern* had concluded that "it was something like infatuation in the Methodist Conference and the Methodist paper to have joined in common cause with Mr. Avery," and suggested:

> [Instead they] should have said to Mr. Avery, if they examined him at all—"Inasmuch as the country has acquitted you of legal liabilities, from the difficulties, as your prosecutors allege, of finding direct testimony, you must therefore prove your innocence by supplying facts voluntarily, under your implied obligations as an honest man and a christian" (*Literary Subaltern*, 2 August 1833).

Other papers were more emphatic. Predictably, James Ford's *Fall River Monitor* proclaimed that "the public will never fellowship a murderer, and every attempt to force them to it will increase the excitement and strengthen the public aversion to the man and his advisors" (*Fall River Monitor*, 21 September 1833). Further, he wrote:

> It will be many a long year before the unwarrantable and unprecedented proceedings of the Conference will be forgotten. It has fixed a stain upon that body and brought reproach upon the whole order, which will take ages to wipe away. And never can the memory of Avery cease to be execrated while time shall last, and history retains any evidence of his suspected guilt (*Fall River Monitor*, 9 November 1833).

It was also predictable that the tenacious Aristides should assume the journalistic lead in attacking the Methodist organization. The final chapter of his *Strictures*, written as an open letter to the New England Conference, berated the Methodists soundly for their endeavors to free Avery and, that accomplished, to reinstate him on the pulpit (Aristides 1833, 93–97). "Gentlemen," he concluded, "I now take my leave of you for the present, perhaps, forever," but it was little more than a month later when he began a new series of articles for the *Republican Herald* entitled "The Methodist Church—Its Government, Its Discipline, And Its Influence" (*Republican Herald*, 16 October 1833). Published over the next month in four installments, Aristides' argument was probably the clearest and best sustained—if, according to one critic, not necessarily the most accurate (*Republican Herald*, 16 November 1833)—attack on the Methodist organization printed that fall. Aristides wrote:

> Christianity [is] outraged, and its pretensions falsified, when those who advocate her doctrines, make use of every means in their power to obtain a preponderating influence in the affairs of state, to convert its powers into instruments of their own aggrandisement, ask for privileges they would withhold from others, and make the laws subservient to their particular views (*Republican Herald*, 16 October 1833).

Speaking of the Methodists and their attempts to preserve Avery's social position, Aristides contended that "It is not religion of which the people complain; it is the foreign garb in which fanaticism has arrayed her" (*Republican Herald*, 16 October 1833). The Methodist church, he said, was organized on the "great principle of despotism" (*Republican Herald*, 20 October 1833) and resulted in an unnatural, antirepublican arrangement in which the lives of many were controlled by the dictates of a few. Just as individual congregations were deprived of the ability to choose their own ministers, Aristides argued that they were made subservient to the interests and ambitions of the Methodist central government. That government, unlike the federal establishment in the United States, was not answerable to the community at large, which had no part in its election (*Republican Herald*, 30 October 1833). The Methodist mode of government, Aristides implied, was inimical to a free society.

Unchecked by internal controls, the Methodist hierarchy was to Aristides a corporate body with almost unlimited potential power. The Avery affair seemed only a prelude to the Methodists' future attempts to control public justice. Fearing that the Methodists had ambitions to convert their social influence into political preferment, Aristides warned that they were "building up a power that will soon allow them to do so, a power that no religious sect has ever failed to wield for the promotion of their own views, when obtained" (*Republican Herald*, 16 November 1833). With their power increasing daily, both in numbers of people involved and amounts of wealth stored up, what effect might the Methodists have on the political future of Rhode Island and, indeed, the nation?

While Aristides pursued the Methodists through the pages of the *Republican Herald*, two more publications were being prepared to add to the attack on Avery. The first, a lithographic tour de force produced by David Melvill of Newport that appeared in mid-

November (*New England Galaxy*, 16 November 1833), reproduced the letters offered in evidence at Avery's trial (Melvill 1833). Theoretically a neutral document designed to let the public compare handwriting, Melvill's pamphlet included a helpful list of points of comparison by which readers could convince themselves that Avery was the author of the disputed letters.

The second, perhaps the most ambitious attempt of the year, was the work of novelist and poet Catharine Read Arnold Williams. In 1833 Williams was forty-six years old, divorced, and a fledgling author who had turned to the pen for support only after she was forced to abandon teaching in Providence because of ill health. An avowed enemy of "priestcraft"—perhaps because of the overly strict religious upbringing she had endured at the hands of two maiden aunts—and naturally sympathetic to the plight of a working woman, Williams was hardly an impartial reporter. Though she asserted that the identity of the person who proposed that she write a book about the trial was of "no consequence" (Williams 1833, 3), it was probably one of the Fall River Committee, for she enjoyed remarkable cooperation when she spent a week in Fall River at the beginning of July (Williams 1833, 73). She toured the town's factories, interviewed more than three hundred people (Williams 1833, 11), and was introduced—probably by mail—to Nancy and Grindall Rawson, from whom she acquired a file of letters that Sarah Cornell had written home.

The only thing denied to Catharine Williams was time; for her book to gain wide distribution—and if she was working to support the committee by producing a propaganda weapon—it had to appear quickly. For this reason, when *Fall River, An Authentic Narrative* was published late in 1833 it appeared disjointed, part semifiction, part journalism, part transcription of records, and part partisan argument against Avery. It was, however, sufficiently readable to go into a second edition in 1834, and it provided an admirable defense of the Fall River Committee's position.

The book owed its success to two things. First, it collected most of the history of Ephraim Avery, Sarah Cornell, and the trial into a loosely chronological narrative in which the welter of confusing, often contradictory information was resolved into an intelligible story. Second, and much more important, she addressed the basic question that had kept the two sides of the controversy battling: Who was responsible for the moral decline, and thus the death, of Sarah Cornell?

Was it the manufacturing community of Fall River? At the very outset of her book, Williams made it clear that that could not possibly be the case. Describing the town's dramatic economic development since 1812 and linking it to the "character for bravery, generosity, and independence of mind" that its present inhabitants had inherited from their revolutionary predecessors (who had fought the Battle of Fall River against a handful of British soldiers sent from Newport to destroy the gristmill), she embedded the community in the highest mythic tradition of the country. "Among all the changes which the increase of population causes," she reported, "the primitive virtues of simplicity and hospitality are still eminently conspicuous. Whoever goes to reside there seems to adopt readily the manners of the inhabitants. Even the labouring part of the community in the manufactories, as well as in other departments, is positively distinguished by a degree of refinement and courtesy of manners" (Williams 1833, 10–11). In a community of such high tone, even the seemingly oppressive work of the mills became benevolent. Williams wrote:

> I shall always recollect with pleasure one little incident in one of the weaving rooms of the manufactory, where the noise was very distracting arising from a vast number of looms going at once. The machinery suddenly stopped, and a strain of music arose simultaneously from every part of the room, in such perfect concord that I at first thought it was a chime of bells. My conductor smiled when I asked him if it were not, and pointed to the girls, who each kept their station until they had sung the tune through (Williams 1833, 11).

Could this be the environment that bred moral decay, crime, and death? Nothing could be more unjust, said Williams, than such a belief. There was, in fact, no better place for grown girls to work— no better environment and certainly no better wages. That there were a few bad girls in the mills was undoubtedly true, but they were assiduously hunted out and expelled, "that is, where they had no meeting to shelter them—where backslidings and recoveries, expulsion and reinstation, were a common thing" (Williams 1833, 196).

The factories and Fall River were faultless; more than that, they were admirable. It was the girl's religion that had failed her. Williams hoped that her book would serve as a "salutary and timely warning" to young women in Sarah Cornell's station that would put them on guard against the "baneful disposition to rove" and "that idolatrous regard for ministers, for preachers of the gospel, which at the present day is a scandal to the cause of christianity" (Williams 1833, 4). Fanatic devotion to ministers, particularly to those of weak mind who were unable to withstand the pressures and temptations of flattery (an obvious slap at the less than intellectual tradition of the Methodist clergy), could have no beneficial result. It was this, thought Williams, that led Sarah Cornell, converted by the personal energy of Edward Taylor, charmed by the foppish attractions of John Maffitt, and finally seduced by the authority of Ephraim Avery, to her demise.

If idolized ministers who could not resist the possibilities of their position were the wolves that young women had to fear, camp meetings were to Williams their most fruitful hunting grounds. Separated from their relations, thrown into the company of "drunkards and gamblers, and horse jockies and pickpockets, and offenders of every other description" (Williams 1833, 168) without adequate protection, their own natural reserve shattered by fatigue and tumult, women at the camp meetings could more readily find personal disaster than religious fulfillment. Williams ended *Fall River, An Authentic Narrative* with a lengthy appendix describing her impressions of a camp meeting, by which she hoped to make clear the environment that had led to Sarah Cornell's fall. The excitement and confusion she observed seemed to have nothing to do with religion.

> The first object that met our eyes upon coming within the barrier was a young woman of extreme beauty, who was staggering through the camp, with her clothes torn and her locks dishevelled, wringing her hands and mourning that the people were not more engaged. She was a girl of about middling height, rather fat, with large, languishing black eyes, and a profusion of raven hair which floated on her shoulders and reached below her waist, with the fairest complexion that could be imagined. She appeared to excite great attention whenever she moved through the crowd. We observed, as she passed along, that the young men exchanged winks and jogged each others elbows (Williams 1833, 177).

Later Williams saw the same girl, swooned in what others told her was religious ecstasy, in a tent where three young men hovered in close attention (Williams 1833, 185). If the open fate of such dissolute creatures were not sufficient, even respectable women were not safe. There was constant pinching, joggling, and looking under

18. An idealized version of a New England Methodist camp meeting.
From James Mudge, *History of the New England Conference of the Methodist Episcopal Church 1796–1910* (Boston: The Conference, 1910).

bonnets in the crowds that left some pretty girls with black and blue arms and every reasonably intelligent woman with the conviction that she had better not close her eyes when praying in public.

The contrast between the pleasant harmony of Fall River's factories, where well-ordered young women worked under the benevolent protection of men schooled in the healthful mental discipline of their forefathers, and the chaos of the camp meeting, where the regular structure of society was shattered and its fragments collected or dispersed at the whim of conceited but inferior minds, made it clear where the fault in Sarah Cornell's death must lie. More than any specific argument about a point of testimony, more than any deposition by a new witness, it was this comparison that was compelling. Combined with traditional perceptions of female character, it resolved the ambiguities of the case—and resolved them in favor of Fall River.

Though the hostile press had continued to pour out articles, pamphlets, and books denouncing him, Avery's silence since September had resulted in a virtual end to public demonstrations against him, making it difficult for Methodists to gauge the level of actual public resentment that remained. Consequently, early in December it was decided that he should attempt a short speaking tour. On the twelfth, Avery, his wife, and their infant child arrived

in Saugus. When no public outcry erupted, he preached two sermons on the following Sunday, both obviously related to his recent
history. In the morning the text was from Proverbs 14:26: "In the
fear of the Lord is strong confidence; and his children shall have a
place of refuge." In the afternoon, he spoke from Psalms 1:15:
"And call upon me in the day of trouble; I will deliver thee, and
thou shall glorify me." Both sermons were attended by large, orderly crowds. Trouble was reported in neighboring Lynn, where an
effigy was burned, but it was discounted as the work of boys and
drunks, who at the same time had similarly honored a temperance
leader (*New England Christian Herald*, 25 December 1833).

Saugus, however, was only a prelude to what would be the real
test: a sermon in Lowell. If Avery could preach successfully there,
to a congregation made up predominantly of mill girls, then the
New England Conference might reasonably hope to bring him to
any pulpit in the region—at least, to any pulpit except that in Fall
River.

Avery arrived in Lowell on Tuesday, December 17. His welcome was apparently less than hearty, but no overt displays of public hostility dissuaded him from remaining in town. On Saturday it
was announced that he would preach on the following day; within
hours, he had been burned in effigy on the commons. Although
the question of public acceptance was, for all intents, settled by that
act, he remained determined to preach. Fearful of an unfriendly
mob in and about the church, Avery allowed the minister on the
circuit to announce Sunday morning that his plans to preach that
afternoon had been canceled; thus no demonstration was organized and the church was filled with none other than the usual congregation when Avery appeared at the pulpit, officiating as he had
originally planned. If he could carry off his secret public appearance and leave without incident, Avery might claim a friendly reception and gain a valuable propaganda victory for himself and his
church. Word of his subterfuge, however, quickly leaked out and a
large mob gathered to begin a rowdy search of prominent Methodists' houses in hopes of finding the refuge to which Avery had retired after completing his service. Fortunately for the unloved
preacher the mob was unsuccessful, but when dawn broke the next
day, an effigy of Sarah Cornell was found hung on the town commons, flanked by a stack of hay and a black-robed effigy of Avery
(*New England Galaxy*, 4 January 1834). This time there was no mention of drunks and children; the community was up in arms and it

was clear that a successful ministry for Avery in industrial New England was impossible.

In January, probably prompted by the unqualified failure of Avery's attempt to return to Lowell and his subsequent silence, a rumor surfaced in Maine that the New England Conference had prohibited him from further preaching (*Zion's Herald*, 22 January 1834). It was exceedingly embarrassing for the New England Conference in that a Methodist publication, the *Maine Wesleyan Journal*, was spreading the rumor; seemingly, the conference had repudiated the unpopular minister when, in fact, it was on the verge of publishing its defense of him. The way to stop the story was clear; Avery was requested to give a sermon in Boston at the Bennett Street church where he had always been well received. Accordingly, he made the trip and preached on January 26 (*Zion's Herald*, 5 February 1834, 26).

The conference had set the stage for the presentation of a final explanation of Avery's involvement with Sarah Cornell, but had not considered that a publication other than its own might be issued. No sooner had the minister returned home from Boston than a small pamphlet that purported to be his confession appeared in the streets of New York. The Methodists, with good reason, were outraged at the forgery, printed Avery's repudiation of it, and assured the public that the minister's real work, his *Vindication*, would be available in a few days. "If this *unparalleled wickedness* will not awake public indignation against the malign miscreants who are seeking the ruin of this abused and insulted man," asserted the *Zion's Herald* (5 February 1834), the successor to the *New England Christian Herald*, "we know not what will."

The forgery was clever; the first word of its title, *Explanation*, was sufficiently similar to *Vindication* to ensure confusion with Avery's real work, and it used constructions, like the interjection "alas!," that the public had come to associate with the minister. Although admitting that the prosecution's case against him was substantially correct—that he had seduced Sarah Cornell, had been in correspondence with her over the ensuing pregnancy, and had met her on the night of December 20—the counterfeit Avery was made to claim that the court's verdict was correct; he was technically innocent of murder. Sarah, he said, had died while he attempted abortion as a result of the "general shock given to the nervous system" (Pseudo-Avery 1834, 14) during the operation, but he had never intended her demise. Like Catharine Williams and Aristides, the pamphlet's author portrayed Sarah Cornell as a victim, a woman whose only crime was fanatic devotion to her minister, her admissions to other affairs and venereal disease being nothing more than "generous sacrifices" designed to give Avery an ironclad defense against charges of adultery (Pseudo-Avery 1834, 8). Avery, on the other hand, appeared as a cold exploiter who was willing to accept her sacrifice and to exonerate himself of her murder on the flimsiest pretext.

The counterfeit confession had one major flaw; it made Avery assert that by the time of publication he would have taken a new name and fled to the west, when in fact he was still in Bristol. Still, given public expectations, it was a fairly plausible production, and the Methodists could not be sure that the public would recognize its falsity. They could only hope that the patent superiority of argument in their *Vindication*, combined with its far more extensive distribution, would swamp the forgery's momentary impression.

Their preparations gave them every reason to believe they would be successful. On February 12 the *Vindication* was offered for sale in Boston and simultaneously released by agents in Providence, New York, Philadelphia, Baltimore, Cincinnati, Springfield, Concord (New Hampshire), Portland, Hallowell (Maine), Bangor, and Cazenovia (New York) (*Zion's Herald*, 12 February 1834). Within a month, seven thousand copies had been sold (*Zion's Herald*, 19 March 1834), and the New England Conference could be satisfied that they were to have a reasonable hearing.

The *Vindication* was a long, laborious pamphlet, a compilation of three distinct documents. The first was Avery's own description of his relation to Sarah Cornell (the statement first given to Justices Howe and Haile), of his excursion to the island on the day of her death, and of his experiences during captivity and trial. Recognizing that a catalogue of sufferings might elicit sympathy where simple renewed protestations of innocence could actually amplify disbelief, Timothy Merritt had advised Avery that his narrative "should exhibit a frank & undisguised state of your mind as circumstances turned up from day to day" (Merritt 1833). Consequently, the minister focused on an emotional history of his troubles, recounting his solicitude for his fellow preachers, for whom his "heart bled" (Avery 1834, 18), his family, for whom "his heart was excessively pained," and the church, for whom his soul was "pierced . . . with many sorrows" (Avery 1834, 20). Responding directly to the critics of the New England Conference's involvement in the trial, Avery asserted that his comfort had not come from his presiding elder, who informed him of "his most fervent wish that the truth should come to light, however painful it might be to bear" (Avery 1834, 19), but from the grace of God that he felt showered on him in his cell at Newport. Avery thus gave his rendition of the story, sought public sympathy for his sufferings, and denied that the conference had any dishonest intent in the handling of his case.

The second document, authored by Timothy Merritt and Joseph Merrill, formed the bulk of the pamphlet and bore the lion's share of the argument. "The design of the following pages," they wrote, "is to support the decision in his case by a brief analysis of the testimony at his trial, and to strengthen this by the addition of new evidence" (Avery 1834, 3). Like Aristides, whom they castigated as a monster who "dipped his pen in gall" (Avery 1834, 3) and "loves darkness rather than light, because his deed [*sic*] are evil" (Avery 1834, 27), Avery's defenders had assiduously collected affadavits to support their argument. Though their analysis of the trial's evidence was persuasive, these certificates gave their work its best chance of success.

Most of the statements that the Methodists had collected were rebuttals to what Avery's critics—usually Aristides—had charged. Aristides claimed that Asa Upham could swear that he had seen Avery and Sarah Cornell together at Thompson but had bowed to Methodist pressure not to testify; Merritt and Merrill produced two certificates by witnesses to whom Upham had admitted he was wrong (Avery 1834, 39–40). Aristides implied that Avery had bought pink paper in James Snow's store in Providence on the morning of November 27; Merritt and Merrill provided Snow's statement that he had not (Avery 1834, 43). Aristides offered certificates that Nathan Spencer had said the pink letter was not the same color as the one he claimed to have delivered to the *King Philip*; Merritt and Merrill provided statements that he had not (Avery 1834, 50). Aristides claimed that David Davol, who had testified that Peleg Cranston had told him that Avery had not passed his bridge on December 20, later admitted that he was mistaken; Merritt and Merrill provided Davol's statement that he still believed his testimony to be "perfectly correct" (Avery 1834, 61). The argument that Jane Gifford had been expelled and harassed by the Methodists because of her testimony at Avery's trial was denied by a certificate from two Portsmouth Methodists who swore that she had been expelled from the church in 1831 (when she was fifteen) for being "in the habit of illegal intercourse with men" (Avery 1834, 60). The accuracy of Avery's description of the country he crossed during his Rhode Island excursion was upheld by the statements of seven men (Avery 1834, 8, 62−63).

It was an impressive display that strengthened the Methodist position, but left an important question unanswered: Why, if Avery were innocent, did the weight of circumstance seem to bear so heavily against him? Merritt and Merrill's answer, again supported by affidavits, was to claim that there had been a "deep-laid" plot to make Avery appear guilty (Avery 1834, 56). Justice John Howe wrote to Joseph Merrill—and the letter was subsequently published in the *Vindication*—that he had met a man on the Boston stage a few days after the conclusion of Avery's examination in Bristol who claimed to have seen the minister crossing Slade's ferry (the other route between Bristol and Fall River) on the night of the twentieth. The same story had already been told to him, Howe went on, on Christmas day of 1832 (when Bristol was swarming with men from Fall River) by a man who, when informed that Avery had been proven to have crossed Gifford's ferry, turned to his companion and cried "Worse and worse!" (Avery 1834, 57). The implication was clearly that someone was seeking to create a perjured witness who could place Avery at the scene of the murder. A letter received by Avery while jailed in Newport that offered to prove his innocence for a fee (Avery 1834, 58−59) pointed in the same direction. Only someone connected with a plot to subvert justice, Merritt and Merrill argued, would be in a position to prove the accused man's innocence and be unwilling to do so without pay.

The third section of the *Vindication* was Wilbur Fisk's meticulous review of the evidence concerning Avery's whereabouts on December 20. Fisk's computations led him to conclude that Avery, "if he was the man at the stack-yard at sunset, had travelled from Bristol town since two o'clock, a distance of twelve miles, in little more than two hours, had a weak ankle, wore a coat and a surtout, and travelled, on his return, in the night; and yet he must have accomplished the whole in fifty-three minutes!!" (Avery 1834, 72). It was too absurd, said Fisk, to be believed.

The *Vindication* did everything that the New England Conference could hope. It cleared the church of any wrongdoing in its defense of the minister, responded strongly and convincingly to his journalistic critics, demonstrated how the testimony of the trial pointed clearly to his innocence, and rejuvenated the conspiracy theory as an alternative explanation for Sarah Cornell's death. The Methodists had only to wait to see if it would silence their critics or precipitate yet another round of debates.

What followed its publication was an unearthly calm. Whether it was the product of exhaustion or merely the eye of a storm in which wary opponents watched suspiciously for new signs of hostility was uncertain. The Methodists published a final deposition in March, claiming that Aristides' assertion that Jason Phipps had been kept from testifying at Avery's trial by Joseph Merrill and William Livesay was not true (*Zion's Herald*, 5 March 1834, 38), but they refrained from bringing Avery back to the pulpit, the act that had previously elicited a strong response. In the uneasy spring months, Avery's continued silence gave new fuel to the story that the conference had banned his preaching (*Zion's Herald*, 26 February 1834, 34; 26 March 1834, 50). The rumor was denied, and Avery was advised by members of neighboring conferences to continue preaching lest his withdrawal appear to be an admission of guilt; nonetheless, though there had been no official directive that he give up the pulpit, some of his fellow preachers had privately advised that he do so (*Zion's Herald*, 26 March 1834, 50). Having had what seemed to be the last word, they were anxious that nothing be done to rekindle a flame that was at last on the verge of burning itself out.

When the Methodists' annual conference was held that July, Avery demonstrated that he had accepted the cautious advice of his fellows by asking that he be left without an appointment for the coming year. His departure, however, was not entirely without debate. When Avery sought to gain financial relief from the conference, he found himself violently opposed by his previous comrade, Ira Bidwell. The confrontation seems to have been the final chapter in the disintegration of their friendship. As early as mid-July of the previous year, Bidwell had written to the editor of the Newport *Rhode Island Republican* (24 July 1833) that he was willing to "leave Mr. Avery to answer to the world" without his aid, and it was easy to understand why he hoped to distance himself from the controversy. As the Methodist minister of Fall River, he was buffeted by intense hostility not only emotionally but also financially when defecting members of the congregation reduced the offerings on which his salary depended. To compound his difficulties, although he was never suspected of complicity in the crime by any legal authority, Bidwell had been questioned about his actions on December 20 (Borden 1833) and was forced to tolerate the Fall River gossips who claimed he was "as guilty as Avery" (Bidwell 1839). It was small wonder that his patience with Avery had worn thin when the two met at the 1834 annual conference.

Avery never again was stationed in the New England Conference. His decision not to request an appointment at the 1834 annual conference was amplified in 1835, when he was listed as a supernumerary, and as such was temporarily removed from the rolls of its active members (New England Annual Conference 1835, 4). He almost certainly returned to Richmond, Massachusetts, after the 1834 conference; a year later he was aiding the New York Conference minister in whose district Richmond fell (Griffen 1836). To support his family, Avery became a carpenter and, following that trade, he lived quietly in Richmond until at least 1850. Ironically, late in life he did "escape" to the west, taking up his last residence on a farm in Pittsfield Township, Lorain County, Ohio.

In 1837, the New England Conference dropped his name permanently from its roster, noting that he had "located," that is, settled in one community and taken up other employment (Whittaker 1912, 204). No longer assigned to a circuit by the church, and no longer in its employ, Avery had not lost his certificate to preach. By locating, he had relieved the church of his support and avoided the problems that might have arisen from his continuing ministry in New England, without admitting either guilt or defeat.

Conclusion

Daniel Mowry's *Daily Advertiser and American* was one of the first casualties of the Avery excitement. On February 1, 1833, he ceased publication, claiming that he could not contend against "priest-craft" alone (*Daily Advertiser and American*, 1 February 1833). With his readership defecting after rabid criticism of Ephraim Avery, the Methodist Episcopal church, and Justices Howe and Haile, Mowry found the *Advertiser* a liability. Fortunately, he also published the *Microcosm*, which he planned to send to all his paid subscribers— but without sanguine expectations. "If any wish to discontinue," he wrote, "they will signify it by returning the papers" (*Daily Advertiser and American*, 1 February 1833).

Mowry was not the only individual to have his life changed by the events of Sarah Cornell's death and Ephraim Avery's trial. Justices John Howe and Levi Haile, for their part in the Avery affair, were widely accused of incompetence, partiality, and—by infer-ence—dishonesty. The extent of the damage to their reputations is hard to assess, but the intensity of the attack they weathered from the public press was great. As late as 1961, Howe's great-grandson was still trying to sort out the facts of the case (Howe 1961).

Many Methodist ministers found 1833 and 1834 particularly hard years. Some, previously inured to the public antagonism directed at their ideology or supposed organizational affinity to

Freemasonry, were unprepared to be addressed as "damned murderers" (Avery 1834, 26). Ira Bidwell, stationed at Fall River, found the population hostile and suspicious and had to live in a community where some openly believed him to be the protector of a murderer and an accomplice in the crime. Even when he left Fall River, the onus of the Avery affair followed him (Bidwell 1839). Four years after the trial, the Methodists still found it "inexpedient" to station a minister who had been deeply involved in Avery's defense at Fall River (Webb 1837).

Charles True's Bristol congregation was divided and ultimately fragmented by the controversy when part of the flock rejected Avery and the episcopal government that supported him. Described as "pestulent and pugnacious" by some of those who did not defect (Upham 1891, 84), Bristol's "Reformed Methodists" established a congregational form of government similar to that represented by Avery's earlier opponent, the Reverend Thomas Norris.

Asa Kent, stationed at Newport, was thrust into the controversy when Avery was imprisoned there in February 1833. Almost immediately, more than half of his congregation disappeared as reports damaging to the Methodist church were circulated (Worth 1888; Mudge 1910, 231). Those who did not defect were intimidated by the jeers and threats that followed them to meeting. Only one man, Jeremiah Hazard, was steadfast in his support of the church and his minister. Although Asa Kent received $470 for his two years at Newport, the trial drove his expenses far beyond that and the excess had to be made up out of his private resources (Worth 1888). The end of Avery's trial was only the beginning of Kent's castigation in the Newport *Rhode Island Republican* (3 July 1833); with his financial and social position tenuous, his congregation scattered and intimidated, and his church reviled by many as an antidemocratic institution, Kent patiently set about the difficult task of rebuilding.

For the New England Conference as a whole, the Avery affair required sacrifice and endurance. Kent, appointed by the conference as its agent to settle the expenses of the trial, spent three years wrestling with the problem. In July 1836 he finally reported that he had "with great difficulty brought the business to a close" (Kent 1836). Unexpected and unprecedented lawyers' fees, he wrote, had involved the conference in "pecuniary embarrassment, & filled our Zion with indescribable affliction." Nathaniel Bullock offered his services to the conference gratuitously, but other lawyers were not so generous. Mason, who originally set his fee at five hundred dollars, demanded two thousand after the trial consumed more time than he had anticipated. Negotiations at the conference's 1833 annual meeting settled his account at fifteen hundred dollars. Unfortunately, Richard Randolf had heard the two-thousand-dollar figure from Mason and was determined to receive fifteen hundred himself. Joseph Blake, also after consultation with Mason, demanded one thousand dollars. The matter was finally settled by Nathaniel Bullock, who as a disinterested party trusted by both the conference and the lawyers was allowed to set the fees. Randolf received a thousand dollars, and Blake received five hundred. Henry Cranston and George Turner, who had taken notes during the trial, were each offered seventy-five dollars. Cranston accepted, but Turner countered with a bill for one hundred and forty dollars. After an attempt at compromise failed, Turner was given seventy-five dollars and his further demands ignored. Including an extra hundred and fifty dollars to Randolf for his work at the Bristol hearing, and almost two hundred dollars for travel during the trial, the lawyers received over three thousand dollars (Kent 1836). With the combined costs of legal assistance, of ministers' expenses in at-

19. Fall River from across Mount Hope Bay. The Durfee farm, where Sarah Cornell was found hung, lies south of the village. From John Warren Barber, *Historical Collections* . . . (Worchester: Warren Lazell, 1839).

tending the trial, and of fees paid to witnesses whose testimony had been solicited, some estimates of the defense's total expenditure ran as high as ten thousand dollars (Mudge 1910, 200).

The New England Conference, at its 1833 and 1834 meetings, subscribed a total of $1,767 toward trial expenses. Their sacrifice was an example followed by the New York, Philadelphia, Baltimore, Washington, Alexandria, Maine, New Hampshire, Troy, and Oneida and Genessee conferences, which pledged an additional $3,156. With these funds, and apparently aided by a firm resolve to pay no more than necessary, Kent was able to pay all the creditors who had presented him with bills up to 1836. Mentioning that demands were still coming in, Kent reported that all his funds had been expended, and he asked that the conference cancel his agency and consider the matter financially closed (Kent 1836).

However difficult the period might have been for Methodist clergymen and their church, they probably suffered no more than the private individuals who were caught up in the events of the trial and its aftermath. The extent to which idle suspicion and unlikely speculation gained credence in Fall River during the excitement is amply illustrated by Dr. Thomas Wilbur's offer to publish an alibi for himself for the night of the murder (Bidwell 1839). If the doctor felt threatened, how insecure might less prominent citizens feel? Sarah Jones, whose testimony had been sought by both sides, lost her position in—and the good will of—the Portsmouth Methodist community. If her loss was adequately compensated by a new position in Borden's cotton mill at Fall River, Jane Gifford, the ferryman's daughter, was not as fortunate. For her, testimony at Avery's Bristol hearing and Newport trial led to a public debate about her honesty. It is not hard to imagine a long period of strained relations in Portsmouth as the assertions of lax moral character made at the trial were remembered in ensuing months. Other witnesses shared a similar fate as they heard themselves contradicted by neighbors, relatives, and friends. Annis Norton, who thought she saw Avery walking north in Tiverton on the twentieth, Peleg Cranston, the gatekeeper at Howland's bridge, and Mary D. Borden, all became targets of minor controversies that inevitably must have caused friction and realigned friendships long after the trial.

In Bristol, where the "Christmas invasion" directed by the Fall River Committee had produced strong factions on both sides, the controversy carried over into politics. Ichabod Davis, a local representative to the state legislature, an alienated Methodist, and a firm believer in Avery's guilt, was accused of producing and suspending one of the minister's effigies found hanging in Bristol in the days following his acquittal. Davis's effigy, inopportunely hung from the rafters of the Episcopal church then under construction in Bristol, naturally turned the outrage of the community's Episcopalians toward him and momentarily redirected anti-Avery feelings toward the unfortunate politician. When his guilt in the matter had been satisfactorily established, Davis felt the power of traditional New England methods of indicating communal displeasure; openly insulted in the street, he found his business in a disastrous decline and his house "besmeared with filth" (*Providence Journal*, 1 January 1883). Turned out of his political office in August, Davis soon sold his Bristol holdings and moved to Pennsylvania.

For Grindall Rawson the trial struck at familial and communal bonds. The only man present at the trial who was specifically accused of having had sexual intercourse with the allegedly promiscuous murdered woman, Rawson must have found composure difficult to maintain as he watched his wife listen to stories of his infidelity. Catharine Williams later questioned Lucretia Rawson about the effect of the trial on her marriage. Lucretia reportedly answered:

> Had I been at all addicted to jealousy, or had the least cause to be so, or possessed as weak a mind as they imputed to my sister, what might not the consequences have been. They might have broken up my family and perhaps driven me to distraction or suicide, but to disturb my peace in that way is beyond their power (Williams 1833, 65).

No matter how strong Lucretia's faith in Grindall, the nationwide assertion that he was an adulterer could not have failed to test their marriage.

These negative effects were not the trial's only product. Albert C. Greene, though he lost the case, was widely praised for having conducted the trial admirably. In June 1833 his brother Elihu wrote from Cincinnati that he had "witnessed with honest pride and pleasure the reputation & honor Albert had reaped in the management of Avery's trial" (E. Greene 1833). For Jeremiah Mason, whose reputation was already firmly established in civil law, the trial provided a rare opportunity to demonstrate his ability in a sensational criminal case (Clark 1917, 360).

Fall River's industrialists also benefited from their participation in the trial. Sarah's murder and the alleged circumstances of her life provided a potentially disastrous contradiction to the ideological position on which the manufacturers depended for their labor supply and a favorable legislative environment. Fortunately, by turning public attention toward Avery and the Methodist church, the manufacturers were able to sidestep responsibility for Sarah's deviance and death. Labeling the Methodists as radicals with philosophies of both government and salvation that were dangerous innovations, the manufacturers reinforced their association with good morals and traditional society by working within the bounds of time-honored institutions. It was Orin Fowler, a Congregationalist minister, who preached Sarah's funeral sermon. It was the Congregationalist church that housed two of the public meetings of the Fall River Committee, and a soon-to-be Congregational deacon who chaired one. The structure, composition, and operation of the committee were patterned on the town meeting as the basis for governmental action, and the close ties of the committee with the attorney general gave it a further semblance of legitimacy. As the nullification crisis was giving American manufacturers the opportunity to identify themselves with the preservation of the Union, so the Avery case allowed Fall River's manufacturing community to express its allegiance to New England's traditions.

This entrenchment in traditional social forms, combined with an effective barrage of pro-industry, anti-Methodism propaganda—culminated in Catharine Williams's *Fall River*—insured that Sarah Cornell's murder would provide scant ammunition for those who thought to question the propriety of factory labor. The battle had been successfully fought, and Fall River's textile industry continued to grow unchecked for another four years, until the nationwide panic of 1837 brought economic rather than ideological hard times (Lamb 1935).

The Methodists, though they won the court case, fared worse in the months that followed. Mistrust of their enthusiasm and centralized government coalesced after the trial, leading to defection, schism, and social antagonism, but while church leaders agonized over their troubles in Bristol, Newport, and Fall River, the damage to their organization was neither as widespread or irreparable as they feared. The New England Conference grew by fewer than 100 communicants in 1833, reaching barely over 15,600 members, but 1834 saw the healthy addition of 1,700 (Mudge 1910, 453). In the

same way that the industrialists managed to avoid responsibility for
Sarah Cornell's career, the Methodists were able to recover their
position. The opening of Wesleyan University in September 1831
had already provided the basis for an answer to the charge that the
passions of Methodist ministers were unbridled by a developed intellect; enthusiasm was thus compromised with the intellectual tradition of Congregational New England, and it was easy to find
other more radical and threatening groups to oppose. Quick to
seek out a common enemy, the Methodists claimed that the assault
against them was part of a larger scheme to destroy all organized
religion in America, and the fate of Daniel Mowry's *Daily Advertiser
and American* demonstrated how many people were willing to believe
them. In the years that followed, by establishing themselves strongly
against radical religion—the Universalists and Unitarians—(and,
for some, by joining the rising abolitionist movement), the Methodists were able to unite with the community against other groups
whose ideologies were more threatening to New Englanders' per-
ception of an acceptable social order. Thus, while they suffered a
momentary defeat at the hands of the Fall River industrialists in
1833, in other battles soon to follow the Methodists proved capable
of supporting and, finally, becoming part of New England's traditional culture.

Avery, of course, was a liability to the church, which could
neither abandon him with honor nor maintain him with credit.
His graceful withdrawal to Richmond, where he became an
unofficial aide to a New York Conference minister, was a perfect
solution to the New England Conference's problem. They had
not bowed to public pressure by expelling him, yet he would no
longer be present to stir up further contention. When he finally
moved to Lorain County, Ohio, bordering on Lake Erie just west of
Cleveland, the controversy was long behind him, and he was able to
find a degree of acceptance and success in a profession—farming—
that he had always tried to avoid. Though he was certainly not a
wealthy man when he died, on October 23, 1869, he had sufficient
resources to be able to afford some luxuries. Among his prosaic
wagons, his estate listed a two-horse sleigh and a carriage, both
valued at ninety dollars. His personal estate was valued at four
hundred and fifty dollars, and he was owed another thirteen hundred and sixty. Though there was a mortgage on ten acres of his
land, that was paid off soon after his death. The estate was sufficiently endowed to provide his widow, Sophia, seven hundred dol-

lars for her support in the year following her husband's demise (Lorain County Probate Court 1869).

For Sarah Cornell there was no second chance. After the second autopsy her mutilated body was returned to the unmarked grave that became, in the summer of 1833, a popular attraction. Eager both to do something for the dead woman and to accommodate the tourists, some locals—perhaps members of the Fall River Committee—offered to erect a handsome stone monument, "detailing the sad tragedy of her death" (Williams 1833, 73), on the site. Lucretia and Grindall Rawson declined the gift and instead commissioned H. L. Price of Providence to carve a plain white marble tablet with the inscription:

IN
MEMORY OF
SARAH M. CORNELL
DAUGHTER OF
JAMES AND LUCRETIA
CORNELL
WHO DIED DEC. 20, 1832
IN THE 31ST YEAR
OF HER AGE

When the excitement waned the grave ceased to be more than locally significant, and even that interest faded with the passage of time. At the turn of the century, the Durfee farm was engulfed by the expanding city and converted into South (now Kennedy) Park. Few remembered Sarah Cornell's story, and none were willing to take responsibility for her remains. Once again she was left to the charity of Fall River residents, who were obliged to move her grave to the community's prestigious Oak Grove Cemetery, where it presently occupies lot 2733 on Whitethorn Path. The cemetery, like Fall River, has neighborhoods, and Sarah's is not of particularly high status. The acid rain of this century has almost washed away the inscription on her stone, and it is only faintly legible when an oblique sun casts wavering shadows in the disappearing letters. Her humble station and anonymity, however, have at last come to her aid, for the vandals that delight in mutilating the elaborate stones of Fall River's elite have left her completely alone.

Bibliography

Bibliographic note: The contemporary literature generated by the death of Sarah Cornell was, from the very beginning, partisan, and is best read with that in mind. Luke Drury's *Report of the Examination of Rev. Ephraim K. Avery*, the first pamphlet on the case, was seen by many as an attempt to disguise the inadequacy of Justices Howe and Haile's decision by distorting the testimony given at the Bristol hearing. William Staples's *A Correct Report of the Examination of Rev. Ephraim K. Avery* was the prosecution's rejoinder. In the same way, both sides produced transcripts of the trial in Newport: Benjamin Hallett's *A Full Report of the Trial of Ephraim K. Avery*, his *The Arguments of Counsel in the Close of the Trial*, and his *Avery's Trial (Supplementary Edition)* were, in effect, the prosecution's version, while Richard Hildreth's *A Report of the Trial of the Rev. Ephraim K. Avery* was that of the New England Conference. The arguments against Avery in the months after his trial are most easily found in Aristides' vitriolic articles collected in his *Strictures on the Case of Ephraim K. Avery*, and in Catharine Williams's remarkable *Fall River, An Authentic Narrative*. Williams's book is of particular interest, far beyond its limited literary merit, because it concisely combines the favored themes of the Fall River Committee: the public virtue of Fall River and the private virtue of Sarah Cornell, contrasted with the personal guilt of Ephraim Avery and the social culpability of his church. Avery's defense of his innocence and the New England Conference's defense of its actions are most ably presented in Avery's *Vindication of the Result of the Trial of Rev. Ephraim K. Avery*. Perhaps the most unusual pamphlet was the Pseudo-Avery's *Explanation of the Circumstances Connected With the Death of Sarah*

Maria Cornell, a totally fictitious but cleverly written confession that was circulated early in 1834.

Newspapers throughout the country reported and commented on Avery's
case, usually adopting an obvious controlling bias in their selection and
presentation. It is hardly surprising, however, that the clearest statements
of partisan feeling came from those editors most closely related—by organization or location—to the principals in the controversy. Inevitably, Fall
River's two newspapers—the *Monitor* edited by James Ford (of the Fall
River Committee) and the *Weekly Recorder* edited by Noel Allen Tripp—
assumed and asserted Avery's guilt. The best sustained attack on the minister and his church, however, was printed in the more widely circulated
Providence *Republican Herald*, published by William Simmons, Jr., and the
Newport *Rhode Island Republican*, published by F. B. Peckham. The leader
in Avery's defense was the New England Conference's own *Zion's Herald*
(previously the *New England Christian Herald*), published in Boston.

Even the manuscript collections that survive share in the biases of their
time. Although documents exist in many libraries, the two major collections are housed at the Library of the New England Methodist Historical
Society in Boston and at the Rhode Island Historical Society in Providence,
whose Avery Trial Papers are mostly prosecution documents but include
one important and impartial piece: the trial notes (unfortunately damaged
by water and partially illegible) of Chief Justice Samuel Eddy.

Later publications about the case have done little to resolve the controversies of their predecessors. In 1877, apparently in hostile response to the
evangelical successes of Dwight Lyman Moody and Ira D. Sankey, the case
was rehearsed in a pamphlet entitled *Life and Trial of the Rev. Ephraim K.
Avery*. Primarily a work of imagination, the pamphlet erroneously paints
Avery as an influential evangelical figure as well as a proven adulterer and
murderer. James Mudge's *History of the New England Conference* (1910),
biased in the opposite direction, briefly outlines the story and asserts
the minister's innocence. Fifty-one years later George Howe, the great-
grandson of Justice John Howe, retold the story in "The Minister and the
Mill Girl," an article unfortunately marred by many factual errors and perhaps influenced by family pride. In the 1980's, two novels have used Avery's
trial as their base—Mary Cable's *Avery's Knot* and Raymond Paul's *The Tragedy at Tiverton*—but, as works of fiction, both books deviate considerably
from historical fact.

Widespread interest in Avery's trial was part of a larger pattern of obses-
sion with violence in Jacksonian America. A survey of that period's newspapers demonstrates the accuracy of the statement, attributed to Black
Hawk as he toured the United States after his unsuccessful war, that "there
is nothing these people, especially the women, run after with such eagerness as a murderer" (*Georgia Messenger*, 11 July 1833). Of all the murders
recorded in the popular press of the era, probably the archetype—and best

remembered because of literary renditions by Edgar Allen Poe, William Gilmore Sims, and Robert Penn Warren—is the killing of Solomon P. Sharp by Jereboam O. Beauchamp. The best contemporary description of what came to be called the "Kentucky Tragedy" is Beauchamp's *The Confession of Jereboam O. Beauchamp*, composed during a stay of execution granted for that purpose. In 1832 and 1833 two other murder trials vied with Avery's for public favor: that of Lucretia Chapman and Lino Amalia Espos y Mina for the murder of Lucretia's husband, William, and that of Joel Clough for the murder of Mary Hamilton. The first is described in William E. Du Bois's transcript of the *Trial of Lucretia Chapman, Otherwise Called Lucretia Espos y Mina*, and the second in Clough's *The Only True and Authentic Life and Confession of Joel Clough.*

Most Americans in the 1830s believed that women's physical nature dictated a unique psychological balance that, while extremely sensitive to moral issues, limited their rational capacities and made them the inevitable wards of males. Avery's trial was thus a threatening propaganda event to both the Methodist church and Fall River's industrial community because it would affix blame for Sarah Cornell's fall on one of the male institutions on which she had depended for support—either the church or the factory. The basis for this theory of female nature—which led inexorably to the idea that there were distinct spheres of male and female endeavor and was at the root of the concept of female domesticity—can be seen in psychological treatises like Thomas Upham's widely read *Elements of Mental Philosophy* and *Outlines of Imperfect and Disordered Mental Action*, R. C. Dallas's *Elements of Self-Knowledge*, and Ezra Stiles Ely's *Conversations on the Human Mind.*

The world in which Ephraim Avery and Sarah Cornell lived, one that was beginning to change under the impact of industrialization and population growth, has attracted the attention of many scholars. The impact of the idea of a link between female physical nature and psychology is explored in Sara Delamont and Lorna Duffin's *Nineteenth-Century Woman: Her Cultural and Physical World*. The social position and self-image of New England women in the 1820s and 1830s are described in Nancy Cott's *The Bonds of Womanhood*, which draws on the personal documents of the women themselves rather than on the moralizing tracts they presumably read. The political avenues toward reform open to women enmeshed in the "female culture" of that time are discussed in Barbara Epstein's *The Politics of Domesticity*, as are the links among economy, demography, reform associations, traditionalism, and the transformation of the American middle-class family in Mary Ryan's *Cradle of the Middle Class*.

The history of New England's early industrialization is presented in Caroline Ware's *The Early New England Cotton Manufacture*. The story of the industrial community at Lowell is told in Hannah Josephson's *The Golden Threads*—like Caroline Ware's book an older work, but one that is very readable. The history of the rural mills throughout the villages and hamlets of New England, as important as that of Lowell in Sarah Cornell's life, has begun to emerge in works like Jonathan Prude's *The Coming of Industrial Order*, which studies the process of establishing mills in Dudley and Oxford, Massachusetts. Comparative data for a mid-atlantic community, where no dramatic event like Avery's trial forced evangelical religion and industrialism into opposing camps—and where members of these groups were allies—can be found in Anthony F. C. Wallace's *Rockdale*.

The condition of workers in industrial centers of the 1830s often has been viewed from the perspective of the unrest of the decades that followed. The Lowell mill girls are best known, for example, for their literate outcry against the worsening conditions of the 1840s, which has been presented in their own words in Philip Foner's *The Factory Girls*. Norman Ware's *The Industrial Worker 1840–1860* looks at the same period of defensive labor organization on a broader geographic scale. The earlier origins of the self-conscious labor groups of the 1840s, however, have begun to attract more attention. Paul Faler's *Mechanics and Manufacturers in the Early Industrial Revolution* traces the evolution of class consciousness among shoemakers in Lynn, Massachusetts, while Thomas Dublin's "Women at Work" does the same for the workers at Lowell, noting significant links among the dormitory system, a feeling of community, and the factory girls' ability to unite in concerted opposition to their employers.

Although several other histories of Fall River are available, a clear picture of the town's early years is presented in the work of its original historian, Congregational minister Orin Fowler, who published *An Historical Sketch of Fall River* in 1841. Frederick Peck and Henry Earl's *Fall River and Its Industries* is also a useful source of cultural, economic, and genealogical information, and Robert Lamb's "The Development of Entrepreneurship in Fall River 1813–1859" is invaluable for its care in unraveling the intricate web of marriage and descent that was the basis for capitalizing and running the first generation of Fall River mills.

Most of the numerous nineteenth-century and early twentieth-century histories of American Methodism give a general impression of the church's course of development, though none with the degree of New England detail, perhaps, of James Mudge's *History of the New England Conference*. The religious nature of the eastern United States in the first half of the nineteenth century—the Second Great Awakening—has been analyzed by many authors since Whitney Cross produced *The Burned-over District* in 1950. Most authors generally agree that the political and social implications of American independence and the industrial revolution prompted conversion to a more personalistic religion—and that that change in philosophy promoted new feelings of personal power and responsibility that were expressed in the wave of reform movements that washed over the country. Concise general discussions of the period can be found in William McLoughlin's *Revivals, Awakenings, and Reform* and in Richard Carwardine's

Trans-atlantic Revivalism, while studies of specific events and communities include Paul Johnson's *A Shopkeeper's Millennium* and Glenn Altschuler and Jan Saltzgaber's *Revivalism, Social Conscience, and Community in the Burned-Over District*. What they all show, ultimately, is a society that was conscious of opportunity but ridden by conflicts produced when emerging groups saw those opportunities differently, and that was sobered by a fear that the quest for a better future might destroy the best of what it already had.

Alabama General Assembly
    1828   *Remonstrance of the General Assembly of Alabama, on the Subject of Protecting Duties, and Adverse to an Increase.* 20th Cong., 1st sess., S. Doc. 86.

Alcott, William A.
    1835   *The Young Man's Guide.* Boston: Samuel Colman.
    1846   *The Young Husband, or Duties of Man in the Marriage Relation.* Boston: Waite, Peirce.
    1849   *The Young Woman's Guide to Excellence.* Boston: Strong and Broadhead.

Alexander, William, M.D.
    1779   *The History of Women, From the Earliest Antiquity, To the Present Time.* 2 vols. London: W. Strahan.

Allen, Ralph Willard
    1880   Biographical Sketch of the Rev. Ira M. Bidwell. MSS, New England Methodist Historical Society.

Altschuler, Glenn C., and Jan M. Saltzgaber
    1983   *Revivalism, Social Conscience, and Community in the Burned-Over District: The Trial of Rhoda Bement.* Ithaca: Cornell University Press.

American History Workshop
    1981   *The Fall River Sourcebook: A Documentary History of Fall River, Massachusetts.* Massachusetts Department of Environmental Management, Fall River Heritage State Park, Contract no. 991-80.

Angell, Oliver
    1840   *The Select Reader, Or Union No. 6.* Philadelphia: Marshall, Williams and Butler.

Aristides
    1833   *Strictures on the Case of Ephraim K. Avery, Originally Published in the Republican Herald, Providence, R.I.* Providence: William Simmons, Jr.

Avery, Ephraim K.
    1834   *Vindication of the Result of the Trial of Rev. Ephraim K. Avery, To Which is Prefixed his Statement of Facts Relative to the Circumstances by Which he Became Involved in the Prosecution.* Boston: David Ela.

Barber, John Warren
    1839   *Historical Collections, Being a General Collection of Interesting Facts, Traditions, Biographical Sketches, Anecdotes, &c, Relating to . . . Every Town in Massachusetts.* Worchester: Warren Lazell.

Bartlett, Elisha
    1841   *A Vindication of the Character and Condition of the Females Employed in the Lowell Mills.* Lowell: Leonard Huntress.

Bayles, Richard M.
    1891   *History of Providence County, Rhode Island.* 2 vols. New York: W. W. Preston.

Beauchamp, Jereboam O.
    1966   *The Confession of Jereboam O. Beauchamp.* Philadelphia: University of Pennsylvania Press.

Bidwell, Ira M.
    1839   Letter (June 3) to Edward Mason, Provincetown. New England Methodist Historical Society.

Borden, Alanson
    1899   *Our County and Its People. A Descriptive and Biographical Record of Bristol County Massachusetts.* Boston: Boston Historical Company.

Borden, Nathaniel B.
    1833   Letter (April 8) to William R. Staples, Fall River. Avery Trial Papers, Rhode Island Historical Society.

Boston Atlas
    1833   *Boston Daily Atlas.* Newspaper. Boston. Richard Haughton, ed.

Bowen, Clarence Winthrop
    1926   *The History of Woodstock, Connecticut.* Norwood, Mass.: Plimpton Press.

Brayton, Alice
    n.d.   *Life on the Stream*, vol. 1. Fall River: n.p.

Briggs, Lemuel
    1833   Letter (May 7) to William R. Staples. Avery Trial Papers, Rhode Island Historical Society.

Buckminster, Rev. J. S.
    1814   *Sermons by the Late Rev. J. S. Buckminster.* Boston: John Eliot.

Cable, Mary
    1981   *Avery's Knot.* New York: G. P. Putnam's Sons.

Carey, Henry
    1838   *Principles of Political Economy.* 3 vols. Philadelphia: Carey, Lea, and Blanchard.

Carey, Mathew
    1822   *Essays on Political Economy.* Philadelphia: H. C. Carey and I. Lea.
    1830   *Miscellaneous Essays.* Philadelphia: Carey and Hart.
    1837   *Plea for the Poor, Particularly Females.* Philadelphia: L. R. Bailey.

Carwardine, Richard
  1978   *Trans-atlantic Revivalism: Popular Evangelicalism in Britain and America, 1790–1865.* Westport: Greenwood Press.
Cavin, Joseph
  1843   *A Dictionary of Science, Literature, and Art.* New York: Harper and Brothers.
Chevalier, Michael
  1969   *Society, Manners, and Politics in the United States.* Ithaca: Cornell University Press.
Clark, G. J.
  1917   *Memoir, Autobiography and Correspondence of Jeremiah Mason.* Kansas City: Lawyers' International.
Clement, J.
  1851   *Noble Deeds of American Women: With Biographical Sketches of Some of the More Prominent.* Buffalo: Derby.
Clough, Joel
  1833a   *The Only True and Authentic Life and Confession of Joel Clough.* Philadelphia: Robert Desilver.
  1833b   *The Authentic Confession of Joel Clough, The Murderer of Mrs. Mary W. Hamilton.* Philadelphia: Robert Desilver.
Commonwealth v. Buckingham
  1823   *Trial: Commonwealth vs. J. T. Buckingham, On an Indictment for a Libel, Before the Municipal Court of the City of Boston, December Term, 1822.* Boston: *New England Galaxy.*
Cott, Nancy
  1977   *The Bonds of Womanhood: "Woman's Sphere" in New England, 1780–1835.* New Haven: Yale University Press.
Coxe, Tench
  1787   *An Address to an Assembly of the Friends of American Manufactures.* Philadelphia: Aitken.
Crockett, David
  1835   *An Account of Col. Crockett's Tour to the North and Down East, in the Year of Our Lord One Thousand Eight Hundred and Thirty-four.* Philadelphia: Carey and Hart.
Cross, Whitney Rogers
  1950   *The Burned-over District: The Social and Intellectual History of Enthusiastic Religion in Western New York, 1800–1850.* Ithaca: Cornell University Press.
Daily Advertiser and American
  1833   Newspaper. Providence. Daniel Mowry, ed.
Daily City Gazette
  1833   *Providence Daily City Gazette.* Newspaper. Providence. S. S. Southworth, ed.
Dallas, R. C.
  1805   *Elements of Self-Knowledge: Intended to Lead Youth into an Early Acquaintance with the Nature of Man.* London: J. Swan.

Daniels, W. H.
1887   *The Illustrated History of Methodism in Great Britain, America, and Australia, From the Days of the Wesleys to the Present Time.* New York: Methodist Book Concern.
Delamont, Sara, and Lorna Duffin, eds.
1978   *The Nineteenth-Century Woman: Her Cultural and Physical World.* New York: Barnes and Noble.
De Tocqueville, Alexis
1841   *Democracy in America,* vol. 2. New York: Langley.
Dew, Thomas
1829   *Lectures on the Restrictive System.* Richmond, Va.: Samuel Sheppard.
Drury, Luke
1833   *A Report of the Examination of Rev. Ephraim K. Avery, Charged with the Murder of Sarah Maria Cornell.* N.p.
Dublin, Thomas L.
1975   "Women at Work: The Transformation of Work and Community in Lowell, Massachusetts, 1826–1860." Ph.D. diss., Columbia University.
Du Bois, William E.
1832   *Trial of Lucretia Chapman, Otherwise Called Lucretia Espos Y Mina.* Philadelphia: G. W. Mentz.
Eastern Argus
1833   *Eastern Argus and Tri-Weekly.* Newspaper. Portland, Maine. Thomas Todd, ed.
Eddy, Samuel
1833   Trial Notes. Avery Trial Papers, MSS, Rhode Island Historical Society.
Elsemore, Moses
1848   *An Impartial Account of the Life of the Rev. John N. Maffitt.* New York: John F. Feeks.
Ely, Ezra Stiles
1819   *Conversations on the Human Mind.* Philadelphia: printed for the author.
Emporium
1833   *Emporium and True American.* Newspaper. Trenton, N.J. Joseph Justice, ed.
Encyclopedia Britannica
1771   3 vols. Edinburgh: Bell and Macfarquar.
Epstein, Barbara L.
1981   *The Politics of Domesticity: Women, Evangelism, and Temperance in Nineteenth-Century America.* Middletown, Conn.: Wesleyan University Press.
Factory Girl
1843   *Lights and Shadows of Factory Life in New England. By a Factory Girl.* New York: J. Winchester.

Fairfield, Lincoln Sumner
  1833   "Table Talk." *The North American Magazine* 2, no. 10:256.
Faler, Paul G.
  1981   *Mechanics and Manufacturers in the Early Industrial Revolution: Lynn Massachusetts 1780–1860.* Albany: State University of New York Press.
Fall River Historical Society
  1927   *Proceedings of the Society From its Organization in 1921 to August 1926.* Fall River: The Society.
Fall River Manufactory
  1832   Fall River Manufactory Time Book. MSS, Fall River Historical Society.
Fall River Monitor
  1832–34   Newspaper. Fall River. James Ford, ed.
Fall River Savings Bank
  1978   *Fall River Savings Bank 1828–1978.* N.p.
Fall River Weekly Recorder
  1833   Newspaper. Fall River. Noel Tripp, ed.
Farnham, Eliza W.
  1864   *Woman and Her Era*, vol. 2. New York: A. J. Davis.
Farrar, Mrs. John
  1838   *The Young Lady's Friend.* Boston: American Stationers.
Felch, Walton
  1816   *The Manufacturer's Pocket-Piece: Or The Cotton Mill Moralized.* Medway, Mass.: Samuel Allen.
Fenner, Henry M.
  1906   *History of Fall River.* New York: F. T. Smiley.
Foner, Philip, ed.
  1977   *The Factory Girls: A Collection of Writings on Life and Struggles in the New England Factories of the 1840s by the Factory Girls Themselves, And the Story, in Their Own Words, of the First Trade Unions of Women Workers in the United States.* Urbana: University of Illinois Press.
Fowler, O. S.
  1844   *Love and Parentage, Applied to the Improvement of Offspring.* New York: Fowler and Wells.
Fowler, Orin
  1841   *An Historical Sketch of Fall River, From 1620 to the Present Time.* Fall River: Benjamin Earl.
Franklin, Conn.
  1869   *The Celebration of the One Hundred and Fiftieth Anniversary of the Primitive Organization of the Congregational Church and Society in Franklin, Connecticut, October 14th, 1868.* New Haven: Tuttle, Morehouse and Taylor.
Freeholder
  1833   Letter (May 20) to Albert Greene, Newport, signed "A Free-

holder." Albert C. and Richard Ward Greene Papers, Rhode Island Historical Society.

Georgia Messenger

1833   Newspaper. Macon. S. Rose, ed.

Gill, Thomas, Jr.

1833   Letter (May 25) to Chief Justice Samuel Eddy, Newport. Avery Trial Papers, Rhode Island Historical Society.

Goodwin, Isaac

1834   *Town Officer: Or, Laws of Massachusetts Relative to the Duties of Municipal Officers.* Worcester: Dorr, Howland.

Greene, Charles

1833   Letter (May 1, dated "Wednesday eve.") to Thomas Gill. Avery Trial Papers, Rhode Island Historical Society.

Greene, Elihu

1833   Letter (June 24) to Mrs. D. Greene, Cincinnati. Greene Papers, Rhode Island Historical Society.

Griffen, B.

1836   Certificate of good standing for Ephraim K. Avery (February 29), directed to the "Bishop and Members of the New England Conference." MS, New England Methodist Historical Society.

Hallett, Benjamin F.

1823   *An Exposure of the Misrepresentations Contained in a Professed Report of the Trial of Mr. John N. Maffitt, Before a Council of Ministers of the Methodist Episcopal Church, Convened in Boston, December 26, 1822.* Boston: n.p.

1833a   *A Full Report of the Trial of Ephraim K. Avery, Charged with the Murder of Sarah Maria Cornell, Before the Supreme Court of Rhode Island, At a Special Term in Newport, Held in May 1833.* Boston: *Daily Commercial Gazette.*

1833b   *The Arguments of Counsel in the Close of the Trial of Rev. Ephraim K. Avery. Also a Literal Report of the Medical Testimony of Professor Walter Channing and Dr. William Turner.* Boston: *Daily Commercial Gazette.*

1833c   *Avery's Trial (Supplementary Edition).* n.p.

1833d   Trial: Commonwealth vs. J. T. Buckingham, on an Indictment for a Libel, Before the Municipal Court of the City of Boston, December, 1822. n.p.

Harnden, Harvey

1833a   *Narrative of the Apprehension in Rindge, N.H. of the Rev. E. K. Avery.* Providence: W. Marshall.

1833b   Letter (May 5) to N. B. Borden, Boston. Avery Trial Papers, Rhode Island Historical Society.

Hildreth, Richard

1833   *A Report of the Trial of the Rev. Ephraim K. Avery, Before the Supreme Judicial Court of Rhode Island, On an Indictment for the Murder of Sarah Maria Cornell.* Boston: Russell, Odiorne.

Hooper, Foster
    1833   Letter (February 4) to William R. Staples, Fall River. Avery Trial
        Papers, Rhode Island Historical Society.
Hooper, Robert
    1832   *Lexicon Medicum*. New York: Harper Brothers.
House Committee on Manufactures
    1821   *Protection to Manufactures*. 16th Cong., 2d sess., Doc. 609.
        American State Papers, vol. 3 (Finance), pp. 594–645.
Howe, George
    1961   "The Minister and the Mill Girl." *American Heritage* 12, no. 6:
        34–37, 82–88.
Howe, John
    1832   Letter (December 25) to Albert C. Greene, Bristol. Avery Trial
        Papers, Rhode Island Historical Society.
Humphreys, David
    1794   *A Poem on Industry, Addressed to the Citizens of the United States of
        America*. Philadelphia: M. Carey.
Independent Chronicle
    1826   *Independent Chronicle and Boston Patriot*. Newspaper. Boston.
        Nathan Hale, ed.
Johnson, Paul E.
    1978   *A Shopkeeper's Millennium: Society and Revivals in Rochester, New
        York 1815–1837*. New York: Hill and Wang.
Josephson, Hannah
    1949   *The Golden Threads: New England's Mill Girls and Magnates*. New
        York: Duell, Sloan and Pearce.
Kay, James
    1833   *The American Lady's Pocket-book, and Nursery-Advisor*. Philadel-
        phia: James Kay, Jr. and Brother.
Keller, Charles Roy
    1942   *The Second Great Awakening in Connecticut*. New Haven: Yale
        University Press.
Kemble, Frances Anne
    1835   *Journal (1 August 1832—17 July 1833)*. London: J. Murray.
Kennebec Journal
    1833   Newspaper. Augusta, Maine. David L. Wilson, ed.
Kent, Asa
    1836   Letter (July 19) to the Members of the New England Confer-
        ence. New England Methodist Historical Society.
Kingsley, A.
    1833   Letter (May 11) to William R. Staples, Providence. Avery Trial
        Papers, Rhode Island Historical Society.
Lamb, Robert K.
    1935   "The Development of Entrepreneurship in Fall River, 1813–
        1859." Ph.D. diss., Harvard University.

Lawless, William
  1833   Letter (May 27) to Albert C. Greene. Avery Trial Papers, Rhode
         Island Historical Society.
Leffingwell, Christopher
  1811   Estate Papers. MSS, Connecticut State Library.
Lerner, Gerda
  1973   "The Lady and the Mill Girl: Changes in the Status of Women
         in the Age of Jackson." In Hogeland, Ronald W., and Aileen S.
         Kraditor, eds., *Woman and Womanhood in America*. Lexington,
         Mass.: D. C. Heath.
Liberator
  1833   Newspaper. Boston. William Lloyd Garrison, ed.
Lieber, Francis
  1840   *Encyclopedia Americana*. Philadelphia: Thomas, Cowperthwait.
Life and Trial
  1877   *Life and Trial of the Rev. Ephraim K. Avery for the Murder of the
         Young and Beautiful Miss Sarah M. Cornell*. Philadelphia: Barclay.
Literary Subaltern
  1833   Newspaper. Providence. Southworth and Holroyd, pub.
Logan, George
  1800   *A Letter to the Citizens of Pennsylvania on the Necessity of Promoting
         Agriculture, Manufactures, and the Useful Arts*. Lancaster, Pa.:
         n.p.
Lorrain County Probate Court
  1869   Estate Papers of Ephraim K. Avery. MSS, Lorrain County
         Court of Common Pleas, Probate Div. Lorrain County Court-
         house, Elyria, Ohio.
Mail
  1833   *The Mail*. Newspaper. Hagerstown, Md. Ott and Weber, eds.
Manufacturers and Farmers Journal
  1833   *Manufacturers and Farmers Journal and Providence and Pawtucket
         Advertiser*. Newspaper. Providence. John Miller, pub.
Marshall and Brown
  1833   *The Correct, Full and Impartial Report of the Trial of Rev.
         Ephraim K. Avery, Before the Supreme Judicial Court of the State of
         Rhode-Island, at Newport, May 6, 1833, for the Murder of Sarah M.
         Cornell*. Providence: Marshall and Brown.
Mathews, Donald G.
  1978   "The Second Great Awakening as an Organizing Process
         1780–1850." In Mulder, John M., and John F. Wilson, *Religion
         in American History*. Englewood Cliffs, N.J.: Prentice Hall.
McLoughlin, William Gerald
  1978   *Revivals, Awakenings, and Reform: An Essay on Religion and Social
         Change in America, 1607–1977*. Chicago: University of Chicago
         Press.

Melvill, David
    1833   *A Fac-simile of the Letters Produced at the Trial of the Rev. Ephraim K. Avery, on an Indictment for the Murder of Sarah Maria Cornell, Taken with Great Care, by Permission of the Hon. Supreme Judicial Court of Rhode Island from the Original Letters in the Office of the Clerk of Said Court.* Boston: Pendleton's Lithography.

Mentz, George W.
    1832   *Trial of Lino Amalio Espos Y Mina.* Philadelphia: G. W. Mentz.

Merritt, Timothy
    1833   Letter (July 6) to Ephraim K. Avery and Charles True. New England Methodist Historical Society.

Mirror
    1833   Weekly journal. Vol. 10. New York. George Pops Morris, ed.

Montgomery, James
    1840   *A Practical Detail of the Cotton Manufacture of the United States of America.* Glascow, Scotland: John Niven.

Moore, J. Hamilton
    1807   *The Young Gentleman and Lady's Monitor, and English Teacher's Assistant.* Hartford: O. D. Cooke.

Mudge, James
    1910   *History of the New England Conference of the Methodist Episcopal Church 1796–1910.* Boston: The Conference.

Murray, Lindley
    1829   *Sequel to the English Reader: Or, Elegant Selections in Prose and Poetry.* Philadelphia: S. Probasco.

Napheys, George H.
    1890   *The Physical Life of Woman: Advice to the Maiden, Wife and Mother.* Philadelphia: David McKay.

National Banner
    1833   *National Banner and Nashville Daily Advertiser.* Newspaper. Nashville. Hunt, Tardiff, pub.

National Intelligencer
    1833   *Daily National Intelligencer.* Newspaper. Washington, D.C. Gales and Seaton, eds.

New England Annual Conference
    1833   *Report of a Committee of the New England Annual Conference of the Methodist Episcopal Church, On the Case of the Rev. Ephraim K. Avery, Member of Said Conference.* Boston: David Ela.
    1835   *Minutes of the New England Annual Conference of the Methodist Episcopal Church for the Year 1835.* Boston: David Ela.

New England Christian Herald
    1832–33   Newspaper. Boston. S. W. Wilson and S. O. Wright, eds.

New England Galaxy
    1821–33   Newspaper. Boston. Joseph T. Buckingham and William J. Snelling, eds.

New Hampshire Patriot
>1833 *New Hampshire Patriot and State Gazette.* Newspaper. Concord. Hill and Barton, pub.

New-Hampshire Sentinel
>1833 Newspaper. Keene. J. and J. W. Prentiss, eds.

New Jersey State Gazette
>1833 Newspaper. Trenton. George Sherman, ed.

Newport Mercury
>1833 Newspaper. Newport, R.I. William and J. H. Barber, eds.

Niles, Hezekiah
>1827 "General Convention of Agriculturalists and Manufacturers, and Others Friendly to the Encouragement and Support of the Domestic Industry of the United States." *Niles' Weekly Register* 3d ser., 8: 388–96.

Niles' Register
>1833 Newspaper. Baltimore. Hezekiah Niles, ed.

Norris, Thomas F.
>1833 "To the Public. East-Cambridge, Feb. 1833." Copy in Avery Trial Papers, Rhode Island Historical Society.

North American Magazine
>1833 Philadelphia. Sumner Lincoln Fairfield, ed.

Norwich Courier
>1833 Newspaper. Norwich, Conn. J. Dunham, ed.

Odell, George C. D.
>1928 *Annals of the New York Stage. Vol. III (1821–1834).* New York: Columbia University Press.

Ohio Republican
>1833 Newspaper. Zanesville. Peters and Pelham, eds.

Painesville Telegraph
>1833 Newspaper. Painesville, Ohio. E. D. Howe, ed.

Paul, Raymond
>1984 *The Tragedy at Tiverton.* New York: Ballantine.

Pawtucket Chronicle
>1833 *Pawtucket Chronicle and Rhode Island and Massachusetts Register.* Newspaper. Pawtucket, R.I. H. and J. E. Rousmaniere, pub.

Pearce, Dutee J.
>1833 Letter (March 14) to Albert C. Greene. Avery Trial Papers, Rhode Island Historical Society.

Peck, Frederick M., and Henry H. Earl
>1877 *Fall River and Its Industries.* New York: Atlantic Publishing and Engraving.

Peckham, A. C.
>1927 "Early Physicians of Fall River." In *Proceedings of the Society From its Organization in 1921 to August 1926.* Fall River: Fall River Historical Society.

Pennsylvania Society for Promoting National Industry
    1819   *Address of the Pennsylvania Society for Promoting National Industry.*
           Philadelphia: M. Carey and Son.
Philadelphia Album
    1833   *The Philadelphia Album and Ladies' Literary Port Folio.* Newspaper.
           Philadelphia. Robert Morris, ed.
Phillips, Arthur Sherman
    1941   *The Phillips History of Fall River.* 3 vols. Fall River: Dover Press.
Phoenix Gazette
    1833   Newspaper. Alexandria, Va. Edgar Snowden, ed.
Pierce, Moses
    1833   Letter (May 6) to Albert C. Greene, Fall River. Albert C. and
           Richard Ward Greene Papers, Rhode Island Historical Society.
Post
    1833   *The Evening Post.* Newspaper. New York.
Potter, Elisha R.
    n.d.   Biography of Benjamin Franklin Hallett. MS, Elisha R. Potter
           Papers, Rhode Island Historical Society.
Providence Journal
    1833   *Providence Daily Journal.* Newspaper. Providence. John Miller,
           pub.
    1883   Providence. Knowles, Anthony and Danielson, pubs.
Prude, Jonathan
    1983   *The Coming of Industrial Order: Town and Factory Life in Rural*
           Massachusetts 1810–1860. Cambridge, Mass.: Cambridge University Press.
Pseudo-Avery
    1834   *Explanation of the Circumstances Connected With the Death of Sarah*
           Maria Cornell; By Ephraim K. Avery. Providence: William S.
           Clark.
Raleigh Register
    1833   *Raleigh Register and North Carolina Gazette.* Raleigh, N.C. Joseph
           Gales and Son, pub.
Rawson, Grindall
    1833   Letter (March 19) to William R. Staples, Woodstock, Conn.
           Avery Trial Papers, Rhode Island Historical Society.
Republican Herald
    1832–33   Newspaper. Providence. William Simmons, Jr., pub.
Rhode Island Republican
    1833   Newspaper. Newport. F. B. Peckham, pub.
Robbins, Thomas
    1824   *A View of All Religions; And the Religious Ceremonies of all Nations*
           at the Present Day. Hartford: Oliver D. Cooke and Sons.
Ryan, Mary P.
    1981   *Cradle of the Middle Class: The Family in Oneida County, New York,*
           1790–1865. Cambridge, Mass.: Cambridge University Press.

Sangamo Journal
    1833   Newspaper. Springfield, Ill. S. and J. Francis, pub.
Savage, Sarah
    1814   *The Factory Girl.* Boston: Munroe, Francis and Parker.
Scudder, M. L.
    1870   *American Methodism.* Hartford: S. S. Scranton.
Secretary of the Treasury
    1833   *Documents Relative to the Manufactures in the United States, Collected and Transmitted to the House of Representatives, In Compliance with a Resolution of January 19, 1832,* vol. 1. Washington, D.C.: Duff Green.
Sewell, Thomas
    1833   Letter (July 25) to Albert Greene, Washington, D.C. Greene Papers, January–July 1833, Rhode Island Historical Society.
Shove, Jervis
    1833   Letter (May 22) to N. B. Borden, Fall River. Avery Trial Papers, Rhode Island Historical Society.
Sigourney, Lydia M.
    1846   *Letter to Mothers.* New York: Harper and Brothers.
Simpson, Matthew
    1882   *Cyclopedia of Methodism.* Philadelphia: L. H. Everts.
Smith, Thomas Russell
    1944   *The Cotton Textile Industry of Fall River, Massachusetts: A Study of Industrial Localization.* New York: King's Crown Press.
Southern Banner
    1833   Newspaper. Athens, Ga. Albon Chase and A. N. Nesbit, eds.
Spirit of the Age
    1833   *Spirit of the Age and Journal of Humanity.* Newspaper. Boston. Ford and Damvell, pub.
Stanley, Nancy
    1833   "Providence City, April 5, 1833." MS deposition, Avery Trial Papers, Rhode Island Historical Society.
Staples, William Read
    1833a   *A Correct Report of the Examination of Rev. Ephraim K. Avery, Minister of the Methodist Church in Bristol, R.I. Who Was Charged With the Murder of Sarah M. Cornell.* Providence: Marshall and Brown.
    1833b   Letter (March 4) to Albert C. Greene. Avery Trial Papers, Rhode Island Historical Society.
    1833c   Letter (March 29) to William Remington, Providence. Avery Trial Papers, Rhode Island Historical Society.
Stewart, Dugald
    1831   "Of the Varieties of Intellectual Character." In Upham, Thomas, *Elements of Mental Philosophy.* Portland, Maine: S. Coleman.

Storrs, George
    1833   Letter (January 4) to Albert C. Greene. Avery Trial Papers, Rhode Island Historical Society.

Sweet, Leonard
    1983   *The Minister's Wife: Her Role in Nineteenth-Century American Evangelicalism.* Philadelphia: Temple University Press.

Taussig, F. W.
    1931   *The Tariff History of the United States.* New York: G. P. Putnam's Sons.

Taylor, George Rogers
    1968   *The Transportation Revolution 1815–1860.* New York: Harper and Row.

Thayer Brothers
    1825   *The Life, Trial, Condemnation, and Dying Address of the Three Thayers!!* Buffalo: n.p.

Thompson, Harold W.
    1958   *A Pioneer Songster: Texts from the Stevens-Douglass Manuscript of Western New York 1841–1856.* Ithaca: Cornell University Press.

Trial at Large
    1833   *The Trial at Large of the Rev. Ephraim K. Avery, For the Wilful Murder of Sarah Maria Cornell, At Tiverton, in the County of Newport, R.I.* New York: n.p.

True and Greene
    1823   *Report of the Trial of Mr. John N. Maffitt, Before a Council of Ministers, of the Methodist Episcopal Church, Convened in Boston, December 26, 1823.* Boston: True and Greene.

Turner, William
    1833   Certification of illness (May 30), Newport. MS, Avery Trial Papers, Rhode Island Historical Society.

Upham, Samuel F.
    1891   History of the Methodist Episcopal Church, Bristol, R.I. New England Methodist Historical Society.

Upham, Thomas C.
    1831   *Elements of Mental Philosophy.* 2 vols. Portland, Maine: S. Coleman.
    1868   *Outlines of Imperfect and Disordered Mental Action.* New York: Harper and Brothers.

Virginia Herald
    1833   Newspaper. Fredericksburg. James D. Harrow, ed.

Walker, John
    1819   *A Critical Pronouncing Dictionary, and Expositor of the English Language.* New York: Collins and Hannan.
    1827   *A Critical Pronouncing Dictionary, and Expositor of the English Language.* Hartford: Silus Andrus.

Wallace, Anthony F. C.
    1978   *Rockdale: The Growth of an American Village in the Early Industrial Revolution*. New York: Alfred A. Knopf.
Ware, Caroline F.
    1966   *The Early New England Cotton Manufacture: A Study of Industrial Beginnings*. New York: Russell and Russell.
Ware, Norman
    1964   *The Industrial Worker 1840–1860: The Reaction of American Industrial Society to the Advance of the Industrial Revolution*. Chicago: Quadrangle Books.
Webb, Daniel
    1837   Letter (June 29) to Edward Mason, Fall River. New England Methodist Historical Society.
Webster, Noah
    1846   *An American Dictionary of the English Language*. New York: Harper and Brothers.
Welter, Barbara
    1966   "The Cult of True Womanhood: 1820–1860." *American Quarterly*, 18:151–74.
Whittaker, George
    1912   "Minutes of the New England Conference of the Methodist Episcopal Church. Volume II. Excerpts from the Journals of the Conference made by the Rev. James Mudge." New England Methodist Historical Society.
Williams, Catharine
    1833   *Fall River, An Authentic Narrative*. Boston: Lilly, Waite.
Winebrenner, John
    1849   *History of all the Religious Denominations in the United States*. Harrisburg: John Winebrenner.
Woodville Republican
    1833   Newspaper. Woodville, Miss. William A. A. Chisholm, ed.
Worth, William T.
    1888   Sketch of Asa Kent. MSS, New England Methodist Historical Society.
Young, William, and William W.
    1833   Letter (September 23) to DuPont and Bauduy, and Company. Winterthur Manuscripts, Papers of Victor DuPont, Eleutherian Mills Historical Society.
Zion's Herald
    1824
    –29   Newspaper. Boston. Barber Badger, ed.
    1834   Boston. Shipley W. Wilson, ed.

Index

What was the larger social question posed
   by the trial?
— who supported Avery?
— who was against him?
— who was to blame for Sarah's situation?
   — what had her actions? (296)
What brought Sarah to Fall River?
How did Sarah & Avery know each other?
Why did some people hold the meeting
   Church responsible?
Why did some people hold Fall River
   manufactures responsible?
How could this have happened?
What were the social changes people in
   the area were grappling w/ at the time?

—